AGE OF *SHŌJO*

AGE OF SHŌJO

The Emergence, Evolution, and Power of Japanese Girls' Magazine Fiction

HIROMI TSUCHIYA DOLLASE

Cover image: Fukiya Kōji, *Waga Atelier*. © Fukiya Kōji 2018.

Published by State University of New York Press, Albany

© 2019 State University of New York

All rights reserved

No part of this book may be used or reproduced in any manner whatsoever without written permission. No part of this book may be stored in a retrieval system or transmitted in any form or by any means including electronic, electrostatic, magnetic tape, mechanical, photocopying, recording, or otherwise without the prior permission in writing of the publisher.

For information, contact State University of New York Press, Albany, NY
www.sunypress.edu

Library of Congress Cataloging-in-Publication Data

Names: Dollase, Hiromi Tsuchiya, 1968- author.
Title: Age of Shōjo : the emergence, evolution, and power of Japanese girls' magazine fiction / Hiromi Tsuchiya Dollase, State University of New York.
Description: Albany : State University of New York Press, [2019] | Includes bibliographical references and index.
Identifiers: LCCN 2018021840| ISBN 9781438473918 (hardcover : alk. paper) | ISBN 9781438473901(paperback : alk. paper) | ISBN 9781438473925 (e-book)
Subjects: LCSH: Children's periodicals, Japanese—History—20th century. | Girls—Books and reading—Japan—History. | Japanese literature—20th century—History and criticism. | Japanese literature—Women authors—History and criticism. | Girls in literature.
Classification: LCC PN5407.J8 D65 2019 | DDC 895.6/0992837—dc23 LC record available at https://lccn.loc.gov/2018021840

10 9 8 7 6 5 4 3 2 1

CONTENTS

Illustrations / vii
Acknowledgments / ix
Introduction / xi

1. *Shōfujin* (*Little Women*): Re-creating Jo for the Female Audience in Meiji Japan / 1

2. *Shōjo sekai* (Girls' World): The Formation of Girls' Magazine Culture and the Emergence of "Scribbling Girls" / 17

3. Yoshiya Nobuko and Kitagawa Chiyo: Fiction by and for Girls / 31

4. *Shōjo* Feminism in Semi-autobiographical Stories by Yoshiya Nobuko and Morita Tama / 49

5. *Shōjo no tomo* (Girls' Friend): Conflicting Ideals of Girls on the Home Front / 65

6. *Himawari* (Sunflower): Reimagining *Shōjo* during the Occupation Period / 81

7. Himuro Saeko's *Shōjo* Heroines from Heian to Shōwa / 97

8. Tanabe Seiko and the Age of *Shōjo* / 115

Epilogue / 127
Notes / 131
Works Cited / 171
Index / 189

Illustrations

1.1 Front cover of *Shōfujin*. / 2

1.2 Illustration for *Shōfujin* by Kitada Shūho. / 3

2.1 Cover of the first issue of *Shōjo sekai*. / 18

2.2 "Five Honorable Girls." / 26

3.1 Illustration for Yoshiya Nobuko's "Hana monogatari, Nemu no hana" by Fukiya Kōji. / 34

3.2 Illustration for Yoshiya Nobuko's "Hana monogatari, Sanshoku sumire" by Nakahara Jun'ichi. / 35

5.1 Cover illustration of the June 1940 issue of *Shōjo no tomo* by Nakahara Jun'ichi. / 70

5.2 Cover illustration of the July 1940 issue of *Shōjo no tomo* by Miyamoto Saburō. / 71

6.1 Cover illustration of the January 1947 issue of *Himawari* by Nakahara Jun'ichi. / 82

6.2 How the Nishikawa family spent their Mother's Day (a picture story). / 90

6.3 Girls posing as the March sisters. / 91

7.1 Cover illustration of *Cobalt* 1, no 1, 1982. / 101

7.2 Illustration from the second episode of *Nante suteki ni japanesuku* by Tsuchida Yoshiko. / 107

8.1 Cover page of Tanabe Seiko's *Ubazakari*. / 116

ACKNOWLEDGMENTS

Many people helped me in the years during which I produced this study. First, I would like to express my thankfulness to Eiji Sekine, Sally A. Hastings, Aparajita Sagar, and Siobhan Somerville, who served as advisers for my PhD dissertation, "Mad Girls in the Attic: Louisa May Alcott, Yoshiya Nobuko and the Development of Shōjo Culture" (2003), from which this book project originated.

I would like to express my gratitude to Purdue University, for awarding me the Purdue Research Foundation Grant; and Vassar College, for granting me the Dean of Faculty General Fund, the Susan Turner Fund, the Salmon Fund, and the Emily Floyd Fund, all of which have enabled me to go to Japan yearly to work on my research. This book would not have materialized without the ongoing support of the Dean of Faculty Office, the Grant's Office, and the Library at Vassar College.

I would like to express my appreciation to Christopher Ahn, an editor at SUNY Press, for finding my study interesting and guiding me throughout the publication process. I also owe my deepest thanks to the reviewers of the manuscript who provided extremely valuable suggestions and comments, which helped me look at the whole book with fresh eyes.

I wish to thank the journals *Japanese Studies*, the *Journal of Popular Culture*, *U.S.-Japan Women's Journal*, *Asian Studies Review*, and the *Association for Japanese Literature Studies* for allowing me to reproduce parts of essays that first appeared in these publications. The following publishers, museums, and individuals allowed me to use images: Mineko Miyamoto, Mitsuko Yasuda, Himawariya, Hakubunkan Shinsha, and Shinchōsha, Shūeisha. I would like to thank Yūichi Iwano of Jitsugyō no Nihonsha, and Shizuo Hasegawa of the Fukiya Kōji Memorial Museum for helping me in the process of obtaining permissons. I appreciate the generosity of Tatsuo Fukiya for permitting me to use Fukiya Kōji's beautiful artwork, which perfectly represents the spirit of my book, on the front cover.

I looked at many volumes of girls' magazines at the Center for International Children's Literature in Osaka, the International Library of Children's Literature in Ueno, the Museum of Modern Japanese Literature in Tokyo, and the National Diet Library in Tokyo; without the help of library staff, my study would not have been possible. I am also grateful for the kindness of Taiko Katō, Taeko Emoto, and the members of Kitagawa Chiyo Kenshōkai in the city of Fukaya, Saitama, who shared stories about Kitagawa Chiyo with me.

I always enjoyed the fun and collaborative spirit of the scholars whom I got to know throughout the course of the project and invited me to participate in workshops, conference meetings, and collaborative projects, including Tomoko Aoyama, Jan Bardsley, Nathen Clerici, Catherine Driscoll, Nahoko Fukushima, Barbara Hartley, Rachael Hutchinson, Laura Miller, Amanda Seaman, C. J. Suzuki, Masami Toku, and Patricia Welch. I also thank Kiyomi Eguro, Helen Kilpatrick, Yuko Matsumoto, and Kayo Takeuchi for sharing their girl study research. I would like to express my very special gratefulness to the late Satoko Kan, an extraordinary educator, researcher, and critic, for the friendship and inspiration she provided me. My appreciation also goes to my colleagues in the Chinese and Japanese Department and the Asian Studies Program at Vassar College, in particular, Peipei Qiu, and my research assistants, Sabrina Castillo, Jennifer Novak, Stephanie Seto, Hikari Tanaka, and Alisa Vithoontien.

This book would not have happened without the support of my family in both Japan and the United States; Susumu and Reiko Tsuchiya, Bill and Anna Mae Dollase, and my sisters, Nobuko and Natsue. Last, but absolutely not least, I would like to express my deepest appreciation to Rob Dollase who read multiple drafts of this book and helped me polish the final product. My heartfelt thanks go to him for his patience, constant encouragement, and support.

Previously Published Journal Articles

Chapter 1 was previously published as "*Shōfujin* (Little Women): Recreating Jo for the Girls of Meiji Japan," *Japanese Studies* 30, no. 2 (2010): 247–62.

A section of chapter 3 was previously published as "Early Twentieth Century Japanese Girls' Magazine Stories: Examining Shōjo Voice in *Hanamonogatari* (Flower Tales)," *Journal of Popular Culture* 36, no. 4 (2003): 724–55.

A section of chapter 4 was previously published as "Yoshiya Nobuko's 'Yaneura no nishojo': In Search of Literary Possibilities in Shōjo Narratives," *U.S.-Japan Women's Journal* 20–21 (2001): 151–78.

Chapter 5 was previously published as "Girls on the Home Front: An Examination of *Shōjo no tomo* Magazine 1937–1945," *Asian Studies Review* 32 (2008): 323–39.

A Note on Japanese Names

All the Japanese names from Japanese publications will follow the form in which surname comes before given name.

INTRODUCTION

Little Women, Anne of Green Gables, A Little Princess, Daddy-Long-Legs, Pollyanna, and *Heidi*—for over one hundred years, these stories, though they originated in the West, have resonated with young female Japanese readers like no others. They have been repeatedly translated into Japanese, reprinted, adapted as animated television series and more, continuing to attract new audiences. The origin of Japanese girls' fiction, *shōjo* manga (girls' comics), and even anime can be traced back to these Western stories that inspired little girls, including future fiction writers and manga artists who grew up steeped in them.[1]

The Japanese girls' fiction genre has gone through many transformations over the past century, repeatedly reshaping its themes and the images of its heroines. It has picked up and shed various attributes through the years, but at the core of today's sprawling Japanese girls' culture an evolving force consisting of a pattern of attitudes and processes has persisted. Sparked by girls' resistance against their oppressive fates as females in traditional Japan, this force originally manifested as a passive retreat into fantasy worlds and the attempt to maintain them beyond their practical limits. The strength of these reveries proved durable, generating attitudinal and practical changes in the lives of those they inspired. The soft power of this phenomenon, which continues to expand and advance through generations and throughout the larger culture, is a process we can identify as the "way of *shōjo*."

The "way of *shōjo*" traces back to the introduction of Western girls' stories into Meiji Japan. Great numbers of them were translated during this period, a time when Japan, having just exited its feudal period, was transforming into a modern nation. Wakamatsu Shizuko (1864–1896),[2] best known for her translation of Frances Hodgson Burnett's *Little Lord Fauntleroy*, contributed greatly to the introduction of Western girls' fiction in Japan. One magazine that published her translations was *Jogaku zasshi* (Women's Education Journal),[3] a Christian magazine founded by her husband Iwamoto Yoshiharu. Her original intention was to use these stories to introduce young women to the idea of the Western home and modern women's domestic roles. However, responding to the growing number of juvenile magazines in the late nineteenth century, she gradually widened her intended audience to include children.

Wakamatsu was entrusted with a girls' section in the magazine *Shōnen sekai* (Boys' World, founded in 1895), in which she wrote original fiction for girls. Kume Yoriko sees the birth of girls' fiction here, and states that Wakamatsu's literature—"a mixture of didacticism with fantasy and romance—is the precursor of the girls' fiction that emerged abundantly in the later era."[4]

The age of *shōjo* commenced with the creation of girls' magazines, which proliferated in the 1910s, corresponding with the increase in the number of girls' schools. Girls' magazines normally consisted of educational articles, fiction, and readers' pages. It was frequently a convention to indicate the genre category *shōjo shōsetsu* (girls' fiction), above the title of a story.[5] Judging from the fact that boy's magazines did not feel it necessary to label the gender category of their stories, it seems the editors considered girl readers a subcategory that required special guidance and attention from adults and educators. Girls' fiction was used as a means to promote the *ryōsai kenbo* (Good Wife, Wise Mother) educational ideology, a national policy that was a conglomerate of the ideals of Western womanhood and Confucian female roles. Girl readers, nevertheless, were enthralled by girls' stories and embraced the publications, which they soon turned into their own cultural space. They communicated on the pages of the magazines via submissions of letters and compositions and constructed a girls' community. Some girls emerged as fiction writers from this magazine community. They each aspired to an ideal of girls' fiction suitable for readers of the new era. The result was a dynamic negotiation between authors' intentions and publishers' commercial goals. This book will follow the transformation and development of Japanese girls' magazines, investigating, in particular, the role girls' fiction played in the creation of modern girls' culture.

Shōjo Narrative Study

"*Shōjo*," indicating adolescent girl, is a modern concept. The *Daijirin* dictionary defines *shōjo* as "girls of age between 7 or 8 to 15 or 16": in other words, school age. However, as many would agree, age is not a particularly important factor in defining this concept. The term *shōjo* should rather be understood as a cultural term, formed amid the give and take between modern educational policy and consumer culture. In premodern times, *shōjo* (少女) in kanji was also read as *otome*, which simply indicated the status of unmarried woman. When a girl started menstruation, she was viewed as a woman available for marriage. Later, with the rise of female education in Meiji, the term *shōjo*—female youth—became the counterpart of *shōnen* (少年), for male youth.[6] *Shōjo* may be physically mature and recognized as capable of reproduction during this period, but they are temporarily partitioned in the space of a school. As long as they are in this space, they are free from social obligations, including marriage. Ōtsuka Eiji states that *shōjo* are "exempt from all kinds of production,"[7] including labor and reproduction. John Treat finds the idea of *shōjo* to be uniquely Japanese: "[I]n Japan, one might well argue that *shōjo* constitute their own gender, neither male nor female but rather something importantly detached from the productive economy of heterosexual reproduction."[8] Temporarily excused from social obligations, the culture allows girls to embrace freedom from gender normativity as well.

The study of *shōjo* narratives in Japan has encompassed a variety of approaches, ranging from examinations of their stylistic qualities to political and psychological analyses of their characters. Honda Masuko is regarded as a pioneer in the field of Japanese *shōjoron* (Girls' Study).[9] Her "Hirahira no keifu" (The Genealogy of *Hirahira*), published in 1982,[10] explains the nature of girls' narratives exemplified by fiction writer Yoshiya Nobuko's sentimental prewar stories. According to Honda, Yoshiya's stories are characterized by ephemeral imagery and motifs of flowers and "*hirahira*" (swaying) ribbons; fantasy that enables girl readers to divorce themselves from their social reality.

> In order to gain entry to the world of the girl one must first engage with these "colors, fragrance and sounds." These "signs" are not found in boys' genres.... Boys' culture has been granted a place in ... [the] everyday order with terms such as "boys' idealism" and "guts and grit drama." Girls' culture, on the other hand, has been excluded from all discussion.... As a result, the door of the world of *hirahira* has been closed to all except the girl. Girls have hidden themselves behind this door and let their dreams dance and sway within their closed room.[11]

Girls' fictional world advances different values from those of mainstream culture. Honda contends that the function of girls' fiction is to provide fantasy to the girl audience, and that through reading fantasy stories, girls constantly resist joining the establishment.

Feminist and artist Miyasako Chizuru's *Chōshōjo e* (Towards Super/Beyond-Girl) published in 1989,[12] however, expresses a different judgment on the flowery, frivolous aspects of *shōjo* culture. Miyasako looks at girls as real individuals who may stray outside the stereotype. She criticizes critics' oversimplification in understanding girls' culture.

> *Shōjo* is systematically made. Honda Masuko only explains superficial aesthetics of the self-satisfactory world that is constructed upon the girls' *hirahira* image.... Of course, humans are made up, too, and people are

forced to wear underwear called culture. It is not the aesthetic of *shōjo* culture that we should be discussing today.... *Shōjo* study should focus on *shōjo* by addressing today's women's situation.[13]

Miyasako asserts that *shōjoron* should contain "the message of women's liberation."[14] She considers that not all girls resemble *shōjo*, wearing ribbons and frills, but many of them in fact feel uncomfortable with the stereotypical *shōjo* image. She calls those who cannot accept the conventional image of *shōjo*, *hishōjo* (non-*shōjo*), insisting that these *shōjo* need to be the focus of study.

Yokokawa Sumiko points out that critics attempt to assign a single quality to *shōjo* narratives, as their arguments are sometimes based on binary oppositions such as feminine versus nonfeminine or political versus nonpolitical, debates that merely essentialize the notion of *shōjo*.[15] Literary critic Takahara Eiri's "Shōjogata ishiki"[16] ("The Consciousness of the Girl"), a chapter in his *Shōjo ryōiki* (The Territory of the Girl) published in 1999, introduces a fresh approach to *shōjo* study. He proposes to interpret *shōjo* in terms of attitudes or psyche. Taking works from beyond the boundaries of girls' fiction, written by both male and female authors, in which young women appear as central characters as examples, he addresses *shōjo* characters' propensity for rebellion against the patriarchal system and heterosexual normativity. He coins the psyche of these heroines, as well as that of the writers and readers, "*shōjo* consciousness," characterizing it with the ideas of "freedom and arrogance."[17] Takahara finds the origin of *shōjo* consciousness in the Taishō era (1912–1926), manifested first among young women of the middle and privileged classes, proposing that this consciousness "defied both the national hegemony and economic rationalism."[18] He contends that *shōjo* consciousness is a mode of thinking not confined to girls; therefore, it can be exhibited by men, as well. Takahara's book avoids girls' fiction published in the girls' magazine medium because female gender is premised and normalized in the magazines. Tomoko Aoyama considers that Takahara's theory—*shōjo* as a mode of thinking—can be a "'strategy' to deal with real and important issues."[19] In her "The Genealogy of the 'Girl' Critic Reading Girls," she includes Takahara in the ranks of critics who provide their own unique approaches to the reading of the girl that contest the conventional, patriarchal critical literary framework.[20]

Girls' magazine studies have placed emphasis on readers and the content of magazines, but the personal circumstances of the authors who served as cohorts in the development of magazine culture surely influenced the ideas transmitted by the stories, and therefore are worthy of our attention. One of the goals of this book is to investigate the *shōjo* mentality of these authors and how they expressed it in their stories, expanding the concept beyond Takahara's idea of girls' consciousness. Within the controlled space of magazines, the authors' management of their desires and their educational responsibilities is evident. The girls' genre has been trivialized as being comprised of immature stories for children. However, the low social status of girls allowed authors to deal with socially prohibited opinions and taboos behind the cloak of girls' "immature" narratives. This book will investigate the politics of authors who wrote stories by taking advantage of the social marginality of *shōjo*.

Summary of Chapters

American author Louisa May Alcott's novel *Little Women* is one of the seeds from which the entire history of Japanese *shōjo* fiction grew. Chapter 1 is an examination of the first Japanese translation of *Little Women*, which could be considered the first American work to focus on young adult women.[21] This domestic fiction, published in America at the same time as Japan's Meiji restoration, was translated into Japanese with the title *Shōfujin* (Little Ladies) in 1906, and was regarded as an educational book that taught the marrow of "Good Wife, Wise Mother" ideology. The story follows the development of four sisters who, under the guidance of their wise mother, correct their flaws as they grow into women. Using the vehicle of the Western author's voice, the young female apprentice translator was able to transmit her own dreams and desires. We will examine how she was able to allow *Little Women*'s ambitious heroine Jo March to become a writer at the end of the story, despite how extraordinary this achievement would seem in the conservative culture of Meiji Japan. Over the years, *Little Women* was repeatedly translated into Japanese and serialized in girls' magazines. Each time the portrayal of Jo March was slightly calibrated to fit the audience, and editorial goals, of the period, but the strong, unconventional Jo has always appealed to young female readers and has become a *shōjo* prototype of Japanese girls' fiction, a literary heroine for young female writers.

Jo motivated many young girls who would later become professional writers themselves. They took their first steps into this world as readers and contributing fans of magazines such as *Shōjo sekai* (Girls' World) magazine,[22] which launched in the same year the translation of *Little Women* was published. Chapter 2 examines this magazine and its role in the formation of girls' culture, or *shōjo bunka*. With "Good Wife, Wise Mother" as its educational tenet, this magazine intended to nurture schoolgirls into future domestic women. Editor in chief Numata Rippō, however, also urged young girls to understand the preciousness of the adolescent period they were going through. He attempted to develop ideals for the new concept *shōjo*, and proffered them to his readers in the hope of assisting their smooth growth without being pressured by their future responsibilities. In order to create a family-like atmosphere, he often organized readers' gatherings; a group of enterprising girls, including Kitagawa Chiyo, Yoshiya Nobuko, and Morita Tama, who met at one such get-together soon founded a book reading club and published booklets. These talented young girls eventually flew from his nest to become fiction writers.

The girls' fiction genre was still developing in the 1920s, and writers were trying to come up with suitable material for adolescent girls. Chapter 3 will follow two of the above-mentioned aspiring writers, Yoshiya and Kitagawa, and look at how they contributed to the momentum and diversification of girls' fiction. Although Yoshiya and Kitagawa emerged from the same circle of girls, they each found their own areas of interest and cultivated individual themes and writing styles. Yoshiya depicted tales of same-sex love in her sentimental writings and provided young readers with romantic dreams. Kitagawa wrote about the reality of working-class girls in simple undecorated language, teaching readers about the class inequality of society. Despite their differences, however, Yoshiya and Kitagawa were both motivated by discontent with a society that exploited women, girls, children, and the socially weak. Yoshiya's escapism was a sign of resistance against patriarchy, and Kitagawa's harsh stories about helpless girls were critiques of the class system. Diversity in the genre of girls' fiction pushed girls' magazines forward to further prosperity.

Chapter 4 shifts focus from magazine stories to literary works targeted at a wider audience. Semi-autobiographical works by Yoshiya and Morita display the influence of *Seitō* (Bluestocking), the first Japanese feminist group. This group was born in 1911, and the magazine *Seitō* members published became an arena in which feminist dialogues took place about such ideas as marriage, sexuality, and motherhood. The power of these "new women" stimulated young girls like Yoshiya and Morita. Yoshiya's *Yaneura no nishojo* (Two Virgins in the Attic) and Morita's *Ishikari Otome* (Ishikari Maiden) portray young girls' struggles in patriarchal culture. In these works, heroines refuse to submit to gender normativity or their predefined future roles. They eventually find ways to develop into women without extinguishing their *shōjo* spirits. The words *otome* and *shojo* (*shojo* meaning maiden or virgin, as distinct from *shōjo* meaning "girl"), included in the story titles and both indicating maidenhood, imply the heroines' pledge to be faithful to their *shōjo* identity and the declaration of a modern womanhood different from the conventional. While these stories contain elements of the girls' fiction observed in girls' magazines, the application of *Seitō* feminist discourses can be perceived as well. The examination of these works reveals the potential of girls' fiction to be elevated to *shōjo* literature possessed of political and artistic distinction.

Eventually, dark clouds cast their shadow over the landscape of girls' culture. In 1938, the National Mobilization Law was issued and magazines were obliged to support the war. The role of print media was critical in the government's effort to gain the public's support of the war, and tremendous pressure was placed on girls' magazines. Chapter 5 will look at the transformation of *Shōjo no tomo* (Girls' Friend),[23] which was the most popular girls' magazine in the 1930s. Yoshiya Nobuko and future Nobel Prize recipient Kawabata Yasunari were star writers for this magazine, and emerging illustrator Nakahara Jun'ichi's contributions added to the magazine's flowery and modern air. As the war situation intensified, however, the magazine was forced to wipe fantasy and Western images from its pages, and instead to publish war propaganda. The readers, editor, and writers were initially confused and frustrated, but they eventually succumbed to war culture. For example, although Yoshiya alleged the peaceful nature of women and opposed male violence in her stories, she cooperated with the government's efforts to colonize Asia during the war. Other writers ended up collaborating with the government as well. Kawabata Yasunari, who had worked for children's education, eventually became a promoter of Japanese-language education in Japan's colonies throughout Asia during the war. Kitagawa Chiyo and her contemporary Tsuboi Sakae, both socialists, came to support the military state through their stories published in *Shōjo kurabu* (Girls' Club), which instructed girls how to contribute to the war through labor. The image of a dreamy *shōjo* was transformed into a *gunkoku shōjo*, a girl of the military nation.

The war ended with the defeat of Japan in August 1945. On the world stage it was the end of the old and the beginning of the new, and the same applied to the realm of girls' culture as the next generation decided its direction. The allied forces led by the United States of America occupied Japan to rehabilitate the Japanese. Media was utilized to introduce American democratic values into Japanese society, and girls' magazines were no exception. Chapter 6 will examine *Himawari* (Sunflower),[24] a girls' magazine founded by Nakahara Jun'ichi, the beloved illustrator from the prewar era. Respected writers and educators, including Yoshiya (who wrote an inaugural essay), Kawabata, and Muraoka Hanako (who is famous for her translation of *Anne of Green Gables*) joined the magazine. The stories and articles mirror some of the writers' ambivalent feelings toward the American presence in Japan and its influence; they knew that it was necessary for Japan to change, but could not help lament the disappearance of old culture. Kawabata's

Hana to kosuzu (Flower and Small Bell) is saturated with his escapist nostalgia for the purity and beauty of traditional Japan through the portrayal of a melancholic young dancing girl. But contrary to the reluctant adults, girl readers, who welcomed American culture, proceeded enthusiastically toward the new Japan. The sales of *Himawari*, a magazine that had been an arena in which the writers and editors struggled through the acceptance of Japan's Western future, declined, and it ceased publication in 1952, the last year of the occupation.

With the passing of a few decades, the wheel turned again, and a new generation of young female writers, arising from the ranks of magazine readers as had their forebears, shifted from wholeheartedly embracing to critically examining the state of their new society. Chapter 7 will look at girls' fiction written in the 1980s, an era that was called the "women's age." Shūeisha's *Cobalt* magazine[25] was originally created to celebrate the increasing independence of and career opportunities for women. Although the new social and economic strength of women, approaching materialistic extremes, gained attention in the media, in reality young women were still bound by the notion of traditional Japanese family and pressured by their families to marry. Himuro Saeko, who wrote many stories for *Cobalt* and its book series, was one such woman.[26] Her *Za chenji* (The Change) and *Nante suteki ni japanesuku* (How Splendid Japanesque) could be read as her reactions to traditional female gender roles and social conventions. She shifts the setting of her stories to the distant past of the Heian period but satirizes the new excess, as well as the persistent conservativeness, of contemporary Japanese society, filtered through the cultural sense of 1980s girls. Her works were entertaining and funny; they were written in colloquial language and accompanied by illustrations that could be enjoyed much like those in *shōjo* manga. These features function to mitigate the harshness of her social criticism, becoming important features of the evolving *shōjo* literary style.

The way of *shōjo*, surviving several variations to its form, had persisted on the pages of girls' magazines for the better part of a century, nurturing and influencing women writers even outside the girls literature domain and beyond the topic of young girlhood. Chapter 8 looks at mainstream writer Tanabe Seiko, an ardent fan of Yoshiya Nobuko who had immersed herself in girls' magazine culture in her youth. Her *Ubazakari* (Blooming Old Woman) series of short story collections gives us an opportunity to investigate the influence that girls' culture and fiction have provided Tanabe in her writing. At seventy-six years of age, the series heroine Yamamoto Utako is no child, but elderly women have some commonalities with young girls; *shōjo* and *rōjo* (elderly women) are both treated as marginal beings in society. Although she herself lives comfortably, Utako's role is to be a listener for those who suffer at home due to the heavy domestic responsibilities that aged women shoulder in the present modern family system. Humor, supporting the fantasy of Utako's fortunate and idealized lifestyle in contrast with others in her social group, is utilized as Tanabe's literary tool to vividly criticize Japanese cultural conventions. As in the stories that had come before, fantasy is used to mitigate the harshness of the commentary on society by characters on its periphery.

The notion of *shōjo*, which was "discovered" at the turn of the twentieth century with the introduction of Western girls' education, has developed and diversified in meaning in today's consumer culture. *Shōjo* culture is no longer owned by schoolgirls, but is appreciated by women of all generations. Clothing and goods bearing illustrations and designs of Nakahara Jun'ichi are purchased even today by women of all ages. Prince Edward Island in Canada, the travel destination for fans of *Anne of Green Gables*, is even more popular among mothers and daughters because of the 2014 NHK morning television drama *Hanako to An* (Hanako and Anne).[27] A 2014–2016 exhibition tour of the *shōjo* manga magazine *Margaret* (founded in 1963 by Shūeisha)[28] was a tremendous success; women young and old swarmed to its venues. These phenomena suggest that the *shōjo* imagination cultivated in girls stays with them forever. *Shōjo* culture has served as an important realm that allows girls and women to explore thoughts and ideas that are alternative, radical, revolutionary, and fun. Girls' narratives, which have constantly exhibited values different from the mainstream, have influenced women's culture, art, and literature. This book will showcase the coherent historical and cultural trajectory of Japanese girls' magazine culture. We will start with the dawn of the age of *shōjo*, observing its eventual growth beyond boundaries of time and place.

CHAPTER ONE

Shōfujin (*Little Women*)
Re-creating Jo for the Female Audience in Meiji Japan

In 1868, after over 200 years of isolation, Japan ended the feudal system and opened its borders to other countries, ushering in a period of rapid westernization and industrialization. This same year saw the publication in America of *Little Women* by Louisa May Alcott (1832–1888),[1] daughter of Amos Bronson Alcott, a leading figure of the American transcendentalist movement.[2] The heartwarming story of the four March sisters' growth into womanhood at the time of the absence of their father during the American Civil War is a semi-autobiographical work. It became a best seller and created a sensation on the American literary scene, proving to the public that a woman could be successful in the male-dominated world of the publishing industry.[3] *Little Women*'s reputation traveled around the world, and the work was translated into various languages, including Japanese.

This section will examine *Shōfujin*, the first Japanese translation of *Little Women*, to see how its female translator strove for the best means to render the world of the novel without deviating from Meiji cultural female codes and to fulfill her directive to deliver the *ryōsai kenbo* educational ideology. The translation nevertheless conveyed the potential of adolescent girls through its introduction of the ambitious heroine, Jo March (translated as Shindō Takayo) to the young female Japanese audience.

As early as 1897, Louisa May Alcott was introduced as the most celebrated American fiction writer in *Jogaku zasshi* in Japan.[4] *Shōfujin*[5] was adapted in 1906 by a novice female translator named Kitada Shūho.[6] Kitada must have been a well-educated woman. She might have been an artist, judging from the fact that an illustration in this book is drawn by Kitada. Unfortunately, no information about Kitada is available today. Although hers was the first translation of the book, *Little Women* has been translated many times since then, usually under the title *Wakakusa monogatari* (Stories of Young Grass),[7] and the fact

1

Figure 1.1. Front cover of *Shōfujin*. The text on the upper right credits forewords by Tsubouchi Shōyo and Aeba Kōson. The publisher's name, *Saiunkaku*, is written on the left. The stamp on the lower right indicates the date, December 28, 1906, when a copy of the book was provided to the Imperial Library by the Department of the Interior. Courtesy of Kokuritsu Kokkai Toshokan.

that Kitada's version exists is hardly known. *Shōfujin* is not a skillfully translated work. However, when viewed in the light of the Meiji era, this abbreviated translation can teach us much about girls' education during that period.

Good Wife, Wise Mother Ideology in *Shōfujin*

Shōfujin was published at a time when girls' schools were proliferating. Most schools upheld the *ryōsai kenbo* ideology as their educational goal.[8] Women's *ryōsai kenbo* education substantially aided the government in the creation of an industrialized and militaristic nation, particularly during the Sino-Japanese War (1894–1895) and the Russo-Japanese War (1904–1905). Stronger family unity equated to stronger state unity,[9] and the wars required women to encourage patriotic sentiment at home. Home life, therefore, was put in service of the state, at the cost of women's independence. Sharon H. Nolte and Sally A. Hastings state that during these years, "[s]tate propaganda exhorted women to contribute to the nation

Figure 1.2. Illustration for *Shōfujin* by Kitada Shūho. Courtesy of Kokuritsu Kokkai Toshokan.

through their hard work, their frugality, their efficient management, their care of the old, young, and ill, and their responsible upbringing of children. The significance of these functions did not entitle them to political rights, however."[10] They argue that "the Japanese cult of productivity... was significantly different from the American cult of domesticity"[11] of Alcott's era, which identified the home as a female sphere and expected women to be religious and virtuous.[12] According to Fukaya Masashi's research, the *ryōsai kenbo* ideology was a historical amalgam of Western ideals, Japanese Confucianism, and nationalism.[13] Home was designated as part of the nation; the concept of "Familial Nationhood" (*kazoku kokkakan*) was created, which situated the Emperor as the "father" and the whole nation as one big family. Women were still forced to accept unequal hierarchical relationships in society and confinement to the sphere of domesticity. Not only that, but the *ryōsai kenbo* ideology taught women their new responsibilities as Japanese citizens. The goal of *Shōfujin* was not to show women's domestic power or independence, but to emphasize that their place was in the home, implanting in readers' minds the awareness that they were not only *ie no musume* (daughters of domesticity) but also *kuni no musume* (daughters of the nation).[14]

Women's education was strictly for the purpose of domestic reform, a national priority that was explicitly entrusted to women. Gender roles in domesticity came to be defined and demarcated. Child rearing in Japan was not originally defined as a woman's role.[15] Kathleen S. Uno elaborates: "[f]rom the Tokugawa period into the mid-twentieth century, both productive work, which sustained the *ie* (stem-family household) by producing essential goods and income, and reproductive work (childrearing, cooking, and housekeeping), which maintained *ie* members, took place at home. The proximity of production and reproduction allowed men, women, and children alike to participate in tasks crucial to the household's survival."[16]

However, in the Meiji era, a division of labor based on gender—husbands working outside the home and wives staying home, in charge of domestic chores and child nurturing—was introduced, defining women as domestic beings. After the Meiji period, domestic work came to be the responsibility of women. Women were to utilize what they had learned at school to manage the chores and home economy as good wives, and, as wise mothers, deliver home education, called *katei kyōiku*, in order to raise children who would shoulder responsibility for the country's future. We can assume *Little Women* was utilized for the development of qualities of ideal womanhood in Japanese schoolgirls.

This educational aspect is emphasized in the two prefaces written by respected fiction writers and translators Tsubouchi Shōyō[17] and Aeba Kōson.[18] They endorsed *Shōfujin* as a good home novel (*katei no yomimono*) worthy of recommendation to its female audience. It is interesting to see that *Shōfujin* was supported by these significant literary figures.[19] Aeba describes this "pure and beautiful" book as suitable for "*fujoshi*" (young women and children), continuing that "although the translation is careless and still immature, it is unique in the sense that it truthfully portrays innocent little ladies."[20] As literacy increased around the turn of the twentieth century, the target audiences of home novels were women and children, newly emerging readers at that time. Aeba demarcates women's literature from men's, "authentic" literature, corralling women and children within the confines of domesticity and segregating them from the mainstream literary world. Despite their favorable views of *Shōfujin*, an attitude of male patronization by both Aeba and Tsubouchi toward female writers, translators, and readers is evident. Kitada Shūho translated *Little Women* without deviating from literary conventions or social norms, perhaps doing her best to loyally play her role as a "female translator" for a "female audience."

Kitada's statement of the goal of *Shōfujin* in her preface conforms closely to the principles of *ryōsai kenbo*.

> This book is an abridged translation of *Little Women*, written by Miss Alcott, who is very famous in the American literary world. The original work is full of great writing.... This beautifully written book should be taken as a home primer which teaches *shūshin* (morals) and *seika* (wise governance of family affairs).[21]

Shōfujin introduced the Japanese female audience to Western lifestyle and the image of a Western home. It also taught female virtues and modern women's expected roles and enhanced responsibilities at home.

Introduction of the Idea of Western Home and Women's Roles

The novel contains descriptions of an ideal Western culture from which Japanese people at that time were trying to learn. The parts of the original that touched on educational issues such as women's virtues and morals were translated faithfully, so that readers could learn and internalize them as they read the story.

The idea of "home" was a focus among intellectuals in nineteenth-century America. The role of the white middle-class American woman prior to 1860 had been encapsulated in the concept of the "cult of domesticity." While accepting the notion that their position was in the home, women later maneuvered this role into one of power. Daniel Scott Smith states,

> [I]nstead of postulating women as an atom in competitive society, domestic feminism viewed woman as a person in the context of relationships with others. By defining the family as a community, this ideology allowed

women to engage in something of a critique of male, materialistic, market society and simultaneously proceed to seize power within the family.[22]

Little Women was written amid this social change. Alcott put forward a new image of young women and illustrated how their powerful and attractive qualities were cultivated at home.[23]

These ideas of "home" and women's domestic leadership were new for Japanese in the early Meiji period. The Japanese *ie* system, based on Confucian principles, originated in the samurai class in the Edo period and came to be institutionalized in a patriarchal sphere controlled by the hierarchized relationships of family members.

> The *ie* is not simply a contemporary household as its English counterpart suggests, but is conceptualized in the time continuum from past to future, including not only the actual residential members but also dead members, with some projection also towards those yet unborn.[24]

In the *ie* system, the primary concern of the family members was to hand down their family name to the next generation. The role of women was to serve their husbands, parents-in-law, and sons, their primary responsibility being reproduction.

The concept of the Western home was first introduced to Japan by Protestant reformers around 1880.[25] Iwamoto Yoshiharu, editor of the *Jogaku zasshi*, was a prominent figure in this effort. An editorial in 1889 explains the difference between a Western "home" and a Japanese "*ie*" thus.

> When I look at Japanese homes, they look like administrative offices. When I look at a Western home, it looks like a hot spring resort. In the former image, guests are welcomed by a host in formal attire, and in the latter, the host sits in a rocking chair and chats with guests at ease.[26]

The following passage from an article published in *Chūō kōron* (Central Review) in 1902 describes the importance of the family getting together.

> Family mealtimes must always be harmonious and taken together.... Indeed, when all family members eat together at one big table, it can be called a true harmonious family ... certainly this will foster a sense of equality in the family.[27]

That family members would gather at the same table and dine while talking to each other was a new and unimaginable concept to Japanese people. However, the terms *katei* (家庭: *ka* 家 meaning home and *tei* 庭 meaning garden) and *hōmu* (ホーム: home), each of which signifies a friendlier sphere than *ie*, were widespread by 1890.[28] By 1900, these concepts were probably no longer new to Japanese readers, but *Little Women* was a perfect reinforcement for the values of this new home or *katei*.[29] In *Shōfujin*, Kitada uses expressions such as *hōmu suīto hōmu* (home sweet home) and *madoi* (happy home), which abounded in *Jogaku zasshi* and other young women's magazines of the time.

The fun and intimate atmosphere of home portrayed at the beginning of *Little Women* is faithfully translated in *Shōfujin*. The story starts with a scene in which the four sisters gather on Christmas Eve[30] and wait for their mother to return home. When the mother arrives, they joyfully crowd around her. In a homey and peaceful atmosphere, the mother takes out a letter she has just received from her husband, who is serving as a chaplain at the battle front, and reads it aloud. Missing their father, the daughters listen to it with restrained emotion. Home is characterized here as an intimate space in which the characters emotionally support each other and ease each other's fear and loneliness. The special atmosphere of home is symbolically illustrated by the next-door neighbor, Toshio. He describes how he sometimes enjoys looking at the Shindō family home and seeing through the window, with a touch of envy, the family gathered around the fire.[31] Like a mother, the female space of the home protects children and provides a sense of security.

A mother was expected to be "guardian of the interior" and "queen of the home" (*hōmu no jōō*): "Her mission in life was to make a nurturing shelter for her children and a blissful refuge for her husband, a sanctuary where he might come to escape the violent challenges of the outside world."[32] Western books on education were translated in great numbers at this time,[33] and Japanese mothers were expected to become experts in the knowledge of modern child-rearing.

Shōfujin illustrates an ideal image of a mother, teaching its readers exactly how mothers should behave at home and educate their daughters. As in *Little Women*, the mother's main responsibility is assigned as training her daughters to become future housewives. She teaches them the importance of domestic chores such as cooking, cleaning, and sewing.[34] In one scene the girls say they are tired of doing the same chores every day. The mother lets them abandon their daily chores for a week; as a result, the home becomes a mess, and the girls start to feel uncomfortable in their idleness. Consequently, they change their minds and come to appreciate their work. The mother states that "work is wholesome, and there is plenty for everyone; it keeps us from ennui and mischief, is good for health and spirits, and gives us a sense of power and independence better than money or fashion."[35] From her statement, we can perceive her sense of domestic feminism and pride in her ordained job. The story's sundry episodes emphasize values such as hard work, frugality, and philanthropy.[36]

Another role of the mother is to listen to her daughters and give advice. The mother cautions Kikue (Meg), who has a materialistic streak and is fascinated with wealthy society, explaining that money is not the most important thing in this world, and teaching her the importance of self-respect and honesty. In another scene, Takayo(Jo) discloses to her mother that her weakness is her inability to control her temper. The mother tells her to pray to God, easing Takayo's restless mind (in the original, the mother goes on to explain how she herself fights and overcomes her own temper, revealing her weakness as a human. However, in the Japanese translation, this part is omitted, presumably to emphasize the authority and strength of the parent). The mother is portrayed as a respected female role model, *ryōsai kenbo*. She is the moral and religious center in the home. The mother's compassion and love guide her daughters along the righteous path, turning them into good, moral human beings.

Overcoming numerous trials and hardships, the daughters of both *Shōfujin* and *Little Women* cultivate sisterhood and come to appreciate the value of home. Despite some minor omissions and occasional paraphrasing, the parts of Kitada's translation that touch on women's education and the role of the mother follow the original faithfully.

However, Alcott's vision of the ideal home only corresponded with the new Meiji way of thinking up to a point. A fundamental gap between the Western notion of home and that developed by the Japanese still existed. In some sense the Japanese home remained a public sphere, under the control of the Meiji government even after the introduction of the Western home, a friendly and relaxing private space.

In the final chapter of *Shōfujin*, Kitada clearly presents this Japanese ideal of home, which is quite different from Alcott's. In both American and Japanese versions of the final chapter of part I, the heroine's younger sister, who has suffered from scarlet fever and lingered between life and death, finally gets better thanks to her sisters' care and fervent prayers during the absence of their parents. In the American version, the parents' return in this chapter is almost a reward for the girls, for it brings them ultimate happiness. Their father is warmly welcomed by them. Witnessing the changes in his daughters, whom he has not seen for a long time, he comments on each girl's development with praise. For instance, he remarks, "I don't see the 'son Jo' whom I left a year ago.... I see a young lady.... I rather miss my wild girl, but if I get a strong, helpful, tender hearted woman in her place, I shall feel quite satisfied."[37] The mother's home education has transformed the tomboy, Jo, into a virtuous woman who meets the father's standards, and likewise the other sisters have matured. The March family dines and sings happily together at the end. With the return of the father, home becomes complete, and with the father's comments on the girls' development, their journey to womanhood ends.[38]

However, unlike in *Little Women*, the father's comments on the four sisters' growth are omitted in *Shōfujin*. At the end of the story, the father briefly states, "It must have been difficult for you without me. Also, the past few weeks, your mother was away from home. You really stuck to it. Now, the hardship is over and you can have a moment of joy."[39] The father does not touch upon the daughters' development, but only praises their domestic perseverance. The story hastens to a conclusion with these words: "Sunset shone through the window glass, as if to give this happy family a moment of fun. They surrounded the hearth and each told her story in turn. It was just like paradise on earth."[40] Despite this happy ending, it can be understood that the four girls of *Shōfujin* are still confined within the sphere of the home, never being allowed to grow up into mature women. As Kishida Toshiko (1863–1901), writer and political activist for women's rights, stated in her lecture, "Daughters in Boxes," Japanese girls are like "creatures kept in a box. They may have hands and feet and a voice—but all to no avail, because their freedom is restricted."[41] As if the translator is assuring the reader that she will not allow the girls too much power, she keeps them under the surveillance of their parents. The second volume of Alcott's book, in which the girls start to marry and leave home, is not included in Kitada's translation. Home, ostensibly a safe haven for women and children, was, at a deeper level, a cloaked arm of the state, limiting their lives in Meiji Japan.

In Kitada's rendition, *Little Women*'s American setting was changed to Japan, following one of the translation conventions of the Meiji period. The consolidation of the concept of modern literature and the technique of translation was still at an early stage. The characters' ages are counted according to traditional Japanese reckoning in which one year is added at every New Year. Meg, originally sixteen, is changed to seventeen years old, and Jo, originally fifteen, to sixteen. In another example, the ballroom dance party that was held on New Year's Eve in the original is changed to January 15, which was the traditional Japanese New Year according to the old calendar. The Western names of characters and geographical locations are replaced by Japanese names, instead of merely phonetically converting them into Japanese katakana characters. The March family name is changed to Shindō; it would not have escaped readers' attention that the first character chosen for this name (*shin* 進) commonly appears in words with the sense of "progress" or "moving forward." Margaret, the beautiful oldest girl, is named Kikue (*kiku* 菊

means chrysanthemum). Josephine, the tall and skinny tomboyish heroine, is called Takayo (the character for *taka* 孝 means duty to parents; this interpretation of her name will be discussed later). Just as Josephine prefers to be called by the boyish name Jo, Takayo goes by the male name Takashi. Elizabeth, a shy and sickly girl, is named Tsuyuko (*tsuyu* 露 means dew). But the youngest girl, the precocious Amy, is named Emiko, simply for the phonetic resemblance. Some of these changes introduce contradictions, which contributes to the technically unsophisticated impression that *Shōfujin* gives. The beautiful hair of Takashi is described as full and "blond,"[42] despite the fact that she is supposed to be Japanese and should have black hair. Also, in a scene in which Takashi has an argument over a croquet game with an English boy who tries to cheat, she tells him that "(we) Americans will never lie,"[43] instead of "Japanese." Backgrounds of culture and nationality are left ambiguous and not completely harmonized.

Shōfujin is simplified for the young audience (presumably schoolgirls[44]), stripping the story of many characters and narratives. References to classical British literary works are either omitted or explained in simple language. The sections that touch on *Pilgrim's Progress*, which represents the subtext of the sisters' journey toward womanhood, are cut. Also, the subject of romantic love is dropped. In the original story, Meg (Margaret) falls in love with Mr. Brooke, the private tutor of her neighbor, and they eventually get married. The development of their romantic relationship is an important part of the story and a significant factor in understanding the character's growth into a mature woman; however, the romance and its implications are completely erased from *Shōfujin*. Even the part in which the mother discusses her image of ideal marriage is omitted. At the time in Japan the idea of chastity loomed over schoolgirls. Both physical and spiritual purity before marriage were emphasized in girls' school textbooks and magazines. As girls stayed longer at school, the average age for marriage rose. According to Watanabe Shūko, the state power felt it necessary to control female sexuality to avoid the risk that illegitimate sons would bring disorder to the patriarchal family system.[45] It appears that Kitada erred on the side of caution and avoided the issue of romance entirely. Through omission, simplification and modification, *Shōfujin* became a somewhat different text from *Little Women*.

Transformation of Jo into Takashi

Due to its modification and simplification, not only did *Shōfujin* become a different text from *Little Women*, but it also lost some of the richness of the portrayal of the original characters. Nevertheless, Takashi survives as an interesting figure in the sense that Kitada shows her special attachment to this character by adding her own interpretation of her.

Jo March in *Little Women* is illustrated as an ambitious young girl who aspires to become a writer. She is a tomboy, refusing to behave like a woman. An active and free-spirited character, Jo is considered one of the first heroines to break away from the image of vulnerable heroines of nineteenth-century sentimental literary tradition.[46] The emergence of a tomboy character is related to the cultural changes of the time. During the Civil War women were encouraged to be healthy and active. The importance of physical exercise for young girls was stressed for the sake of creating vigorous mothers of the future, who would provide resources for the nation.[47] The tomboy quality was in fact encouraged. Jo was consequently accepted as a prototype American heroine for the new era.

Shindō Takayo (Takashi) in *Shōfujin* is similarly depicted as a tomboy, which Kitada translates as *otenba*. *Otenba*, before 1900, had never been seen in a positive light.[48] *Otenba* characters in girls' stories were portrayed as wild and unsophisticated. Their unwomanly behavior often ended up being punished.[49] Kume Yoriko explains that stories which dealt with *otenba* were mostly cautionary tales, teaching the readers that they could never escape the idea that they were the "daughters of home."[50] Around the start of the Russo-Japanese War, however, this view changed. Just like in America, the health and physical strength of girls became a center of attention for educators. For the creation of strong future mothers, the government encouraged girls to exercise and be more active. Educators also showed concern for Japanese girls' physical inferiority and psychological vulnerability compared with Western girls. In 1909, in an article called "Shōjo no chikara" (The Strengths of Girls) in *Shōjo sekai*, an anonymous writer encourages girls to be active, studious, and independent.

> The term *shōjo* has come to be acknowledged recently.... It is important for girls to read many books and widen their knowledge and, at the same time, they should improve their behavior. They can be equal to boys, so they should try their best to show their power. If girls can behave modestly and beautifully, and also excel in study, it is fine whether they are called *otenba* or *haikara* (stylish).[51]

Being *otenba* was acceptable as long as girls understood traditional female virtues and social roles. Their lively quality was believed to positively influence society. An article titled "Beikoku no jogakusei" (American Schoolgirls) published in *Shōjo sekai* in 1907 explained how relaxed, cheerful, and active American schoolgirls were in contrast to Japanese girls, who were extremely shy.[52] It encouraged girls to be more active. Japanese schoolgirls were considered a sort of gauge in measuring the level of advancement and civilization of Japan; thus, they were strongly encouraged to catch up to the level of Western girls both physically and mentally.

Both Takashi and Jo's portrayals as active and strong-willed characters were acceptable, partly due to the political circumstances of each country at the time of the story's release. Nevertheless, if we examine the description of their tomboy qualities in detail, there are important differences between the two. Whereas Jo is described as having boyish qualities, there is much more emphasis on Takashi's maleness and rejection of femaleness. In the opening chapter of the story, the four sisters are introduced to the readers. Jo (Takashi) behaves in an unwomanly fashion; she puts her hands in her pockets and begins to whistle. She is scolded by her sister Amy (Emi) (emphasis in corresponding words and sentences are mine).

"Don't Jo, it's so boyish." [a] "That's why I do it."

"I detest rude, unladylike girls!"

"I hate affected, niminy-piminy chits! [b] . . ."

". . . you should remember that you are a young lady."

"I'm not! [c] And if turning up my hair makes me one, I'll wear it in two tails till I'm twenty," cried Jo, pulling off her net, and shaking down a chestnut mane. "I hate to think I've got to grow up, and be Miss March, . . . [d] It's bad enough to be a girl, anyway, when I like boys' games and work and manners! I can't get over my disappointment in not being a boy." [e]⁵³

—*Little Women*

Emi: "Stop, Takashi, You are like a man." [a]

Takashi: "What's wrong with that?"

Emi: "You are so rough. You are unladylike. . . . I hate it!"

Takashi: "It's none of your business. I hate affectation and weakness. That's nonsense." [b] . . .

Kiku: ". . . You should remember that you're now . . . a young lady."

Takashi: "I hate being a lady [c] . . . If turning up my hair means that I am a lady, I'm not going to do it. I'll wear it in two tails till I'm twenty"; she pulled out her hairpins and shook down her full blond hair.

Takashi: "I feel terrible to think that I have grown up . . . I hate it so much that I can't stand it. [d] I love childish games. I hate to be called Miss . . . I wish I were a man." [e]⁵⁴

—*Shōfujin*

Jo and Takashi's rejections of their development into women and hatred of being viewed as ladies are both emphasized. But the Japanese text places more stress on the strength of Takashi's rejection, using additional expressions such as "that's nonsense" (*bakabakashii*) [b] and "I hate it so much that I can't stand it" (*iyade iyade tamaranai*) [d], and using strong words such as "detest" (*daikirai*) [c]. Also, Jo's boyish quality is replaced in Takashi's case by a mannish one as we can see in the statements "you are like a man" (*otoko mitai*) [a][55] and "I wish I were a man" (*otoko ni umaretakatta*) [e].[56]

Takashi's virile quality is further emphasized in the text. In characterizing Takashi's appearance, Kitada writes that she is "big and male-like,"[57] while Alcott describes Jo as "big, harum-scarum."[58] Similarly, Takashi is described to be a girl with a "dark face" and a kind "masculine voice";[59] contrastingly, the original text says of Jo that "her face was very friendly and her sharp voice unusually gentle,"[60] making no mention of Jo's masculinity. Jo retains some girlish quality, but Takashi is sketched to be rather androgynous.

In these corresponding passages from the two versions, Takashi's physical maturation into a woman is denied, while Jo's physical development as an adolescent girl is hinted at. The following is from *Little Women* (emphasis mine):

> Her long, thick hair was her one beauty, but it was usually bundled into a net, to be out of her way. Round shoulders had Jo, big hands and feet, a flyaway look to her clothes, and the uncomfortable appearance of a girl who was rapidly shooting up into a woman and didn't like it.[61]

In *Shōfujin*, however, the underlined parts above are arranged as follows (emphasis mine):

> Takashi's only beauty was long and thick hair, but she did not care for it, and she usually put it in a net. She did not have any maiden-like quality; she rather hated to be feminine.[62]

The phrase "uncomfortable appearance of a girl who was rapidly shooting up," the indication of a young female adolescent body, is omitted in *Shōfujin*. Takashi does not show any sign of physical femininity.

The quality of beauty is omitted in the portrayal of Takashi, as well. Takashi denies her beauty by stating that "I am neither quiet nor pretty,"[63] whereas in the original text, Jo simply says "I am not quiet and nice."[64] According to Watanabe Shūko, caring about one's own beauty was thought to be important etiquette in Japanese *ryōsai kenbo* education. Female beauty, called *biiku* (cultivation of beauty), was often discussed in women's magazines. A woman's appearance was regarded as being connected to her inner beauty. It was deemed important for women to improve their appearance as well as their spiritual aspects in order to become perfect women. Women, after all, needed to be loved and chosen by future husbands.[65] Takashi's denial of beauty, therefore, is unconventional. What was the intention of the translator in painting her that way?

In a way, Takashi's symbolic action of cutting her hair answers the question. As in the original story, in order to make money for her mother's trip to see her sick husband, Takashi sells her long hair to a barber shop. Cutting hair is a motif commonly used to describe a woman's absolute love and sacrifice. In Japanese culture, Takashi's action carries additional meaning. The way women's hair was pulled up and arranged indicated a woman's age, social level, marriage status, and so on.[66] It was even illegal in 1872 for women to cut their hair short without legitimate reason.[67] Although in the 1920s bobbed hair started to become a symbol of modern girls, in the late Meiji era, short hair was still rare, particularly as *hisashigami* (low pompadour hairstyle) or braided tails tied with a ribbon was a typical schoolgirls' fashion. Takashi's action is regarded as outrageous; she is ridding herself of her identity as a young girl. Nevertheless, Takashi's action is not reproached. That is because her strong will, courage, and selfless love were favorably received in the context of wartime society. Takashi's self-sacrifice for her parents is seen as being in the same spirit with that of the barber's son who is enlisting in the war. Takashi bears two important virtues, *kō* (duty to the parents) and *chū* (loyalty to the nation), Confucian virtues which had been held as precious since the premodern era. Interestingly, the Chinese character, *kō* 孝, which also reads as *taka*, is used for Takashi's name. It must be Kitada's intention to portray Takashi as a loyal and patriotic character through her name, which means a dutiful child. Takashi's patriotic sprit is also witnessed in her statement that "if I were a man, I could have gone to the battlefield with my father."[68] Takashi's courage is viewed in a positive light, even though her statement sounds too mannish. She deviates from the conventional female image, yet she is forgiven because of her loyal, devoted, and self-sacrificial nature.

At the same time, Takashi's drastic action of cutting her hair short has another meaning. It foreshadows the fact that she will follow through with her original intention of becoming a professional writer and live in a male world. The translator, Kitada, depicts Takashi as a masculine character, so that Takashi can achieve her dream to become a writer, a profession still categorized in the male domain.

In America, the late nineteenth century might be called the age of "scribbling women";[69] many female professional writers emerged and made names for themselves. Although they were trivialized by male writers, their books sold very well and helped support the American publishing industry. Alcott was the very model of a successful female writer. She had her protagonist, Jo March, follow a path similar to her own.

Although in smaller numbers than their American counterparts, Japanese women also started to choose fiction writing as an occupation in the Meiji era. In 1895–1896, *Bungei kurabu* (Literary Club) magazine published two special issues that introduced emerging young female writers, calling them *keishū sakka* (talented literary women).[70] Such writers as Higuchi Ichiyō, Wakamatsu Shizuko, and Miyake Kaho were introduced and their photos published. Despite the fame of these female writers, the publishing world was still controlled by men and their standards. As Kan Satoko points out, women writers were commercial products and were viewed as targets of desire; people were interested in their appearance instead of their talents.[71] In order to keep writing, they could never deviate from the literary genres assigned to them; that is, literature for women or children. Their priority was to perform their mission "within the boundaries of their 'domestic realm.'"[72]

We find that Kitada supports Takashi's dreams as much as she can in *Shōfujin*. She tries to truthfully translate Jo's ambition and passion for writing. She even pushes the envelope by allowing Takashi to express her *risshi* (ambition), desire for fame and success; "I want to do something splendid... something heroic or wonderful that won't be forgotten after I'm dead.... I think I shall write books, and get rich and famous."[73] At a time when only men and boys were "candidates for '*risshin shusse*' [establishment and advancement of the public self],"[74] Takashi's ambition for success could have been received as conceited or disgraceful. Nevertheless, without hesitation, Kitada conveys her own excitement for writing. When Takashi's story is finally published in a newspaper, Kitada herself seems to celebrating by writing "*keishū sakka Shindōjō banzai!!!*"[75] which in the original text reads, "Hurrah for Miss March, the celebrated American authoress!" "American authoress" is replaced by "*keishū sakka*," the previously mentioned term, which had recently become popularized in Japan. We also see Kitada's excitement in the additional exclamation marks found in the translation. Interestingly, however, while in *Little Women* Jo's publisher tells her that although this time she won't be paid for her story, she would "get the next paid for,"[76] the statement of his promise is omitted in *Shōfujin*. Kitada probably tried to make sure that Takashi would not look conceited or violate the womanly codes by stepping into the male world too assertively. Takashi's portrayal is a compromise between Kitada's own desires and the patriarchal culture of Meiji Japan.

Thus, Jo March, a realistic American heroine, is transformed into Shindō Takayo, an unconventional adolescent Japanese girl. *Shōfujin* is seemingly a book of precepts for its young female readers, but on examination we find in it the translator's textual scheme and even her own ambition.

Kitada Shūho was an apprentice translator whose name did not survive in literary history to influence later generations. By and large, she did not resist Japanese conventions, and translated within the system. However, despite the original editorial intention of domestic education, the world of *Shōfujin* provided its young readers with dreams and stirred within them strong yearnings for Western ways of life. The readers must also have been stirred by the bold and free-spirited heroines, and wished to become girls like Takashi. *Little Women* continued to be translated under different titles,[77] always in a way suited to the culture and audience of the time, surviving as one of the classic *shōjo shōsetsu* (girls' fiction). Coincidentally or not, the beginning of "the age of young girls" soon arrived. Shortly after the publication of *Shōfujin*, young readers of the newly created girls' magazines genre eagerly wrote stories and submitted them to magazines, just like Takashi did. They grew up into Japanese "scribbling women," inheriting the spirit of Jo March.

CHAPTER TWO

Shōjo sekai (Girls' World)
The Formation of Girls' Magazine Culture and the Emergence of "Scribbling Girls"

1906 is memorable in the history of Japanese girls' culture not only as the year *Shōfujin* was published, but also as the year *Shōjo sekai*, one of the most influential girls' magazines, was founded. *Shōjo sekai* achieved a remarkable relationship between the chief editor, Numata Rippō, and his readers, and as a result, a sense of communal spirit formed centering on the publication. The space of the magazine encouraged readers' literary ambitions, as well, and self-motivated girls—such as Kitagawa Chiyo, Muraoka Tamako (Morita Tama), and Yoshiya Nobuko—emerged as writers. Kitagawa Chiyo became a juvenile story writer and later joined the socialist women's group, *Sekirankai* (Red Wave Society). Morita Tama became an essayist and later a politician. Yoshiya Nobuko established herself to be a successful story writer both for girls and mature women. They were once devoted readers of and contributors to this magazine. *Shōjo sekai* was the center of the nascent Japanese girls' magazine culture, which nurtured these "scribbling girls."

This chapter will investigate Numata Rippō and his seminal girls' magazine *Shōjo sekai* during the period roughly from 1906 to 1914. As a mentor, adviser, and almost a surrogate father for the readers, he was a great contributor to the education of Japanese girls and, more importantly, a key person in the formation of Japanese girls' magazine culture. He gave readers a space, both virtual and often actual, where they could meet, gather, and unite girl-to-girl. By doing so he engendered the creation of a girls' community, without which girls wouldn't have conceived of an identity beyond that of daughters of domesticity, confined in the space of the home. This community proved to be a fertile ground from which sprang *shōjo* identity and the way of *shōjo*, which inspired girls to propel themselves to successes even beyond the original intentions of the magazine.

Figure 2.1. Cover of the first issue of *Shōjo sekai* 1, no. 1 (1906). Courtesy of Hakubunkan Shinsha Publishers, Ltd.

Creation of Girls' Magazines

The publication of girls' magazines surged in the early 1900s. Besides *Shōjo sekai*, *Shōjokai* (Girls' Society, founded in 1902), *Shōjo no tomo* (founded in 1908), *Shōjo gahō* (Girls' Illustrated, founded in 1912), *Shōjo kurabu* (founded in 1923), and so on began publication. Obviously *shōjo* is a key term of this era. The word *shōjo* is believed to have come into frequent use after the *kōtō jogakkō rei* (Women's Higher School Act), which standardized female education, was issued in 1899. Before this idea was conceptualized, *shōjo* simply meant prepubescent girls. This new concept of *shōjo* was therefore a cultural concept rather than a physical one. *Shōjo* existed in a period of moratorium,[1] which temporarily released schoolgirls from social obligations such as marriage and reproduction. However, it is important to note here that the number of girls who were fortunate enough to go to school was only 2 percent of the adolescent female population at that time.[2] Most girls could not afford to read magazines, nor did they acknowledge that that they were going through a precious period of time called *shōjo*.

The word *shōnen* 少年 (which now means boys) simply meant "young children" before 1900, and included both boys and girls.[3] Although the term *shōnen* was at the time gender neutral,[4] it is clear that the stories in early schoolchildren's magazines such as *Shōnen sekai* (Boys' World, founded in 1895) were written for and about boys. They delivered nationalistic messages through adventure tales or stories that encouraged the ideology of *risshin shusse*. *Shōnen sekai* had a special section called *shōjoran* (girls' section) for female readers,[5] which eventually spun off to become a new magazine, *Shōjo sekai*, in 1906.[6] *Shōjo* were born as *shōnen*'s *différance*.[7] Imada Erika proposes that the development of these magazines at the turn of the twentieth century helped promote greater cultural differentiation between the genders in children.[8]

Shōjo sekai's readers were schoolgirls in their early teens.[9] Obtaining their own magazine space, the young readers of *Shōjo sekai* were thrilled, and their joy is witnessed in the letters published in the readers' section of the first issue. A girl named Hatsuko states: "*Shōnen sekai* used to be dominated by boys, and I always felt uncomfortable reading it. But now that we have *Shōjo sekai*, I can contribute my writings as much as I can."[10] Young girls were always treated as secondary to boys, but in the space of girls' magazines, they could be the central agents. The separation of magazines based on gender helped girls create their own cultural space, *shōjo bunka* (girls' culture), for the first time.

Shōjo sekai started off under the editorship of Iwaya Sazanami,[11] a famous juvenile story writer. From the second volume, however, due to Iwaya's busy schedule as the editor of *Shōnen sekai*, the chief editor's position was transferred to Numata Rippō,[12] who had previously served as an editor of *Nihon no katei* (Japanese Home), a women's magazine. Numata became a driving force of *Shōjo sekai* and developed it into a rich and lively publication. The magazine's editorial goal is spelled out in the first issue by Atomi Kakei (1840–1926), an educator and the founder of Atomi Jogakkō (Atomi Girls' School).

> The reason why you study at school is because you have to become respectful women and supporters of your husbands in the future.... If you don't receive education, you will be looked down upon as useless beings and never be able to contribute to anything.... Some people say that women do not need education, but that is not true. When you get married and have children, they might ask you some questions; it will be embarrassing if you cannot answer them. If you have education, you can also become good conversation partners for your husbands.[13]

Girls' future roles are clearly defined as mothers and wives here. *Shōjo sekai* was an educational magazine and its basic goal was to deliver the *ryōsai kenbo* ideal. The article titled "Shōjo no sekai" (World of Girls) written by an anonymous writer similarly states: "... if you gain knowledge now, you will be able to become great wives and wise mothers. With superior wives, families will prosper.... Eventually the civilization of the whole country will advance."[14] The article continues to emphasize how influential each girl can be, and concludes by stating that it is time for the readers to show the potential of girls' power to the world. It demonstrates not only the *ryōsai kenbo* ideal but also palpable nationalism. Having gone through the Sino-Japan War and the Russo-Japan War, Japan was embarking on imperial expansion. The government found the most urgent priority was to Westernize Japan, to construct a *kokka* (unified state), and eventually to make people into *kokumin* (Japanese citizens). It was important to educate and modernize girls because in the future they would be useful resources for the nation. Girls' magazines were viewed as a tool for molding them into the state's educational ideal.

There is no doubt that Numata was a promoter of the *ryōsai kenbo* ideal and believed that girls' future roles were to become good wives and wise mothers. However, he also searched for a new manner of education befitting the ages of his readers. He tried to establish *shōjo rashisa* (conventional girls' quality), different from *onna rashisa* (mature women's conventional femininity). Having initially emerged as the "difference" from boys, the concept and image of *shōjo* were not wholly defined yet. Numata tried to clarify this still ambiguous notion, and to create codes and standards for *shōjo*. In an article written in 1908, Numata stated that he expected his readers to become girls with "Japanese maiden's gentle hearts" (*yamato otome no yasashii kokoro*).[15] He placed value on internal quality and associated *shōjo* with inner beauty. He also emphasized that they should become *airashii shōjo* (adorable and likable girls), elaborating the idea thus:

> Why are girls so adorable? . . . Adorableness cannot be intentionally created. If you just try to make yourself look likable on the superficial level, you will not be loved. . . . Be the way you are as *shōjo*. . . . Don't buy books you know you cannot read, and don't pretend that you can read difficult books. . . . Such behavior is not *shōjo* behavior and girls who behave like that will not be loved.[16]

The *shōjo* who would be loved were the ones who were not pretentious or audacious. They were to be gentle and kind, and humble enough to listen to teachers and parents. Kume Yoriko believes that the fact that Numata uses the word *aisareru* (to be loved) instead of *aisuru* (to love) is important, because an *aisareru shōjo* (a girl who is loved) will be chosen by a man in the future and welcomed into the patriarchal family.[17] Although Numata does not use words like *mothers* and *wives*, his ultimate goal was to raise his readers into women who would enter domesticity without complaining or questioning and bring harmony and joy into their homes in the future. For Numata, his magazine was "confectionary which contains nutrition"[18] for his readers; the magazine should be entertaining and at the same time educational. As an educator, he wanted to cultivate girls' good natures and watch them grow healthily. He wanted them to embrace the period of *shōjo*, before entering womanhood.

From Didacticism to Sentimentalism in Girls' Stories

Until this point, girls' stories were dominated by tales that taught readers the importance of endurance, self-sacrifice, and submission to their parents. According to Kume Yoriko's research on girls' stories published in *Shōnen sekai* magazine, prior to the arrival of *Shōjo sekai*, the Meiji era stories taught the readers of the importance of *kō* (obligation to parents) and their position as *ie no musume*, preaching to them that they were under the control of their parents (like the messages emphasized in *Shōfujin*).[19] The stories often condemned characters who attempted to leave home or their parents. Such cautionary tales could still be found in the early issues of *Shōjo sekai*. "Ame" (Rain) by Kaiga Hentetsu (1872–1923), a male fiction writer who was involved in the editing of the initial year of *Shōjo sekai*, is an example. It is the story of a schoolgirl who selfishly demands her mother make her a *kairyōfuku* (a kimono refitted as a casual garment), so that she can wear it at a sports festival to be held on the following day. Being told that it is impossible to make it in one day, the girl gets upset, whines, and cries. That night, a monster appears in her dream and punishes her for being "such an un-filial girl."[20] The girl begs forgiveness, promising that she will never be a troublesome child again. Short moralistic tales like this were published under the genre category, *shōjo shōsetsu*, which still had a didactic connotation.[21]

Confucian teachings stressed female modesty, humility, and submission, and girls were taught to be reserved and to understand that they were different from male members of the family. Interestingly, however, there were some adventure stories in the early issues of *Shōjo sekai*. As Japan experienced growing imperial power and expansion, the need for women's strength and participation in society was discussed in public. *Shōjo sekai*, therefore, often taught that Japanese girls should be more active and physically strong like their American counterparts. Biographies of Louisa May Alcott[22] and Florence Nightingale were published because these women served on the battlefields as military nurses and were viewed as models of bravery and selflessness.

Oshikawa Shunrō,[23] a boys' story writer, was asked to be in charge of adventure stories in *Shōjo sekai* in 1906. The stories usually took place in foreign countries, and the heroines were princesses.[24] Although such exotic tales did not directly apply to the lives of ordinary girls, the heroines were certainly proactive, and *Shōjo sekai* was trying to reinforce the active *ryōsai kenbo* (Good Wife, Wise Mother) ideal. However, Oshikawa was ambivalent about the purpose of these stories.

> I was told to write adventure stories about girls, but was quite at a loss. Women are supposed to be gentle in nature and would never go on adventures.... However, as long as we live in tumultuous times, we never know what kind of crisis might occur. When the time comes, women should not just be gentle.... They don't need to pursue adventure forcefully, but they should have the courage to undertake adventure in the case that the country becomes involved in war.[25]

The notion of active girls contradicted Confucian norms. Therefore, only mental strength came to be stressed. The adventure stories took place far from Japanese reality because girls' free actions could take place only in a fantasy realm. Adventure never became mainstream in girls' magazines.

Stories in *Shōjo sekai* gradually started to shift focus from moral lessons to representations of friendship outside the family. Because of the rising numbers of girls attending schools, a new type of story, which emphasized sentimentalism and the emotional interactions between girls, started to emerge in this magazine and others. Emphasis was placed on values of compassion and sisterhood, and these stories contributed to the creation of a sympathetic community of girls. Numata Rippō's "Kokoro no ane" (Sister of My Heart),[26] for instance, is the story of a hardworking fourteen-year-old orphan, Oharu, whose only joy is to see a beautiful and elegant girl named Tamako who passes every morning on her way to school. Watching her, Oharu can temporarily forget her own harsh circumstances. One day, during a heavy rain, Oharu, soaked to the skin, is taken under Tamako's umbrella; after this incident, they become close friends. However, Tamako and her family eventually move to Taiwan[27] for business reasons. Oharu and Tamako promise each other that they will remain eternal sisters in their hearts. Love, compassion, and kindness, rather than submission and patience, are emphasized here, and the two girls' sisterhood, which transgresses the difference of social class, is pictured emotionally. This is a tale of beautiful friendship. In Numata's stories, he defines *shōjo*'s ideal attitude and behavior, teaching his audience that no matter how difficult their lives may be, they should never forget their inner qualities as Japanese *shōjo*.

Numata Rippō's wife, Matsui Yuriko (1885–1974; real name Numata Fuku) was a champion of this trend. Her sentences are always written rhythmically, and the sad feelings of girl characters are embellished with beautiful language. The story "Yūbe no hoshi" (Evening Star) is an example of this effusive style. A lonely girl, Mie, idly spends time watching the evening sky, filled with melancholy. She misses her *onēsama* (bosom sister), with whom she had had a passionate relationship. Her *onēsama* disappeared from Mie's presence without telling her the reason; she even forbids Mie from sending her a letter. Mie's sadness is expressed thus: "*Onēsama*! I want to see you one more time. I want to talk to you the way I used to do . . . . . . I will never forget you. I will call you *onēsama* forever."[28] High emotion is observed in the exclamation mark and abundantly inserted pauses (. . . . .). When Mie finds a composition in a girls' magazine that seems to represent her own feelings ("A star shining in the sky! It looks like the eye of my late mother and makes me miss her so much . . . . . In the misty evening, tears fall on my cheeks, and I feel unbearable sadness. . . ."[29]), she is moved. Mie's sadness is so strong that it is comparable to the feeling of losing her own mother. Mie wants to correspond with the author of the composition so they might console each other's deeply hurt souls. But because she is shy, the letter she writes remains inside her desk. The readers are meant to indulge in the atmosphere of these stories; therefore didacticism and even clear plots are absent. Readers were fascinated by this kind of flowery writing, and the letters and compositions they submitted to the readers' pages reflect a similar style.

Writers like Matsui Yuriko and her contemporary, Izawa Miyuki (who was popular in *Shōjo gahō*)[30] greatly influenced the story writers of the next generation, as well.

Formation of Girls' Community

Readers of *Shōjo sekai* were fascinated not just by the stories, but also by the community of girls that formed around the magazine. Following the convention of women's magazines such as *Bunshō sekai* (Composition World) and *Jogaku sekai* (School Girls' World), *Shōjo sekai* had a readers' section that consisted of editor's messages, readers' compositions, and readers' letters. Girls made new friends in the magazine section called *danwa shitsu* (conversation room) and used it as a means of communication. The readers' space in the magazine was soon extended to outside the magazine. A monthly *aidokusha taikai* (readers' event) gave the readers an opportunity to widen their circle of *shōjo* friends. They were thrilled by the fact that they could actually meet other magazine readers, as well as writers and editors, in person. The first official *aidokusha taikai* was held in February 1908 in Kanda, Tokyo. An article published in the April issue of *Shōjo sekai* reports that the crowd was so large the hall filled quickly and there were people who could not get in. Numata Rippō, Iwaya Sazanami, representatives of *Shōjo sekai*'s publisher Hakubunkan, newspaper reporters, and so forth attended. There were performances by groups of girls and an educational talk by Numata Rippō. The event was reported to be a great success.[31] Thereafter, *aidokusha taikai* was held every month not only in Tokyo but also around the country. *Aidokusha taikai* were culturally important because they united *shōjo* readers from all over Japan, and gave them a sense of belonging to and ownership of their culture. *Shōjo sekai* also created a song called "Shōjo no uta" (Song of Girls) for the audience to sing at the *aidokusha taikai*. This further strengthened the unity among magazine readers. *Aidokusha taikai* were of course created for the commercial purpose of maintaining and increasing readership. However, it seems that Numata also wanted them to be a supplement to school education. He probably wanted to cultivate girls' good nature and watch them grow into fair Japanese women of the new era.

Just as sentimental stories continued to attract audiences, readers employed a similar emotional writing style in both letters and compositions they submitted to the magazine. The fact that their compositions were picked by Numata Rippō and read by other readers was an exciting, honorable, and proud experience for the contributors. Girls' magazines were the only space where they could test their talent and skills. Those who excelled in writing were awarded a prize called *Sendan shō* (Chinaberry Prize) and received a medal. Young Kitagawa Chiyo, Morita Tama, and

Yoshiya Nobuko were all frequent contributors and recipients of the medals. Girls' compositions often waxed nostalgic about schooldays and friends. According to Nakamura Tetsuya's study, the *bibun* (flowery language) style, utilizing pseudoclassical language and widely used in the mid-Meiji by such male writers as Tokutomi Roka[32] and Ōmachi Keigetsu[33] was in vogue among schoolgirls at that time.[34] In the October 1909 issue of *Shōjo sekai*, the composition topic "the sound of insects" was announced; many readers submitted short compositions. They creatively compared the sounds of a cricket with those of *koto* instruments, crystal balls, gold bells, and so on. The following composition was chosen for first place.[35]

> The overwhelming sound of crickets sounds like a stream in the valley. They come close to my bedroom door and awaken me from a deep sleep. How beautiful! I remember that, for several years, in the season in which reeds start to bend down, I heard the sound of crickets in the field of my hometown under the evening crescent!!! . . . [36] (Toyama Girls' High School, Morinaga Matsue)

However, as readers' compositions became increasingly maudlin and pretentious, the publisher began to receive letters that criticized *Shōjo sekai* for encouraging this propensity in its readers. Numata himself at one point wrote to the readers thus: "this month, the majority of compositions were about the death of a friend or mother. I am not saying that sadness is wrong, but intentionally obvious sadness is not appreciated."[37] Readers, however, never stopped. They used the magazines to construct a nexus of sentimentality, a junction point from which they could access their *shōjo* world.[38] Benedict Anderson's theory expounds on the idea that any cultural and social "codes"—languages, behaviors, emotions, and so forth—create imaginary and meta-geographical boundaries.[39] According to Honda Masuko and Kawamura Kunimitsu, ciphers of language and feelings in readers' letters and stories, therefore, united readers with readers, strengthening the "imagined community" of *shōjo*, or in other words, *shōjo bunka* (girls' culture).[40] These tear-jerkers did not create a fragile culture, despite the fears of educators and parents; instead, they produced active girls and strengthened their communal ties.

As part of the observance of the fifth year of publication of the magazine in 1911, five readers who excelled in writing were selected as honorable *Shōjo sekai* readers.[41] Seventeen-year-old Kitagawa Chiyo received the highest number of votes, and a picture of her with four other girls was published. This image reminds us of *keishū sakka*, female writers of the Meiji era, whose pictures were published in literary magazines and introduced as talented beauties. But these five girls are honored as respected *shōjo*. It is important that the pictures of actual readers were

Figure 2.2. "Five Honorable Girls." Kitagawa Chiyo appears on the upper right. *Shōjo sekai* 6, no. 12 (1911). Courtesy of Hakubunkan Shinsha Publishers, Ltd.

published here; they were neither princesses nor girls from prestigious families, but simple and ordinary. This event taught the readers that if they persevered, they could be the ones in the spotlight and receive praise just like these five girls. The appearance of ordinary girls in the magazine allowed readers to acknowledge that *shōjo* was no longer an ambiguous concept or fantasy, but real, and their own. It taught them that they were *shōjo* as well.

If you flip through the issues of *Shōjo sekai* published between 1908 and 1911, Kitagawa's name can be seen often on the readers' pages, but she was known as a reader-contributor in other magazine communities as well. In fact, many talented girls tested their writing ability by submitting their compositions to different magazines.[42] There was, for example, *Shōjo sekai*'s rival *Shōjo no tomo*,[43] which was known for the fact that it featured contributions by famous literary figures such as Yosano Akiko[44] and Ojima Kikuko,[45] and by the well-known artist, Takehisa Yumeji.[46] In 1910, an incident involving Kitagawa Chiyo, who was not yet a professional writer, played out on the pages of *Shōjo no tomo*. The February issue features a letter submitted to the *dokusha dōshi* (readers' column) by a reader named Fumiko.

> Kitagawa Chiyo, Kobayashi Yasuko and Ueno Nariko are called the queens of the contributors to this magazine, but they submit their stories to *Shōjo sekai*, too. . . . It seems like they are writing stories for business. . . . If people did not know them very well, they would call them "*otenba*" (tomboyish) and speak ill of them. . . . It is fine to read more than one magazine, but when they submit stories, they should choose one; what they are doing is like having two hometowns or having two schools. . . .[47]

It was Kitagawa's aspiration that bothered Fumiko. For her, the space of the magazine was not a place intended for writers' pursuits, but a place where girls played and communicated with each other. To play a *shōjo*, commitment and loyalty to the magazine's readers were important. This was how the imaginary community of *shōjo* had maintained its unity. Kitagawa, in the following issue, dissented thus: "Thank you very much for your kind warning, Fumiko! . . . I honestly did not know what people were thinking. . . . By the way I don't think I am so '*otenba*' (tomboyish). Your letter has a tone which makes people feel offended. Be careful."[48] Kitagawa eventually stopped contributing to *Shōjo no tomo*. The debate among the readers continued without the involvement of the editor until May of the same year.[49] The behavioral codes of *Shōjo* were no longer "simply laid down by the editor or the publishers, but molded by the readers themselves."[50]

Many girls found a home in *Shōjo sekai*. At this home base, a number of avid fans formed a group called *shōjo dokushokai* (Girls' Book Reading Circle) in 1910.

It originally started with thirty girls;[51] Kitagawa Chiyo and Morita Tama were founding members, and Yoshiya Nobuko joined later. Although it was initiated by these girls, Numata was deeply involved in this group. They met once a month at Numata's house in Azabu, Tokyo, and read and discussed the books that Numata recommended. They also engaged in fun activities such as playing games and music and sometimes went on picnics. They published booklets called *Hōpu* (Hope, 1912), *Sasayaki* (Whisper, 1913), and *Takane* (Dianthus, a serialized magazine founded in 1915). The members were interested in women's concerns, and were very conscious of *Seitō* (Bluestockings), a feminist group established by Hiratsuka Raichō (1886–1971) in 1911. *Seitō* members published a journal of the same name, which was an arena for exchanging views on social and women's issues as motherhood, marriage, virginity, same sex love, and so on. Their activities sometimes challenged taboos and their radical actions and statements were often reported sensationally in newspapers. Artists and writers, including Yosano Akiko, Tamura Toshiko (1884–1945), Hasegawa Shigure (1879–1941), to name a few, contributed to their publication. In the editorial section of *Sasayaki*, Numata's wife Matsui Yuriko, Morita Tama, and another member criticized *Seitō*, stating that "women should be more serious about the healthy development of children."[52] It is interesting that these two groups were formed by young women, but were working toward opposite goals. Unlike women in *Seitō*, the members of *shōjo dokushokai* believed in women's social roles as mothers and wives. In a way, they grew up as Numata expected, active *ryōsai kenbo*. They thought intellectually and expressed their own opinions, but without forgetting what they saw as their responsibilities as Japanese women.

Numata Rippō cleared a path for talented girls and helped them become professional writers. He not only gave opportunities to affluent girls such as Kitagawa Chiyo, Morita Tama, Yoshiya Nobuko, and so forth to write stories for *Shōjo sekai*, but also helped working-class girls. For instance, he allowed a girl named Kagawa Tsuyuko, who was in a financially difficult situation, to submit a story every month, so that her income from the magazine could cover part of her tuition.[53] She was asked to write episodes from her school life. The realistic portrayal in her stories—the feeling of taking a test, her worry about a friend who has been absent from school, her loneliness on the first day at a dorm, and so on—probably made those who could not afford to go to school imagine what school life was like and feel that they too wanted to be part of school culture. The number of girls who expressed their desire to go to school increased,[54] and there were even girls who visited Numata for help and advice. Stories published around 1914 dealt with this difficulty. "Jikatsu shinagara gakkō e iku shōjo" (A Girl Who Goes to School While Working) written by an author with the pen name Kyōko[55] is an example. It starts with a letter that the main character receives from a poor girl. There is no explanation of the relationship between these two girls (I assume that they are pen pals). The letter from the poor girl states that she wants to continue to study and to go to a school in Tokyo, but she cannot afford it, because her parents are farmers and have many children to support. She asks the heroine to find her a flexible job in Tokyo, which would allow her to go to school during the day. In 1914, school tuition was about 2.5 yen per month and the fee for a dormitory was 2 yen.[56] Judging from the fact that a male teacher's first month salary was 15 yen, we can imagine how difficult it was for working class girls to go to school. In the story, the heroine tries her best to find the perfect job for the poor girl, but does not succeed. The heroine finally consults her *sensei* (like Numata); his opinion is that the poor girl should first concentrate on working in order to save money. He continues: "If she is so serious about studying, why can't she study on her own in her hometown? She does not need to come to Tokyo."[57] This statement may sound harsh, but is a realistic response. This also represented the stance of Numata. This story can be taken as a message to magazine readers who were in a similar situation. Instead of just providing unrealistic hopes and dreams, *Shōjo sekai* tried to show reality to the audience, teaching them to live positively within their limited circumstances.

In line with the governmental promotion of the slogan *risshin shusse* in the 1900s, many Western books teaching how to become successful, such as Samuel Smile's *Self-Help*, were translated and published around this time.[58] Boys' magazines were rife with this term.[59] However, *risshin shusse* was only allowed for boys. While Numata believed that girls should study hard and have high aspirations, he felt that ambition sometimes drove young girls into reckless behavior. Also, he knew that even if a girl had ambition it did not mean that she could eventually get the kind of job—for example, as a government official—that a boy could. Girls' future jobs were limited to teachers, nurses, midwives, seamstresses, salespeople, and, in a very few cases, writers. Girls' ambition should never go beyond the framework of the *ryōsai kenbo* ideology. Therefore, Numata tried to temper the aspirations of girls and transfer the direction of their ambition inward, telling the readers that their efforts should be aimed at strengthening and enriching their inner beauty, a philosophy that is related to the Confucian notion of *shūyō* (self-improvement or discipline). Barbara Sato explains that the term *shūyō*, connoting "character building," "moral training," and "spiritual and cultural growth," was frequently intoned in the Taishō era.[60] In 1908, there was a special issue of *Shōjo sekai* called "shōjo to risshi" (Girl and Ambition).[61] In an article titled "Keibo subeki fujin" (Women Whom You Should Respect),[62] the writer lists the great contributions female educators, including Shimoda Utako (1854–1936: poet and founder of Jissen Girls' School) and Atomi Kakei (artist and founder of Atomi Girls' School), have made to society. However, he also warns the readers:

> It is doubtful that all of you can become women like Shimoda sensei and Atomi sensei, even if you wish to.... Some of you might marry to become wives of farmers or merchants.... Even if you do not become educators or scholars, you can still become great women by serving your husbands and running domesticity wisely with your beautiful heart.[63]

It is clear that *Shōjo sekai*'s editorial goal was to nurture readers into future good wives and wise mothers. It encouraged readers to shed the old-fashioned image of a shy, obedient, and quiet girl, and instead taught them the importance of being active to fit the new era of the modern state as *kokumin* (Japanese citizens). But girls' aspirations were viewed as dangerous when they threatened to transgress socially expected female roles. Barbara Sato states that the "popularization of self-cultivation did not necessarily circumvent the desire to get ahead in the workplace (*risshin shusse*)."[64] Therefore, the magazine sent a mixed message of encouragement and discouragement to the readers (this reminds us of the Japanese alteration of Jo's success at the end of *Little Women*—*Shōfujin*'s Takashi successfully publishes a novel, but unlike Jo, is not allowed to enjoy financial success).

Despite the conservative aspect of *Shōjo sekai*, the important contribution of this magazine to Japanese girls' culture is that it made young readers appreciate the *shōjo* period in their lives. It provided them a girls' community, a safe haven. Numata Rippō defined *shōjo* as neither child nor woman, teaching that as *shōjo*, each reader should enrich her beautiful inner qualities and embrace them as her new identity. He was a teacher and a mentor for Kitagawa Chiyo, Morita Tama, and Yoshiya Nobuko and provided them opportunities to write short stories for his magazine. Between 1913 and 1915 the magazine carried their works frequently. They eventually departed from *Shōjo sekai* in the pursuit of careers as professional writers, and each cultivated new types of girls' stories for the new era. They did not grow up into women who fit into the *ryōsai kenbo* ideal. Kitagawa later became involved in socialist activities, Morita Tama went to Tokyo to become a writer, leaving her husband, who did not agree with her decision, shortly after marrying; and Yoshiya Nobuko never married, but instead, lived with her female partner throughout her life. The girls who listened to Numata's conservative teachings actually developed into unconventional women. Did Numata create these exceptional "scribbling women"? One thing certain is that the magazine, *Shōjo sekai*, allowed them to taste the sweetness of being ambitious, expressing themselves, and connecting with other girls through their stories.

Yoshiya Nobuko and Kitagawa Chiyo
Fiction by and for Girls

Despite some efforts to curtail it, sentimentalism had become firmly established as one of the basic building blocks of *shōjo* magazine culture. Both authors and readers used its common language to consolidate the sympathetic community they were establishing, one of emotional if not physical proximity. One young author who emerged from the ranks of the readership was the embodiment of this spirit and masterfully wielded sentimental power—Yoshiya Nobuko, whose dream was to become an influential writer like Louisa May Alcott.[1] Her story "Suzuran" (Lily of the Valley), published in *Shōjo gahō* in July 1916,[2] created a sensation among young readers. "Suzuran" was an instant success; the chief editor, Wada Kokō[3] asked Yoshiya to continue writing similar stories, which were serialized under the title *Hana monogatari* (Flower Tales),[4] and were published in *Shōjo gahō* and *Shōjo kurabu*, continuing until 1924.

Although *Hana monogatari* made Yoshiya the most popular girls' story writer of that time, girls' culture was not pushed forward by her voice alone. At the same time, Kitagawa Chiyo,[5] who as an amateur had been known as one of the "queens of contributors" among the readership of *Shōjo Sekai*, emerged as a professional writer herself. Like Yoshiya, Kitagawa also drew inspiration from a female American author, in her case social crusader Harriet Beecher Stowe. Her utilization of the power of emotion, though no less skillful than Yoshiya's, was directed toward quite different goals. Whereas Yoshiya's tales contained an air of modern, delicate fantasy, Kitagawa's stories pointed out injustice through the eyes of the socially weak, including women, girls, and children.

This chapter will examine the ideas of girls' stories presented by these two writers. Each cultivated girls' fiction that they believed to be suitable for young readers. Yoshiya and Kitagawa, who both spent a period of apprenticeship in the magazine community of *Shōjo sekai*, grew into leading girls' story writers of the new era and proved through their works what girls' stories can do.

The Flowery World of *Hana monogatari* by Yoshiya Nobuko
Hana monogatari*'s Motif, Tone, and Language*

Yoshiya Nobuko (1896–1973), born in Niigata, was the youngest daughter of Yoshiya Yūichi, the police chief of Niigata. When Nobuko was five years old, Yūichi was transferred and the Yoshiya family moved to Tochigi. Her parents were heirs to a bloodline of the samurai class. As a daughter of samurai descent, Nobuko was taught the importance of submission to her parents and older brothers. Disliking unequal treatment, young Nobuko always resisted her family's old-fashioned views toward women. At the age of twelve, she started submitting compositions to such girls' magazines as *Shōjokai* and *Shōjo sekai*, often receiving prizes for her efforts. After graduating from Tochigi Jogakkō (Tochigi Girls' School) in 1915, she came to Tokyo to write stories professionally, although her parents did not approve of her decision. "Suzuran" (Lily of the Valley) was one of her earliest works as a professional writer.

"Suzuran" takes place in one summer evening. Seven girls gather in a room in a dormitory of a missionary school, and listen to a story told by Fusako who starts her tale in "a soft voice like singing a lullaby."[6] Fusako's story revolves around her mother at a time when her mother was younger and a music teacher at a girls' school. One day, Fusako's mother hears a rumor that someone plays the piano at school at night. She thinks it is strange, for she locks the piano every day. She decides to solve the mystery. When she arrives at the school that night, she hears beautiful piano music that sounds like "a crystal ball rolling down on a rail of coral."[7] When Fusako's mother enters the room, she sees a beautiful Italian girl with blond hair standing next to the piano. Suddenly the girl disappears as if she were an illusion. The next day, the mother finds a flower and a silver piano key with a note in Italian that says, "To you with appreciation for letting me go."[8] Fusako's mother later finds out that the piano originally belonged to an Italian missionary woman who is now deceased and that she had a daughter who had just recently gone back to Italy. When Fusako's story is over, the listeners sigh and, looking at each other's "young, dreamy and moist black eyes,"[9] indulge in the afterglow of their romantic journey.

Like "Suzuran," the other stories of *Hana monogatari*, in particular the early ones, are short and do not have distinct plot development.[10] The stories are made to gratify readers' inclination toward fantasy. Exoticism is one important element that enhances their dreamy air, and Western motifs—pianos, organs, ribbons, attics, rings, and churches—estrange the audience from everyday Japanese society. Evasion of reality is manifested by the characters' pseudonyms such as "Sister Sarah," "Miss Red Poppy," "Nightingale," and "The Girl with Purple Sleeves"; these decorative names function to erase the characters' actual identities. As Kawamura Kunimitsu's study of *Jogaku sekai* details,[11] the employment of fancy names was a convention of schoolgirl magazines. Western imagery and beautiful names were also used by the readership when they submitted their letters and compositions to decorate their world.

Yoshiya's works always detailed the characters' appearance to help her audience visualize a *shōjo* image. In "Wasurenagusa" (Forget Me Not), a female beauty is described thus:

> The girl had soft and full black hair.... The two braids, the large black hair pins on the sides of her head, and the tangled hair on her forehead enhanced her pure and likable face. She had a slightly pale face with gentle eyebrows. She had long and moist eyelashes which cast an elegant shadow under her eyes when she blinked with shyness.... She also had small red lips which closed lightly.... She had a tall and slender body. Her slim neck was covered with purple kimono with a white collar. Under her small and young breasts, the brown *hakama* [loose trousers] was tightly wrapped.... Everything looked graceful and suited her.[12]

Shōjo is fantasized, idolized, and celebrated here, meant only to be admired by the readers/viewers. The image of *shōjo* in *Hana monogatari* was further consolidated by the pictures drawn by such artists as Shimizu Yoshio,[13] Kametaka Fumiko,[14] and Fukiya Kōji[15] that always accompanied the installments. Fukiya Kōji's contribution to Japanese girls' culture is important to note here. Through a connection with Takehisa Yumeji, Fukiya started working for *Shōjo gahō*, and his illustrations for *Hana monogatari* (which started in December 1920) made his name. Fukiya's illustrations follow features of *jojōga*, lyrical paintings of weak and dreamy girls popularized by Takehisa. Fukiya's illustration was modern, and matched the flowery world of *Hana monogatari*. Fukiya also drew illustrations for *Reijokai* (Lady's World) magazine, a girls' magazine targeted at a slightly higher age group than *Shōjo gahō*. Mizuki Takahashi states that "[i]llustrations were key to developing a recognizable and appealing image of perfect shōjo."[16] When selected tales of *Hana monogatari* were republished in *Shōjo no tomo* in 1937 and 1938, the iconic illustrations of Nakahara Jun'ichi[17] further stylized the *shōjo* image, adding the characteristics of large dreamy eyes and ribbons. Through reading stories and looking at illustrations, Japanese girls discovered modern *shōjo*.

Frequent usage of "……" and "!" to express the characters' overwhelming feelings of sadness and love fed readers' *shōjo* narcissism. Michiko Suzuki explains that these nonverbal symbols were originally used by literary figures who were involved in the *genbun-itchi* (agreement of speech and written languages) movement to "show a break or shift in the flow of articulation or internal monologue."[18] Yoshiya utilized the emotional signs of "……" and "!" abundantly as girls' narrative tropes to construct a world of feelings and senses. These semiotic signs recall French psychoanalyst Julia Kristeva's idea of *jouissance*, the pleasurable feelings and senses that infants have in the preverbal phase. Kristeva explains that during this phase, an infant, who does not recognize a border between Self and Other, thinks it simply exists as part of its mother. For the infant in this stage, the "meaning of language is not a symbolic order but is a semiotic realm of sounds, color and rhythms."[19] The emotional signs displayed by Yoshiya could be interpreted as devices to create the sphere of pleasure and to help girls indulge in narcissistic play. Through their emotional agreement, readers strengthen their own cultural space, the "*shōjo*'s imagined community."

Yoshiya's stories were often criticized as unrealistic and excessively mawkish. Fiction writer Tsuboi Sakae[20] complained that "the stories

Figure 3.1. Illustration for Yoshiya Nobuko's "Hana monogatari, Nemu no hana" by Fukiya Kōji. *Shōjo gahō* 10, no. 5 (1921). © Fukiya Kōji 2018.

in *Hana monogatari* are like lullabies.... [which make readers] feel good and forget reality."[21] Yosano Akiko similarly wrote that "I don't like cheap stories that try to curry favor with children.... Sentimental shōjo stories that attempt to invite cheap tears are, in my opinion, harmful to society."[22] Yoshiya's stories were viewed as politically insensitive as poverty, in particular, was utilized for emotional effect. Yoshiya's "Sazanka" (Camellia, 1916),[23] for instance, is controversial because it deals with *hisabetsu buraku* (outcast communities that existed throughout the Tokugawa era).[24] The story starts with a scene in which a schoolgirl walks into the woods with her new camera in hand. She soon finds herself in a poor village and encounters a pretty little girl, who "wears a gold *obi* [sash] just like a *gion maiko* [maiko dancer]."[25] The little girl mistakes the camera bag that the schoolgirl is holding for a doctor's bag, and asks her to come with her to her village to treat her sick mother. When the schoolgirl hears the name of the village, she is stunned, for it is a village of "untouchables."[26] Yoshiya describes the beauty and sadness of the village.

> Oh, the village, full of camellia in bloom. Oh, the neglected village. The girl shed tears sympathetically.... She did not take any pictures of the village, but in her mind, she kept a picture of the sad and pitiful village, such as she had never seen before.[27]

Figure 3.2. Illustration for Yoshiya Nobuko's "Hana monogatari, Sanshoku sumire" by Nakahara Jun'ichi. *Shōjo no tomo* 30, no. 9 (1937). © Junichi Nakahara/Himawariya.

Elegant language, contrasted with their untouchable status, is used to describe the girl and her village, their sad isolation cast poetically. The schoolgirl's camera represents the distance she maintains from the village—never truly entering nor interacting it, only gazing at it from a level of remove. This bridge between "the readers' world" and "the other world" through "a sense of pity,"[28] exists only on the emotional level.

Resistance against Social Reality and Cultural Conventions

When the stories are viewed from the perspective of gender, the characters' refusal to grow up could be taken as a sign of resistance against their future roles as women. The idea of development and loss of girlhood in Yoshiya's stories is always associated with sadness. In "Ukon zakura" (Saffron Cherry Blossoms), Sister Sarah, who will soon leave school to get married, tearfully tells her younger roommate to "stay in girlhood forever. Never grow up."[29] Once girls leave school, they can no longer maintain the identity of *shōjo*. They are destined to enter society and to change their identity from *shōjo* to *onna* (women). Growing up is not simply a physical change for girls, but is loss of self-identity. "Fukujusō" (Adonis) explores the confusion of female identity. In the story, Kaoru, a second-year schoolgirl, is shocked to learn that her sworn "*onēsama*" (literally sister, but in this case, future sister-in-law) is now called "*okusama*" (madam, indicating married woman) by her maid. Kaoru questions her.

> "Why do you call my beloved sister '*okusama*'?" Kiyo laughs and says "She is now your brother's wife, so I call her that way." Shaking her head, Kaoru does not want to accept what Kiyo has said: "No! She is my sister. She is not my brother's wife." ... Kaoru is confused and continues: "Which is true, *okusama* or *onēsama*? What should I do if *okusama* is real and *onēsama* is not true?"[30]

"*Okusama*," a married woman, is obviously a foreign identity for a little girl. Her *onēsama* has now become a member of her *ie* (household), and is no longer the *onēsama* that she knew. Kaoru cries over her beloved "sister's" sudden departure from her world, the world of *shōjo*.

"Moyuru hana" (Burning Flower) illustrates the pain of losing the *shōjo* identity through the perspective of a married woman who tries to escape from her *ie* and her domestic and social responsibilities. Omasu is the wife of a rich husband. Feeling something is missing in her life, she abandons her fame and wealth and comes back to her old world, a girls' school. Though a married woman, Omasu sits in class and studies with girls. The girls are fascinated by this mysterious woman, an outcast who evades cultural womanhood and is unable to conform to the family system, calling her "a mysterious witch."[31] With tears in her eyes, Omasu tells one of the students not to grow up.

"Keep the purity of your mind as *shōjo* for ever and ever. . . . Don't grow up. Never grow up into a woman." Omasu sheds her tears on the girl's hand, just as dew accumulates on white rose mallows and drops off in autumn. . . . What is the reason for her sadness? What tortures this beautiful lady? . . . Enigma! It is a mystery for Midori.[32]

The mystery is revealed soon. One day, a messenger from her husband comes to the dormitory to bring Omasu back in exchange for ten thousand yen—though her previous life was comfortable, she is merely an object that is exchangeable for money. Mrs. Wagner, a foreign teacher, tries to protect Omasu. The contrast of Mrs. Wagner and ten thousand yen highlights the confrontation of fantasy and reality. The world of *shōjo*, which is dominated by the unreal air of Western language and images, is intruded on by male power and the language of society. The man intimidates Mrs. Wagner, Omasu, and other girls, and his violence corrupts the fragile *shōjo* world. At the end, Omasu desperately sets fire to the school and kills herself. A woman of fantasy changes into a madwoman, disappearing with her world.

Fantasy is a form of resistance against the real world; the girls' imaginary "cocoon"[33] is supported by antipatriarchal mentality.[34] This resistance is also expressed through tears, and readers are moved and sympathize with what the characters have to go through. Jane Tompkins addresses the value of "tears" in sentimental fiction of late-nineteenth-century America, stating that sentimentalism was used as a political device by female authors to deliver feminism, and that, through emotional scenes, women writers attempted to cultivate in their readers a common moral standard. Tompkins calls this literary device "sentimental power."[35] In *Hana monogatari*, this power is observed. Although Kume Yoriko is skeptical that Yoshiya's dreamy tales have any actual political influence on readers,[36] we can at least say that audiences are unconsciously inclined to Yoshiya's perspective and strengthen their communal tie through tears.

In order to secure the protection of this communal fantasy space, Yoshiya even deconstructs cultural understandings of women's bodies and denaturalizes heterosexual normality in the world of her literature. In "Kuchinashi no Hana" (Gardenia), female adolescent physical features are expressed thus:

> In the steam, a half-naked shadow appeared. It was a noble and beautiful *shōjo*. . . . Her black shining soft hair curled around her white forehead and smoothly covered her gentle shoulder. . . . Her face with lips of flower petals and pale white cheeks was elegant and mysterious. Her body, which was white as a fine cotton cloud, curved softly.[37]

The physical presence of the naked woman is obscured and erased by diaphanous steam, which indicates the ambiguous dreaminess and elusiveness of the body. The description of the girl's erotic beauty does not focus on the conventionally emphasized features of woman's physicality.

According to Kawamura Kunimitsu, in the Taishō period (1912–1926), Western ideas about beauty permeated schoolgirl culture. They changed girls' bodies from vessels of reproduction into "*miserutame no karada*" (bodies to show).[38] Kawamura calls these bodies "*burujoateki shintai*" (bourgeois bodies), explaining that "*otome* [maiden] recognized the eroticism of their own 'bourgeois bodies' and indulged in them narcissistically."[39]

Honda Masuko recognizes the influence of Yosano Akiko's *Midaregami* (Tangled Hair) on *Hana monogatari*, stating that expressions such as "black shining soft hair," "softly curved body," and "lips of flower petals" recall Yosano's poems that celebrated maidenhood.[40] Egusa Mitsuko explains that "Yosano converted male defined female sexuality into female sexuality, instilling women's own wills in these converted images of maidens" and that "female body parts like skin, hair, and breasts, which had been the objects of the male gaze, were 'restructured into female bodies as real individuals' with souls."[41] *Midaregami* and *Hana monogatari* commonly liberated the image of maiden bodies from cultural conventions and helped the authors imagine new expressions of female sexuality.

In *Hana monogatari*, the mainstream idea of romantic love is also re-created in that it involves only a single gender in the terrain of senses. In "Hikage no hana" (Shaded Flower), two girls' intimate love is portrayed with poetic abstractions. Tamaki always looks at the portrait of her deceased mother—"a young lady with a gentle smile as if the sound of a crystal ball rolls out of her lips"[42]—and misses her in solitude. Tamaki one day meets a girl, Masuko, who bears a striking resemblance to her own mother. Tamaki is attracted to Masuko, and the two beautiful *shōjo* start to love each other. Their close intimate relationship eventually develops into a deeper one, transgressing the "fence of friendship."[43]

> Two girls learn the sweet taste of forbidden fruits—how can they go back to their old days? . . . They were wearing a beautiful pink veil called "secret." People say that this secret veil was knitted with rays of midnight moon light by the hands of beautiful witches—The two girls protect and nurture their own small and tasteful round world—
>
> (we are . . . . . . flowers in shade. . . . . .) [44]

Their deep love is confirmed not by the depiction of actual physical activity but through the delicately evocative language used to describe it. Their love is narcissistic—surely Masu who resembles Tamaki's mother resembles Tamaki herself. The excessive use of points (......), signifying a pause, enhances the dreamy atmosphere. Also "the moon" and "a round world" evoke femininity and maternity. Protected by a maternal womb (a soft secret veil), they indulge in *joissance*.

In early-twentieth-century Japan, female-female romantic love relationships were a sort of fashion called the relationship of S (which stood for Sister). Romantic friendship was actually a universal phenomenon.[45] In America around this time as well, schoolgirls enjoyed the thrill of a "crush" and romantic involvement with friends of the same sex. Lillian Faderman's study maintains that Western stories before the 1920s openly dealt with female-female love relationships, which were not viewed as threatening because they were considered "rehearsals in girlhood of the great drama of women's life," and "the friendships of young girls prefigure the closer relations which would one day come in and dissolve their earlier intimacies."[46] Similarly, in Japan, the relationship of S was viewed as an extension of friendship. The all-female *Takarazuka kageki* (Takarazuka revue) helped promote this phenomenon.[47] Schoolgirls were intoxicated by the romantic love portrayed onstage, and particularly thrilled by the mysterious sexuality of "*dansō no reijin*" (beauty in male costume). In the space of the Takarazuka theater, gender was simply a performance; it was not masculine sexuality that attracted the Japanese girl audience but feminine eroticism. In the same way that young girls dreamed about Takarazuka stars, they found targets of admiration at school and enjoyed passionate friendship. The term *lesbianism* was nonexistent both in Japan and in America until sexuality came to be studied from a pathological perspective around the turn of the twentieth century.[48] Schools came to forbid S relationships, and even exchanging romantic letters among students was prohibited. In an essay, Yoshiya criticizes educators who label girls' intimate friendships as dangerous and evil, stressing that their attitude threatens "young girls and makes them doubt the purity of their love, killing the gentle and beautiful natures of girls which were granted by God."[49] Michiko Suzuki explains that "Yoshiya defends same-sex love by insisting that it is part of a broader notion of love"; she believed that it was an "important component of adolescent education."[50] It is known that Yoshiya had a female companion named Momma Chiyo throughout her life. Her stories could be her reaction to negative social understanding of a female passionate relationship and partnership.

"Kibara" (Yellow Rose) also deals with same-sex love. Katsuragi Misao, a schoolteacher, one day receives a romantic poem from Reiko, one of her students. In response, the teacher relates the story of the ancient poet, Sappho,[51] who devoted herself to her female lover but was betrayed by her. Heartbroken,

Sappho threw herself from a cliff into the deep ocean and killed herself. Misao states: "Miss Reiko, Sappho was one who loved a beautiful friend of the same sex and was wronged.... Betrayed by that girl, Melitta, Sappho, in honor of her own deep passion for this girl, cast herself from the rocks of Lucretius into the deep blue sea, disappearing in the waves—the sad woman poet, Sappho—I, I, love her—"[52] Her student, Reiko, suspects the passionate feeling of Misao toward her and exclaims "Teacher!"[53] Through subtle expressions of eroticism and female sensuality, the reader knows that they cross the boundaries of the teacher-student relationship. Promising to be together eternally, they decide to go to America to study at a college together in the future. However, Reiko's mother asks Misao to convince her daughter to accept an arranged marriage. Misao is sad to learn that Reiko's parents believe that marriage is the only goal for women. The issue of marriage intrudes on the ideal world that Reiko and Misao are about to create. Misao eventually breaks her relationship with Reiko. Real schoolgirls were enthralled by romantic relationships with their sisters, but after they graduated from school they quickly accepted reality, married, and settled down in domesticity. Most of them accepted their future social roles as mothers and wives. For them, female-female relationships were limited to while they were at school and were mere playful fantasy.

End of Shōjo *World*

In a short essay called "Shojo dokuhon" (Maidens' Readings), Yoshiya writes about girls' school graduation as a sad event. She describes that what lies waiting for girls after leaving school are future husbands and "a heavy millstone called '*boseiai*' [maternal affection]."[54] And as soon as girls exit the school gate, they face a road leading them to a life of "service and sacrifice."[55] *Hana monogatari*'s episodes get increasingly pessimistic. The episode of "Nashi no hana," (Flower of Pear Tree) is the most tragic one. Two girls climb the stairs of a tower. From the top of the tower, they look at the flowers of pear trees.

> "Pear flowers . . . . . . How beautiful . . . . . . How white and fuzzy. . . . . ."
>
> The girl with the white sash says—"Look—the moon—"
>
> The girl with the blue sash says "moon—oh . . . . . . The pear flowers are fragile. The moon above the flowers is more fragile . . . . . ."
>
> The girl with the white sash—says quietly, "And us . . . . . . ?"
>
> "—I don't know . . . . . ."[56]

Fragility is emphasized throughout the conversation. The story is filled with ellipses and the dialogue is fragmental and incomplete, and the readers sense the oncoming unhappy end of these girls. One year later, the girl with the white sash climbs the stairs of the tower alone, her friend having committed suicide. Like one year earlier, she looks down at the pear trees. Her sight suddenly blurs and she sees the illusion of her friend down behind the trees. Following this vision of her "lover," the girl jumps from the tall tower and kills herself. After that, people call the tower "the witches' tower" and lock its door forever.

By terminating their lives by their own hands, the characters prevent their bodies from growing into those of women. Paradoxically, Yoshiya uses the extreme sadness of the tragedy of these girls to decorate the finale of *Hana monogatari*. Yoshiya finally prays, "May flowers bloom on the ground. May their beautiful *shōjo* spirits rest in peace in heaven."[57]

Despite the melodrama of the final story, *Hana monogatari* is Yoshiya's celebration of this phase of girls' lives; young Yoshiya's dream was shared with and appreciated by her readers. *Hana monogatari*—written by and for *shōjo*—is without a doubt an influential work in the development of Japanese girls' culture.

Kitagawa Chiyo's Stories on Marginalized Girls

Kitagawa Chiyo as a Socialist Writer

Although the term *shōjo* had already become widely used by the 1920s, the percentage of girls who were fortunate enough to be able to study at higher schools was still small.[58] Kitagawa Chiyo (1894–1965) paid attention to the marginal girls who were not included in the *shōjo* community. In the preface of *Kinuito no zōri* (Silk Sandals), a collection of short stories published in 1931, Kitagawa states,

> When I was a girl like you, I used to love girls' stories. However, in every story I read, the girl was depicted to be weak and sentimental, merely shedding cheap tears. I always had complaints about stereotypical girls' stories. I used to think that "a real girl is not like this." ... "a girl should not be like this." ... This is how I became a girls' story writer.[59]

Kitagawa's stories contained class consciousness and social truth. For Kitagawa, girls' magazines were a perfect arena in which to voice her own political ideas. The characteristics of her works are clearly illuminated when they are compared to Yoshiya's works.

Kitagawa Chiyo was born in Fukaya, Saitama, the daughter of Kitagawa Shun, a factory manager of the Brick Corporation of Japan. Her father was a modern and open-minded man, and had studied in Germany when he was young. Raised by affectionate parents, Chiyo grew up happily. She entered Miwada Jogakkō (Miwata Girls' School) in 1905. Inclined to ill health, however, she had to quit school after three years. It was around this time she zealously submitted her compositions to girls' magazines such as *Shōjo sekai* and *Shōjokai*. After she became a professional writer, she wrote stories for many other publications, including *Reijokai, Wakakusa* (Young Grass),[60] and *Shōjo kurabu*, and was also active in the field of children's literature, her work printed in *Yōnen no tomo* (Children's Friend), *Kodomo no kuni* (Children's Country), and *Akai tori* (Red Bird).[61] She regularly contributed to *Shōjo gahō*, and it is interesting that her stories were published in the same volumes as the *Hana monogatari* series.[62] Kitagawa's stories, which were accompanied by the illustrations of Fukiya Kōji, Katō Masao, and Takabatake Kashō,[63] were glamorous, although they often delivered messages different from those in *Hana monogatari*.

Chiyo married Eguchi Kan,[64] a proletarian writer, in 1915, and her marriage led to her becoming one of the founding members of the *Sekirankai* (the Red Wave Society), a women's socialist group (which mainly consisted of the wives of socialists). Their declaration statement was drafted by socialist and feminist Yamakawa Kikue (1890–1980) in 1921.

> The *Sekirankai* is a women's organization that plans to participate in the enterprise to destroy the capitalist society and build a socialist society. The capitalist society turns us into slaves at home and oppresses us as wage slaves outside the home. It turns many of our sisters into prostitutes. . . . The *Sekirankai* declares all-out war on this cruel, shameless society. . . ."[65]

Unable to bridge "the gap between intellectual women and working women,"[66] *Sekirankai* eventually ceased in 1923, and several leading members were imprisoned. However, the spirit of the *Sekirankai* continued to live in Kitagawa's literature in stories such as "Kinuito no zōri" and "Shunran" (The Noble Orchid), which will be discussed below, in which she illustrated how capitalist society enslaves poor children.

The marriage between Chiyo and Eguchi Kan was tumultuous. Chiyo refused to suppress herself and to let her soul as a writer die within domesticity. She considered Eguchi hypocritical—while he worked for social equality, he didn't appreciate Chiyo's hard work at home. Finally, in 1922, they divorced. In the magazine *Josei kaizō* (Women's Reconstruction) in 1922, Chiyo explained that one of the reasons for her divorce was the fact that she was always treated by her husband and the public as the wife of Eguchi Kan: "I always wanted to be treated as Chiyoko, as an individual human being...."⁶⁷ She was a feminist as well as a socialist. Just like the *Seitō* "New Women" of the time,⁶⁸ Chiyo possessed her own *jiga* (selfhood) and wanted to protect her individuality and professional identity.

After separating from Eguchi Kan, Chiyo found a new partner in Takano Matsutarō, a labor activist who is known for his participation in the Ashio Copper Mining pollution case.⁶⁹ Her married life with Takano was financially difficult, but emotionally gratifying. Many of her *shōjo* stories are about marriage, love, and divorce, and many of them are based on her experiences. Sharing pieces of her own life story, Chiyo tried to make her audience contemplate social inequity.

Crossing the Border of Class

Kitagawa's "Kōfuku" (Happiness), published in *Shōjo gahō* in September 1925, not only explores the existence of class in society, but also views the social order through the innocent eyes of a school girl, Seiko. Seiko's aunt once married a rich man from a privileged family, but left him because she felt empty—she felt herself to be a "living doll."⁷⁰ She is now married to a working-class man. Seiko's family, including parents and grandparents, are all upset and blame the aunt for abandoning the "perfect marriage." When the aunt comes back home to visit her family, they treat her rudely; looking at her worn-out *kimono* and *obi*, they say that they are embarrassed. Seiko wonders "why don't they look at just the aunt herself, instead of looking at the clothes she is wearing."⁷¹ It is *sekentei* (public image) that the family is most concerned about. Seiko's aunt is viewed as the shame and disgrace of the *ie*, in which marriage is believed to exist not for personal happiness but for the prosperity of the family. Seiko's aunt had experienced a situation similar to the sad predicament faced by Omasu in *Hana monogatari*'s "Burning Flower." But unlike the desperate Omasu, who killed herself because of her miserable marriage, Seiko's aunt breaks out of the situation and searches for a new life.

The aunt is eventually disinherited and never allowed to visit the family again. A kind grandmother who feels sorry for the aunt one day asks Seiko to deliver her a new *kimono*, which the grandmother has secretly made. Seiko travels from Kōjimachi (located in *yamanote*, uptown), where she lives, to Honjo (in *shitamachi*, downtown),⁷² by train. For the first time, Seiko crosses the geographic border of social class. What she sees there is very different from the world that she is familiar with; she is surprised to see that all the *nagaya* (old-fashioned tenement houses) look the same and are all shabby and dirty. Soon she hears cheerful laughter from one of the houses. When she peeks inside the house, she finds her aunt holding a baby. Next to her is her husband with "muscular shoulders and a tanned neck,"⁷³ features that announce his job involves physical labor. Looking at the poor but happy aunt, Seiko feels that their place is like "heaven filled with clear air,"[74] and realizes that her aunt is much happier than any other member of her family. If Seiko's family represents *ie*, the old Japanese family system, the aunt's place represents *katei*, a warm home where "the two individuals are united with love"[75] without being "trapped by annoying conventions."[76] Seiko is enlightened, realizing that true happiness cannot be achieved by fame, social status, or money.

Nevertheless, Kitagawa understands that financial difficulty is a serious and realistic challenge for poor families and that it is unrealistic to say that happiness transcends money. "Mikan" (Tangerine Orange) published in *Wakakusa* in January 1928, discloses Kitagawa's awareness of the naïveté of the notion that "money doesn't matter." In this autobiographical work, she writes about a newlywed couple; the wife is a children's story writer and her husband is a political activist. The wife was from an affluent family just like the aunt in "Kōfuku," but because of her political beliefs, she shed her "old shell"[77] and came to this workers' town. Although they are poor, their life is blissful in a modest *nagaya* tenement. His name on a political "black list," the husband has only recently, with difficulty, been able to find a job. However, the wife becomes sick due to the unsanitary living environment and her fatigue from domestic work. The husband gives up his job in order to care for her. She has mentally transgressed the border of social classes; however, physically she was not capable of adjusting to the new environment.

A doctor in the neighborhood, who feels sorry for the wife, starts visiting her. The husband goes to the clinic to ask about the fee, but the doctor tells him that he does not need any payment. The husband joyfully comes back home, stopping off to get tangerine oranges on the way. He tells his wife that the doctor "trusted us," continuing, "that is because you still have a bourgeois aura."[78] The doctor's kindness and generosity come from a sense of affinity for someone who is from his own social class. Having seen that she has many books, he understood that the wife is also well educated—the help he gives her is a special case. The notion of the poor being able to rely on those better off for help seems to be, realistically, muted.

No doubt Kitagawa learned the practical limits of ideological fervor from actual experience. Kindness to and understanding of the poor is important, but there is a limit to what one can do to help. Kitagawa expresses this unfortunate fact in "Tamago hitotsu" (One Egg; no information on the original publication), a story about a woman who adopts a poor girl, Teru, out of pity. The woman, however, soon realizes that there are hundreds of children who are similarly suffering from poverty.

> Behind Teru there is Toshiko. Behind Toshiko, there are plenty of girls like Teru and Toshiko. Will these poor girls be all saved if I keep saving them?

> Teru and Toshiko are like bubbles coming out of social deficiencies. As long as the deficiencies are there, poor children are born one after another even if I keep picking them up.[79]

The story ends as the woman "smiles sadly because of the irony" of this situation.[80] Kitagawa believed that society and its members had to change in order to eliminate class differences. She realized that what she could do was to keep writing stories and keep moving her audience in the hope that eventually, her readers would grow up and alter society. Kitagawa's stories, therefore, tend to portray innocent children who face horrible incidents. Through the chronicles of their agonizing lives and their hapless conditions, Kitagawa attempted to shock the audience. She believed in the power of the emotional impact that a single story could make.

"Shunran," published in *Reijokai* in 1929, is one of her most wrenching and powerful stories. This graphically written tale, full of anger, speaks the value of Kitagawa's literature. The story starts with a scene in which a poor seventeen-year-old orphan, Fuji, gives birth to a baby girl. Fuji is about the same age as schoolgirls who are called *shōjo*, but without knowing that there is such a phase, she has become pregnant. In a society that forbids women to bear children before marriage, she is convinced to take medicine to terminate the pregnancy. Upon discovering that the father is marrying a different woman, she becomes distraught and fails to take the full dose. Regrettably this results in the baby, who Fuji names Aguri, being born with a deformity on her face; instead of a normal nose, there are just two nostrils where her nose should be.

Society is cold and merciless to Fuji and Aguri. Fuji's aunt and uncle, who treat her as if she were a servant, say to her that the baby was deformed as punishment for her promiscuity. Calling Aguri, "*obake*" ("demon"), people in the village despise her and tell Fuji that "having such a freak is a punishment for your sinful behavior."[81] The mother and the child face *mura-hachibu*, social ostracization; they are viewed as having disturbed the order of the village and consequently are treated as outcasts. It is interesting to contrast this work with Yoshiya's "Sazanka," the story about the poor girl in the outcast village. Yoshiya's story objectifies the girl and views her through the "camera eyes" of a bourgeois girl, treating the poor girl as a target of fantasy and curiosity. Kitagawa's story, on the other hand, does not employ this curious "gaze"; the glorification and idolization of the poor are not witnessed. Kitagawa only shows the harsh and merciless world to her readers.

One day years later, Fuji and Aguri go to the circus and enter a tent. There, they see a picture of a pregnant mother and a "crab girl," an unfortunate child whose body is deformed. On the picture is published the phrase "poor crab girl, born as retribution to her mother."[82] Ashamed of her own situation, Fuji eventually commits suicide by slashing her wrist. Her death is reported in a small corner of the newspaper next to the picture of *hanami* (cherry blossom viewing), which describes how people are enjoying parties under the cherry trees and celebrating the arrival of spring. The cheerfulness of the parties and the darkness of the life of Fuji and her daughter are harshly contrasted. Through this contrast, Kitagawa attempts to make her readers realize that what is ugly is not the child, but the society that views the poor child as ugly. Her works crystallize the essence of *Sekirankai*, which encouraged "all-out war on this cruel, shameless society." The name "Aguri" is traditionally given by parents, who already have many children and want this child to be their last. Perhaps Kitagawa is expressing her desire that there be no more mistreated women and children like those portrayed in her tale.

Subverting the World of Hana monogatari

There is definitely an eminent distinction in the attitude toward girls' fiction between Kitagawa and Yoshiya. Yoshiya and many other girls' story writers pursued beauty and girls' fantasy even in the context of social class and poverty, but Kitagawa used the "shock effect" by projecting unremitting social actuality in her stories to influence her young audience. In "Shōjo shōsetsu no kōsei to gijutsu" (the Structures and Techniques of Girls' Fiction), Kitagawa criticizes conventional girls' fiction, the goal of which, according to her, is to invite readers' tears. She states: "Girls' fiction emphasizes cheap sentimentalism and tears.... Cheap sentimentality makes girls' fiction trivial."[83] This could be taken as Kitagawa's criticism of Yoshiya, whose hallmark is her sentimental writing.[84] However, as "Shunran" illustrates, Kitagawa herself employed melodramatic and emotional tactics no less manipulative, though undeniably powerful. They differ mainly in their political, outwardly directed, rather than inwardly directed, agenda.

Kitagawa's "Kinuito no zōri" (no information on the original publication) can also be taken as the antithesis to the tales represented by *Hana monogatari*. "Kinuito no zōri" has a format similar to that of the first seven tales of *Hana monogatari*, in which a narrator relates an episode to young listeners within the story. In "Kinuito no zōri," five schoolgirls gather around their female teacher to listen to her story. Kitagawa's story revolves around a tiny beautiful silk sandal that the teacher always carries with her. The sandal was given to her by a poor man named Shōsaku, her acquaintance, who used to run a horse carriage business. Because of the rising use of automobiles, his business was in decline and his life was very difficult. He had a fourteen-year-old daughter named Ofumi, a hardworking girl who helped her father's business. One day, she was seriously injured while she tried to pull a horse to the barn. Ofumi needed to be treated, but the family was so poor that the father did not have money to buy medicine. Desperate, he stole money that he happened to find on the coach, knowing that it belonged to his rich customer. He was soon arrested and imprisoned.

In this story, the description of Ofumi, the adolescent girl, is minimal. Unlike Yoshiya's "Suzuran," which described the beauty of the Italian girl, Kitagawa's story only focuses on the father's tormented mind and his unfortunate situation. Day after day in jail, Shōsaku collected silk lint from the floor and weaved a sandal, believing the superstition that one's dream would be granted if one makes a sandal while praying earnestly. Finally, he finished the sandal; however, on the same day, he found out that his daughter had already died. "Shōsaku was outraged, and he shed tears which ran like a waterfall."[85] Sympathizing with him, the chief manager of the jail invited the lonely Shōsaku to live with his family. The chief manager had a daughter who was around Shōsaku's daughter's age. Shōsaku adored her and she became a reason to keep on living. The teacher concludes the story: "You must already know who this daughter is. The reason I keep this sandal with me all the time is for this reason. Whenever I look at this sandal, I talk to the late Shōsaku in my mind, saying 'Look, I am fine and very happy.'"[86] Unlike Yoshiya's "Suzuran," which concludes with the listeners' lingering indulgence after listening to the fantasy story of an Italian girl, Kitagawa's sad tale of the poor man and his daughter makes the listeners consider the plight of the underprivileged and the fact that they themselves are truly fortunate. If each character in one of Yoshiya's luxurious tales is a petal of a beautiful flower, the characters in Kitagawa's stories of the socially weak are pieces of lint found on the ground, which are invisible and unnoticed, but when they are picked up and pieced together, they become a beautiful work (story) competitive with a gorgeous flower.

Kitagawa uses various tactics to expose the existence of social class by juxtaposing two worlds—the world to which her readers belong and another world with which they are not familiar. Her fiction helps readers acknowledge how deep the gap between the two classes is.[87] The following passage from Kitagawa Chiyo's preface to her 1960 translation of the antislavery novel *Uncle Tom's Cabin*[88] states her attitude as a story writer.

> From childhood, I loved this work. . . . Even though she [Harriet Beecher Stowe] is a woman, she worked for the abolition of slavery and played an important role in the world by using a single pen. When I learned about her, I felt encouraged.[89]

Kitagawa knew the power of the pen. She also knew the power of *shōjo*; her characters suffered assorted forms of cultural disadvantage but their weak social status connected them empathetically to her young female audience, who occupied the lowest level of social hierarchy, below adults and below boys. Yoshiya exploited a different yet equally inherent quality of her young readership, their dreamy emotional passions. These two authors, who emerged from girls' magazine culture, each used their chosen avenue to deliver subversive messages against unbearable reality—Yoshiya spoke against patriarchal control and Kitagawa against social injustice.

CHAPTER FOUR

Shōjo Feminism in Semi-autobiographical Stories by Yoshiya Nobuko and Morita Tama

The girls' group *Shōjo dokushokai*[1] (Girls' Book Reading Circle), to which Kitagawa Chiyo, Yoshiya Nobuko, and Morita Tama, among others, belonged, eventually grew into a women's study group called *Takane fujinkai* (Takane Women's Group) in 1920.[2] Its mentor, Numata Rippō, was always of a conservative bent, with a belief in the traditional role of women as domestic caretakers.[3] The young members of this group often expressed their disagreement with the liberal philosophy of *Seitō* feminists as they discussed issues such as marriage, women's labor, motherhood, and so on, on the pages of their magazine *Takane* (Dianthus).[4]

But some members of *Takane* eventually diverted from the group's beliefs. Yoshiya, for instance, joined the feminist group *Seitō*. Kitagawa, who became involved in *Sekirankai* and *Haishō undo* (the Movement to Abolish Licensed Prostitution), worked for the liberation of women and children from social and domestic oppression. Morita, in the postwar era, became active in promoting the idea of democracy.[5] They departed the circle to grow into progressive women.

This chapter will examine two semi-autobiographical novels, Yoshiya Nobuko's *Yaneura no nishojo* (Two Virgins in the Attic) and Morita Tama's *Ishikari otome* (Ishikari Maiden). These stories, based on what the authors experienced during their transitional period between girl and woman, are interpretations of patriarchal society viewed from the perspective of *shōjo*. The authors seem to have processed *Seitō* discourses on topics such as the idea of *jiga* (self) and *shojo* (virginity) as they wrote. The books were aimed at a general audience; this allowed the authors to exercise their *shōjo* feminism without being trapped by magazine publishers' educational constraints. The autobiographical stories *Yaneura no nishojo* and *Ishikari otome* widen the definition of *shōjo shōsetsu*, demonstrating that girls' stories can be both entertaining and politically powerful, and are examples of the developed form of girls' fiction which embodies literary and feminist potential.

Yoshiya Nobuko's *Yaneura no nishojo*
Attic as Girls' Space

1920 was a memorable year for Yoshiya, because her *Chi no hate made* (To the Furthest Ends of the World) won first place in a literary competition organized by *Asahi shinbun*.[6] With this story, she started her career as a *bundan* (literary circle) writer, while still writing fiction for girls' magazines. This year also saw the publication by Rakuyōdō of *Yaneura no nishojo*, about a romance not unlike the one Yoshiya Nobuko had with her female lover when she was living in the YWCA in Tokyo. It is a transitional work for Yoshiya in which her literary ambition and girls' fantasy coexist. Yoshiya's ideas of "development" as a writer, however, contradict her continued use of *Hana monogatari*-syle fantasy. The story highlights Yoshiya's attempt to negotiate between these two opposing impulses that makes *Yaneura no nishojo* unique and political.

Yaneura no nishojo starts with a scene in which the heroine, Akiko, leaves her school because she cannot tolerate its strict religious education.[7] Neglecting her studies and school regulations, she had been labeled lazy and even insane by teachers. Her rebellious personality results in solitude and discordance with others. She feels different from other adolescent girls and finds herself unable to adjust anywhere. Akiko's fretfulness is symbolically expressed by the image of spilled rice. She tries to feed rice to birds, but suddenly the bottom of the bag is broken: "In a split second, rice started to spill out. She tried to stop it with her hands, but it did not stop. The more she touched the bag, the larger the hole expanded and rice kept falling on the ground."[8] This image recalls Oriki, a *geisha*, in Higuchi Ichiyō's *Nigorie* (Troubled Waters),[9] whose uncontrollable life is similarly compared to rice that she spills in a ditch. Falling rice aptly evokes the feeling of the gradual decay of dreams and the emptiness after they are gone. Without a goal in her life, Akiko can do nothing but let her life slip away from her.

Akiko soon finds a new place at the YWA (YWCA). In the YWA dormitory, she is assigned a triangular room in the attic on the fourth floor. The attic represents Akiko's marginality and the strangely shaped room symbolizes her peculiarity. Despite its odd shape, however, Akiko falls in love with this room and is thrilled by the sound of the word *yaneura* (attic): "'*Yaneura!*' translated from the English 'attic,' a term which for ordinary people . . . is unnecessary. . . . '*Yaneura*'—in this word, Akiko sensed overwhelming richness, freshness, ambiguous horror, mysterious suspense and timid curiosity."[10] As she goes up the narrow stairs leading to the fourth floor, her heart leaps, and she feels "she is leaving reality and entering a mysterious territory."[11] Influenced by the unique atmosphere of her room, she feels herself becoming a princess held captive in a tall tower. Just like the *shōjo* characters in *Hana monogatari*, Akiko finds happiness in this fantasy space and feels that she has finally found a place where she really belongs.

However, in this piece, Yoshiya constantly affirms the gap between fantasy and reality. For instance, in a scene in which Akiko plays the piano, she fantasizes to herself being a talented musician and, in her imagination, stands in front of an audience in a gorgeous concert hall. In her reverie, after her dramatic piano performance the audience members are moved and with tears in their eyes ask for an encore. A young man suddenly proceeds to the stage. His red eyes "mysteriously shone with passion and his hands shivered.... Proceeding toward the stage weakly, he cried and muttered with tears in his eyes 'Oh, Beethoven...' Then he fainted."[12] The exaggerated emotional scenario is similar to those of *Hana monogatari*. However, unlike the characters in *Hana monogatari*, Akiko cannot stay immersed in her dream. It is broken by the sudden intrusion of the real world.

> Now rich illusion and mirage were all gone. The light of the hallway suddenly showed a shabby girl who carried an old piano book and stood under the light.... "A girl of fantasy" miserably accepted the loneliness of reality into her body—and she cried in her attic.[13]

Realization of the fragility of her world makes Akiko feel abandoned. Akiko's sorrow equates to the feeling of losing her girl's days. Yoshiya explains,

> In her *shōjo* days, she created a fantasy world inspired by the diary of a nun, Clara, and the tale of priest, Francis—However, when the girl entered the sphere of womanhood—beautiful illusion gradually diminished.... After the illusion vanished, there was no shadow of it left.... Her soul was empty inside. It only shed troubled tears of ennui.[14]

Akiko now lives in the attic, a marginal space, and tries to adhere to her dream of *shōjo*. Her fantasy, however, is always threatened by reality close at hand outside the border of her world.

Akiko's encounter with Akitsu Tamaki,[15] her new dorm mate and another outlaw, introduces hope into her life. Tamaki is portrayed as a girl with strong will and a rebellious sprit. Akiko admires her and comes to embrace romantic feelings toward her. Akiko's same-sex desire is uniquely expressed in a scene that takes place in the bathroom.

> In the steam . . . . . . fragments of strangely postured human bodies appeared and disappeared. . . . Akiko heard a pretty voice. A beautiful white arm appeared from the steam and reached toward Akiko with a soft circular movement. It was Tamaki. . . . She said, "Let's go to the balcony together." . . . The moon cast dim light on them. Tamaki held a tiny glass bottle of perfume in her hand, squeezed its rubber top, and then sprayed it . . . . . .[16]

Identically to the similar scene in *Hana monogatari*, the steam in the bathroom erases the physical bodies of the women; signs of reproductive functions, which are irrelevant for girls, are also hidden by the steam. Tamaki's eroticism is limited within a dreamlike air. Tamaki and Akiko eventually become lovers and their lovemaking scene also takes place in a dreamy way.

> . . . . . . Akiko felt a warm body behind her . . . . . . Gentle and soft arms held Akiko's shivering shoulders feverishly . . . . . . Akiko felt quick breath on her cheek . . . . . . Fragments of words came in intervals with a shivering voice . . . . . . "How . . . . . . pure and honest . . . . . . you are . . . . . ." Akiko felt a burning focus on her forehead . . . . . . Tamaki's feverish lips were pressed on Akiko's forehead and were wet with tears . . . . One teardrop muttered, "I am lonely." Then the other teardrop muttered, "I am, too." The two teardrops melted together and became a bigger drop.[17]

Their bodies symbolically change into fluid, by which the physical border between them is erased and they become one. They become only their senses. Their expression of love is poetic and sensuous. They create their *shōjo* utopia in the room in the attic, a secret space hidden from society.

Yoshiya's Shōjo Feminism

Unlike *Hana monogatari*, which eschewed realism, in *Yaneura no nishojo* Yoshiya inserts her feminist perspective of the world. The character Kudō Takako plays a key role in the story. Takako appears as a friend of Tamaki from school—humorous, active, and brave. Feminist critic Yoshikawa Toyoko speculates that Takako is modeled after Hiratsuka Raichō, the founder of the *Seitō* feminist group, as evidenced by the fact that Takako always wears her *hakama* (trousers) lower than the norm and wears *geta* (wooden sandals) like Raichō, who needed to do so in order to assume the kneeling posture of the meditation she practiced.[18] Through Takako, Yoshiya blends *Seitō* discourses into her story. In one scene, Tamaki invites her friends to an "apple party" she organizes in their room in the attic. In the beautifully decorated room, they eat apples, the symbols of knowledge and taboo; symbolically they taste the sweetness of feminist power and ensure an alliance of girls. Takako calls this group of friends "*'black hand' no onna kessha*" (the Black Hand Female Group). The girls put on black gloves and stroll through the town. These black gloves can be seen as a parody of the *Seitō* "blue stockings," and the girls' parade through the town reminds us of an incident during which some *Seitō* members made a show of patronizing establishments in their city's pleasure quarter, which was reported as a scandal in newspapers. This scene can be interpreted as the birth of *shōjo* feminism. Male autocratic attitudes and behavior are scrutinized by these girls' critical eyes. For instance, in a scene in which Akiko tries to get on a train in the morning rush hour, she sees young college students and soldiers pushing women aside. Akiko contemplates the men's behavior toward "the young virgins ... who are someday destined to be chosen by them as their wives. Thinking about this miserable fate of women, [she feels] anger and the unfairness of life."[19] Another example of rude men's behavior is observed in a scene in which the girls go to see a play, where they witness men making fun of a female dancer and smoking cigarettes despite annoying others. Takako bravely confronts them by taking a cushion and swinging it left and right as if she is trying to get rid of the smoke. Yoshiya's criticism of men is harsh. In order to emphasize male oppressive power in society, she depicts girls and women as victims.

In the story, the characters' feminism starts to stall; the girls face increasing challenges. Takako, who becomes acquainted with a poor male artist and supports his artistic aspiration (which reminds us of Hiratsuka Raichō's relationship with her artist partner), suddenly dies from a fever.[20] Losing her friend, Akiko is depressed, realizing that "after all we belong to the dark attic.... For girls like us ... this grey attic is a shelter and a place of comfort."[21] Akiko, however, senses that the protective world of the attic is fragile in nature. Soon, the relationship between Akiko and Tamaki starts to go wrong. Akiko discovers that Tamaki is seeing a woman named Mrs. Ban, who used to be Tamaki's lover. Disappointed in her marriage, Mrs. Ban has come back to Tamaki asking her to die together with her. Unable to understand such a situation, Akiko feels jealous and struggles irrationally. Losing control of her feelings, she madly tortures Tamaki's doll which was a gift from Mrs. Ban (emphasis mine).

> Akiko could not stand looking at the doll, imagining how Tamaki held it in her arms.... *Terrible abominable rage* boiled in Akiko's mind—.... "Stupid! Go away!" Akiko shouted and glared at the doll.... She pulled the hand of the doll roughly. She was treating it not as a five inch doll but as a real human—so she pulled the doll up with all her force, after throwing it on the floor.... "This girl!" She twisted its arm and broke it—She found the broken arm of the doll in her hand and fingers—....[22]

This scene not only spotlights Akiko's anger, but also suggests her symbolic departure from the realm of *joissance*. Akiko's "terrible abominable rage" can be interpreted as the moment of splitting the self, *abjection*, as coined by Julia Kristeva.[23] As abjection is a natural ordeal through which an infant develops and comes to recognize Others, so Akiko reconfirms Tamaki's Otherness through this "terrible abominable rage." Through the ritualistic moment of abjection, Akiko transfers from the world of senses and is reborn as "I." Akiko as "I" desires the love of Tamaki as "Other." Akiko begs her: "Come back to me—I cannot live without you."[24] She hits Tamaki as if pounding on the wall between human and human. Akiko realizes the teardrops, which melted together before, now repel each other, never becoming one again. She notices that there is a border between her and Tamaki that she can never cross. Akiko sees blood on her hands in her imagination; blood symbolizes rage and menstruation. Akiko enters womanhood.

Yoshiya's Development as a Writer

Because of her violent behavior, Akiko is ordered to leave the YWA. She is driven out of her attic, her primary space. While Akiko is packing her things, Tamaki suddenly comes into her room. Under the moonlight, Tamaki appears sublime and beautiful, and in a soft voice, she tells Akiko that she has decided to take Akiko over her ex-lover and will leave the YWA together with her. The tone of the story abruptly changes, which gives readers the impression that Tamaki has suddenly transformed into a superior mentor whose role is to empower and guide Akiko.

> ... Akiko's *jiga* (selfhood) was crying to live with Tamaki. ... The time had come when Akiko recognized the fire inside her mind. ... She was actually a girl with strong *jiga*. ... Tamaki said: "Is there life without self?—No there is not—. ... Akiko, let's become strong women. ... We should live strongly in society with this attic as our starting point. Even if our actions are against social codes, our life is given just for us. ... We should look for our own way—"[25]

The concept of *jiga*, imported from Western philosophy and literature, was a popular and modern idea that sparked conversation among intellectuals.[26] *Jiga* was sometimes viewed as a dangerous concept that threatened the social order. Poet and educator Shimoda Utako warns female readers in *Katei* (Home) that "if you consider home important, you should exterminate the idea of *jiga*."[27] The term was also frequently debated by feminists in *Seitō* magazine. The modernity of the concept of *jiga* manifests in Tamaki, who changes herself not only into a guide for Akiko, but into a modern individual as well. The story is concluded in a theatrical tone of voice.

> The time had come to say goodbye—.... The maidens left their blue triangular room in search of their own destinies holding each other's hands—.... Goodbye! The attic which had become a wine bottle fermenting two maidens' "destinies".... Goodbye! Kissing the wall of the attic, the two virgins finally left the room. In search of their new destiny! In search of the way they should take![28]

Yoshiya may have used this dramatic effect in order to emulate Nora's departure from the house in *A Doll's House* by Henrik Johan Ibsen (1828–1906), which was first performed in Japan in 1911, and was analyzed by *Seitō* feminists of the time. Just like Nora, Akiko and Tamaki leave their old sphere behind to establish their selfhood.[29] The ending of the story is a conglomerate of *Seitō* discourse.[30] Michiko Suzuki pronounces the radical aspects of this growing-up story, as it "portrays same-sex love as an integral aspect of self-discovery and progress, not as something transitory, platonic, distant, or dangerous."[31] In other words, Yoshiya related the achievement of modern selfhood without accepting heteronormativity. The portrayal of sensual same-sex love, however, is now subdued, in exchange for the modern discourse of *jiga*.[32]

Around the time she wrote this story, Yoshiya "was beginning to have doubts about the world of *shōjo* publishing, which increasingly narrowed the possibilities for the meaning of girlhood."[33] Illustrator Fukiya Kōji explains that "Yoshiya was disillusioned by the world of Japanese girls' fiction which, [in her words,] '[did] not acknowledge the value of her work, even if I wrote something comparable to Alcott's *Little Women*.'"[34] The dramatic and invigorating ending of the story connotes Yoshiya's efforts to craft a narrative that would be more in alignment with mainstream acceptance than her earlier works, and her departure from the world of *Hana monogatari*. Although she continued to write for girls' magazines, after *Yaneura no nishojo* Yoshiya began to shift her primary focus to stories written for housewives.[35] Many of her works were published in *Shufu no tomo* (Housewives' Friend) magazine. The pattern of her later works is that a heroine, struggling after discovering her husband's love affair, overcomes her troubles and grows up to become strong with the support of her female friends. However, if we look at the stories she wrote for a mature audience, Yoshiya's essential stance toward readers and literature actually remains the same. Although the latter stories are more realistic and politically articulate, as Kan Satoko notices, Yoshiya's idolization of *shōjo* or young women is still evident.[36] Beautiful female characters such as those portrayed in *Hana monogatari* are transformed into a new female prototype known as *kuon no josei* (eternal women), a refined image of *shōjo*, continuing to provide the female audience (who in a way grew up with Yoshiya) with idealistic dreams.

Sarah Frederick states that the "references to and rejections of the typical romance and marriage plots were no doubt among the reasons for Yoshiya's... popularity among many of *Shufu no tomo*'s typical middle-class readers."[37]

Yoshiya ended up leaving the space of attic behind for the sake of her own development as a writer. However, the narrative inside the attic—free, sensual, radical, and revolutionary—is an artistically rich and intriguing alternative form of female writing. The space of the attic in *Yaneura no nishojo* is the politically dynamic intersection point between lesbianism and feminism. *Yaneura no Nishojo* embodies the dynamism of *shōjo* writings.

Morita Tama's *Ishikari Otome*

1. The casual gatherings of a group of female writers including Yoshiya Nobuko, Uno Chiyo,[38] Hayashi Fumiko (1884–1945), Sata Ineko (1904–1998), Enchi Fumiko (1905–1986), and Harabayashi Taiko (1905–1972) resulted in the establishment of *Joryū bungakushakai* (Japanese Women Writers' Association) in November 1936. It grew into an important organization that fostered the development of Japanese women writers until it dissolved in 2007. Morita Tama (1894–1970), the first female writer from Hokkaido, was a member of this group. Her friendship with Yoshiya Nobuko remained unchanged from the time they were both magazine contributors through their careers as professional writers.

Tama was an enthusiastic girl who became one of the most admired *shōjo* in the girls' magazine community; however, behind this positive public image, she faced many hardships, such as a failed marriage and an illness, which forced the end of her education. Born Muraoka Tama in Sapporo, Hokkaido, the northern island of Japan, her father was the wealthy and well-educated owner of a shipping business. American biologist William Clark's[39] famous phrase, "Boys, be ambitious!" was his cherished motto,[40] and he believed that "ambition" was not assigned to boys alone. He was a modern man open to the idea of gender equality. Recognizing Tama's talent and intelligence at an early age, he always encouraged her to study. Young Tama loved to read and write, and started contributing stories to girls' magazines when she was in Sapporo Kōtō Jogakkō (Sapporo Girls' High School), where the future fiction writer Shiraki Shizu[41] was her classmate. Tama soon became one of the most frequent contributors to *Shōjo sekai* magazine and became a favorite of the editor, Numata Rippō. At the age of seventeen she entered an arranged marriage. Unable to give up her dream to become a writer, she left her husband behind in Hokkaido and embarked on an apprenticeship with author Morita Sōhei[42] in Tokyo. Her first work as a professional writer was "Katase made"

(To Katase), which was published in *Shin seiki* (New Century) magazine in 1913. Her husband was indifferent to her ambitions and their marriage deteriorated; in 1916, she dissolved the union. That same year, Tama married Morita Shichirō, a student at *Keiō gijuku* (later Keio university), after a whirlwind romance. With this marriage, she retreated from the literary world into domestic life. It was not until the age of thirty-eight that Tama started writing again with the support and encouragement of her friends, Uno Chiyo and Yoshiya Nobuko.[43] Morita Tama made her name with her *Momen zuihitsu* (Cotton Essays), published by Chūō Kōronsha in 1936, and thanks to her excellence in crafting essays she was called the "modern Sei Shōnagon" (the author of *The Pillow Book*, a collection of essays from the eleventh century).[44]

It was not easy to be successful in the male-dominated literary world of the time. Morita related how poet and literary critic Kubota Mantarō (1889–1963) told her that her writings were "immature" because she neither smoked nor drank.[45] He was trying to imply that if she wanted to be successful, she had to behave like a man. Similarly, Komiya Toyotaka (1884–1966), a fiction writer, told her that she was someone "who lives by eating dreams"[46]: "you may not be able to write literature [for adults]. But you will be able to write pure and gentle fantasy stories like Hans Christian Andersen's tales."[47] Komiya seems to suggest that women are best suited to write for children. Morita writes that her "disillusionment in the male world got deeper" after these incidents.[48] Women writers, regardless of their nationalities, went through difficulties in the male-oriented literary world, including Louisa May Alcott, who was labeled a "scribbling woman." The portrayal of the strong-willed heroine of *Ishikari otome*,[49] who never gives up her dream to become a writer, resonates with Tama's own story.

Portrayal of a Realistic Adolescent Girl

Ishikari otome, published in 1940 by Jitsugyō no Nihonsha (the publisher of *Shōjo no tomo* magazine), has a mature writing style and deals with adult concerns such as marriage. It therefore goes "beyond the framework of the girls' story genre"[50] and its didactic youth-oriented confines, and is highly regarded by critics including Endō Hiroko, who states that it embodies the elements of *junbungaku* (pure literature).[51] *Ishikari otome* is a bildungsroman. Through the eyes of an adolescent girl, the story also imparts Japanese patriarchal reality. The heroine manages her development into a woman without abandoning her selfhood or dream to become a writer.

The novel starts with the description of the heroine, Nomura Yukiko, whose natural beauty is compared to the grand nature of Hokkaido.[52]

> Just as fruits are grown by storm, soil and sunlight, the girl, born in this land, grows up. The cheeks of the Ishikari maiden... are blushed just like the white petals of apple blossoms are tinted red. The innocent eyes looked blue, mirroring the shadow of the deep blue sky. Her slim neck, resembling the branch of an apple tree, supported a heavy looking head with bobbed hair. The girl stood at the gate watching the mountains far away....[53]

Hokkaido, which became part of the Japanese nation state in the Meiji era, is an important locale in modern Japanese literature. The work of Meiji writers such as Kunikida Doppo[54] made it a place onto which readers were able to "project their desires and a place of escape from whatever fetters had constrained them in Japan proper."[55] Hokkaido "played a prominent role in the establishment of modern literature by providing a space to experiment with new concepts and alternative views."[56] Unlike girls in big cities such as Tokyo, ten-year-old Yukiko is natural and unbound by rigid cultural convention. Similar to Hokkaido, the land of experiment, Yukiko is portrayed as an uncultivated entity, her future still unset. Morita's goal appears to be to follow the process of the heroine's development into a modern woman who refutes the Japanese traditions that diminish girls' potential. *Ishikari otome* details the heroine's struggle between the forces of her inherent nature and Japanese culture as she progresses toward adulthood.

Growing up into a woman is a disquieting metamorphosis for an adolescent girl. Simon de Beauvoir, French philosopher and writer, explains the sensitive interior lives of girls who are going through bodily changes, evocatively illuminating feelings of embarrassment, inadequacy, and resentment.

> ... at the moment of puberty boys also feel their bodies as an embarrassment, but being proud of their manhood from an early age, they proudly project toward manhood the moment of their development.... The little girl, on the contrary, in order to change into a grown-up person, must be confined within the limits imposed upon her by her femininity. The boy sees with wonder in his growing hairiness vague promises of things to come: the girl stands abashed before the "brutal and prescribed drama" that decides her destiny.[57]

In the story there is a scene in which Yukiko, now fifteen years old, is teased by a college student named Ichirō who temporarily lives with Yukiko's family. He calls her a future "*vanpu*" (vamp), because he thinks that Yukiko naturally knows how to entice men. He states,

> "She will become a wonderfully attractive vamp in the future. I guarantee you.... She will attract men one after another, and when the men start to feel that they cannot live without her anymore, she will abandon them. The colder men are treated, the more will they want to chase after her. Eventually, they will end up killing themselves."[58]

Yukiko is sexualized and viewed as a seductive *femme fatale*. For Yukiko, being defined as a sexual object for men is nothing but insulting. She is so angry that her face turns red. She feels that her "innocent precious jewelry-like-memory has been stolen by vulgar male eyes, and she has been ridiculed by his vulgar language."[59] Yukiko, for the first time, discovers the male gaze, which insensitively sexualizes an innocent girl like herself. After this incident, Yukiko becomes cautious of men. When she is touched by Ichirō, even only on her kimono, she becomes uncomfortable, as if "a hairy caterpillar" is crawling over her.[60]

Morita also expresses an adolescent girl's bewilderment and feeling of discomfort using metaphors. Throughout the story, Morita evokes worms and caterpillars when describing the heroine's disgust with men. There is a scene in which Yukiko learns that her friend, a poor servant girl, has been sexually abused by a young man. The servant girl states: "I screamed, but nobody heard my voice. After the violence, he always said 'don't think that I love you. You are like a worm to me.' "[61] Yukiko's repulsion at her friend's victimization is expressed as she expands on the previous worm metaphor with her own memory of a large worm chopped in half and tangled under her sandal.

> On the black and damp soil, the dirty worm's pink surface—which reminded her of human flesh—kept twitching, even after it was chopped in half. The image did not disappear from her for a while. Whenever she remembered this image, it was as if she smelled something that had spoiled.[62]

Her disgust at male lust is expressed through invoking odor and vivid physical imagery somewhat suggestive of the body horror endured by adolescent girls. Yukiko experiences an aversion to her own sexual future, trying to exclude this abominable element from her world.

Throughout the story, Morita portrays girls who are mistreated and sexually exploited by men. Yukiko's friend Keiko is one such girl. Keiko becomes close with a flamboyant schoolboy and starts to be influenced by him. Wearing makeup and styling her hair in a classical manner favored by him, she transforms into a sexually mature woman. Labeled as a corrupted girl, Keiko is eventually expelled from school and accused of having been promiscuous and careless. Yukiko feels sad for her change and angry at the man who has deprived her friend of her precious girlhood, accusing him of having contaminated Keiko's beautiful *shōjo* days and her *junketsu* (physical purity).

Junketsu was an important virtue that supported the "Good Wife, Wise Mother" education. The ideology of female *junketsu*, sexual purity, was a "strategy to control girls' sexuality."[63] Protection of physical purity until marriage was girls' own responsibility, and if this purity was violated, they themselves were held accountable. Yukiko's mother therefore warns Yukiko: "You always make yourself look like you want to be talked to, so people approach you and take advantage of you."[64] She tells Yukiko not to give men the opportunity to easily approach her. Morita uses Yukiko's realization that culture requires her to preserve her body and sexuality for her future marriage as a commentary on the disappearing freedom girls experience as they grow into adults.

Yukiko's mother wants Yukiko to grow up into a domestic woman like her older sister. She sees Yukiko as a troubled girl and is not happy with the fact that Yukiko likes reading and writing. Yukiko is viewed as precocious at school, as well. Yukiko stands out because of her maturity, intelligence, and ambition. There is a scene in which her male teacher condemns the lament for Kunikida Doppo's death that Yukiko writes in her journal. The teacher states: "Kunikida Doppo and you have nothing in common. He is not your uncle. Why do you cry over his death? You mentioned that his death is a huge loss to the Japanese literary circle. But you have nothing to do with the literary circle."[65] Her schoolteacher believes that female students should read what is appropriate for their age and gender, and that literature for mature adults is poisonous for young girls (the same message *Shōjo sekai* delivered in the 1910s). Thus, school and home are places that prepare her to become a future good wife and wise mother, trying to mold her into the ideal woman. However, the more she is oppressed, the stronger grows her desire to become "someone who is allowed to talk about literature someday."[66] Mirroring young Morita Tama, Yukiko starts contributing compositions to a girls' magazine called *Girls' Country*, and making a series of booklets called *Seven Grasses* with her friends. She aspires to become a fiction writer.

Fate of a Domestic Daughter

The end of Yukiko's girlhood is symbolically conveyed by her exit from school and home. Yukiko's health starts to decline, which eventually forces her to quit school. Soon after that, a fire destroys their house, and it is decided that Yukiko will temporarily live with relatives in Akita on the northern end of the mainland, across from Hokkaido. There she will also meet her arranged fiancé, Yoshisuke, for the first time. Yukiko crosses the channel to go to *naichi* (mainland). She had always thought that *naichi* must be "a paradise, the center of culture."[67] Her excitement is expressed thus:

> "*Naichi—Naichi—*Oh, every time my father, mother, and deceased grandfather uttered this word, they always looked excited.... They said, 'I hear that cherry blossoms have already bloomed in *naichi*.' 'People are already wearing early summer *kimono* in *naichi*.' After people get caught up on the news of *naichi*, they talk about their memories—the wonderful play that they observed, the tasty red sea bream they ate and the beautiful ladies that they encountered in *naichi*."... Yukiko has been longing for *naichi* for such a long time![68]

In a reflection of Meiji writers who portrayed Hokkaido as mainland Japan's cultural inferior, Yukiko idealizes *naichi* as a space that possesses cultural superiority. To Yukiko, *naichi* is "not a physical place but somewhere [she] longs for."[69] Akita, however, is not the *naichi* that she envisioned. Upon seeing the town from the outskirts for the first time, she thinks: "This town surely doesn't have beautiful tree lined boulevards [like Hokkaido], and this town surely doesn't have brick buildings with fashionable shop windows.... This town looks old and shabby."[70] Yukiko is disillusioned and realizes that her image of *naichi* was an illusion. In Akita, Yukiko encounters the real *naichi*. In the story, *naichi* is a symbolic space permeated by the deeply rooted Japanese customs and mentalities of the old-fashioned patriarchal *ie* household tradition.

Yukiko meets her fiancé Yoshisuke, a college student, and his extended family. Yoshisuke is intelligent and knowledgeable, but socially awkward. He only communicates with Yukiko through memos or letters and does not directly speak with her. Yukiko is disappointed; not only is she unimpressed by him but also finds they have nothing in common. She feels lonely, sad, and unable to adjust to her new environment.

Kojirō, Yoshisuke's oldest brother and the head of the family, feels sorry for Yukiko, and recognizing that she soothes her loneliness by reading, tells her that she can read the books in the *kura* (old-fashioned storehouse) whenever she wants. Yukiko quickly becomes close with Kojirō, who is well educated and knowledgeable about literature. Kojirō says to Yukiko, "Since you came to this village, I am getting more cheerful. I am happy that I have someone I can talk to in this house."[71] Eiko, Kojiro's wife, is not happy about their close relationship, but her *honne* (honest feelings) and desires have been suppressed in the realm of traditional culture. The issue of the silent suffering of Japanese wives has long been a common theme in Japanese literature. The misery of a wife trapped in the *ie* system is best represented by the character Tomo in Enchi Fumiko's[72] *Onnazaka* (Waiting Years, 1957) who endures the humiliation of being asked to look for a mistress for her husband. Tomo's final rejection of the family on her deathbed by refusing to be buried in the family grave attests to the level of remorse and anger she has hidden for years behind her calm face. Like Tomo, Eiko also seeks a means to express her unhappiness. One day, when Yukiko and Kojirō are merrily talking about literature, Eiko purposely interrupts their conversation by noisily slamming a dresser drawer in the next room. In the *ie* household, the wife is a prisoner of domesticity, and required to selflessly serve and live harmoniously with her husband, parents-in-law, and the rest of her husband's family members. As even Kojirō, who has the responsibility to maintain the familial prosperity, mentions to Yukiko: "There is history here.... But history is a burden for us."[73]

Eiko's strong emotion is hidden behind the facade of a well-mannered, beautiful woman from a good family. But one night a fire destroys the house and symbolically burns away the superficiality of Eiko's domestic mask. As they escape into the darkness outside, Eiko scolds Yukiko for being too slow in bringing a lantern, and roughly grabs it out of Yukiko's hands, causing it to extinguish, for which Eiko further blames Yukiko. Upset by this episode and by Eiko's general mistreatment of Yukiko, Yukiko's aunt tells Kojirō that he should divorce Eiko. Neighbors who used to admire Eiko's beauty quickly change their attitude, calling her "a fox" who has a "fierce mind" behind her "beautiful face."[74] Witnessing the fragile position of *yome* (daughter-in-law of the family) saddens Yukiko: "Even if she seems to be the center of domesticity, her parents-in-law may find reasons to chase her out."[75]

In Japanese folktales and traditional literature, women with fierce emotions are viewed as dangerous and driven out of community and society. To avoid this fate, Eiko apologizes and gains reacceptance as a *yome*. Before returning to Hokkaido, Yukiko visits the couple. Yukiko is surprised by Eiko's change back into a beautiful and calm woman. Yukiko cannot believe that "the same woman can be gentle like this but also can be fierce."[76] However, rather than transforming, Eiko merely seems to have succumbed to her fate, while still looking wistfully at the freedom offered outside the *ie* system. Eiko, who had once stayed in Hokkaido near Yukiko's family, tells Yukiko; "when I was in Hokkaido, it was the happiest time for me."[77] She pleasantly remembers her days in Hokkaido, a frontier whose culture is still in a nascent stage of development and less contaminated by oppressive tradition.

Ie no musume (daughter of a patriarchal family) is destined to become *ie no yome* (housewife of a patriarchal family). If Yukiko marries Yoshisuke, her future will be the same as Eiko's. Yukiko promises herself that she will "never become a *yome*."[78] Yukiko goes back to Hokkaido at the end of the story. Leaving *naichi*, she symbolically sets herself free from Japanese tradition and patriarchal culture. By going back to Hokkaido, the land of hope and experiment, she returns to her original spirit of independence and searches for a new womanhood.

Development as Shōjo *and* Otome

The words *shojo* (処女virgin) and *otome* (乙女maiden) included in the titles (*Yaneura no nishojo* and *Ishikari otome*) are actually interchangeable, meaning girls around marriageable age.[79] These two terms are also connected to feminist discourse. *Shojo ronsō* (virgin debate) famously took place among *Seitō* members in the 1910s and the 1920s.[80] This discourse was triggered by an essay in 1914 by a *Seitō* member, Ikuta Hanayo (1888–1970), who claimed that "virginity and chastity were less important than being able to feed oneself, a conclusion she drew from her own experiences as a poverty-stricken writer."[81] However, others, including Hiratsuka Raichō and Yosano Akiko, equated physical virginity to spiritual purity, insisting that virginity should be kept until a woman finds the man she truly loves.[82] Michiko Suzuki explains that "[a]s the debate continued in a number of journals and mainstream newspapers, both male and female intellectuals jumped into the fray, exploring virginity and chastity from a variety of perspectives."[83] Despite the opposition of Morita and Yoshiya to the cultural control of young women's bodies and sexuality, the words *shojo* and *otome* utilized in the titles of *Yaneura no nishojo* and *Ishikari otome* evoke the heroines' spiritual integrity, nobility, and pride as untouched maidens.[84] Referring to Akiko in *Yaneura no nishojo*, Sarah Frederick states that "by rebelling against natural imperatives to marry men and reproduce, she becomes a more civilized human," and, therefore, "purity" and "chastity" became "something women, both individually and as a cultural unit, construct as a positive quality, one that is not conservative but in fact rebellious."[85] Espousing *Seitō* discourse, these stories trace the trajectories young girls take as they develop into modern, awakened women.

Feminism rarely touches on the experiences of girls.[86] However, Yoshiya Nobuko and Morita Tama, through semi-autobiographical stories,[87] describe the importance of selfhood by focusing on the period in their lives, and their fictional characters' lives, when selfhood was most at risk—the threshold of leaving girlhood to become a wife. Thus, the experience of *shōjo* becomes a fulcrum for feminist awakening.

CHAPTER FIVE

Shōjo no tomo (Girls' Friend)
Conflicting Ideals of Girls on the Home Front

By the late 1930s, the specter of militarism had loomed over Japan for decades, and the country was on the path to global war. War history rarely focuses on the lives of young girls at the time. Girls' magazines provide valuable media in which are recorded not only the transformations of their editors and writers, but also the actual voices of their audiences. Understanding the influential nature of girls' magazine media, the Japanese government controlled and manipulated it, inserting war propaganda by which to educate young girls to become patriotic citizens. Influenced for the first time by a formidable external power, girls' popular media was pushed in a new direction, but at the same time given added legitimacy and recognition as a cultural force. Therefore, the status of girls' media was raised, and the "way of *shōjo*" gained strength even as, for the moment, the magazines bent to government control.

This chapter will focus on *Shōjo no tomo*, the preeminent girls' magazine of the 1930s and '40s, and how it was enlisted by the government to reeducate girls into *gunkoku shōjo* (girls of a military nation). Close examination of the magazine suggests that the editor and writers expressed their frustration and resistance against the government's excessive control in a subtle way, despite their avowed support of the war. For example, Yoshiya Nobuko utilized her girls' stories to challenge the government and to assert her own political stance as a pacifist, a promulgator of universal sisterhood. As an article mentioned in this chapter shows, she believed in the value of female culture and the power of women's collective sentimentality, and tried to challenge male culture (which she believed instigated war). But eventually she became a war abettor herself; her interpretation of peace was naive enough to be easily absorbed into the scheme of the government. Some girls' story writers wanted the sphere of girls (who had little social obligation) to be a fort in which to escape from war society. However, it in fact became a heavily supervised governmental precinct. The record of this friction between the goals of the government and the various aims of the authors is encrypted on the pages of *Shōjo no tomo* from the tumultuous war era.

Golden Age of *Shōjo no Tomo*

The 1930s was a transitional period in the development of Japanese girls' magazine culture. *Shōjo sekai*, which had been the leading girls' magazine, ended its run in 1931. In July of the same year, as if to announce the arrival of a new era, *Shōjo no tomo* welcomed new chief editor, Uchiyama Motoi,[1] who introduced fresh ideas and innovations and established its "golden age."[2] The magazine became more modern, glamorous and entertaining. With the arrival in 1935 of young artist, Nakahara Jun'ichi,[3] who decorated it with his beautiful illustrations, *Shōjo no tomo* secured its status as the most influential girls' magazine.

Shōjo no tomo's success was at its peak in the early 1930s. Stories revolving around beautiful and modern *shōjo* continued to attract a large audience. Kawabata Yasunari,[4] who became involved with the magazine in 1937, and Yoshiya Nobuko were particularly popular and were regarded as the "faces of *Shōjo no tomo*." Nakahara Jun'ichi illustrated girls with big dreamy eyes who always wore ribbons in their hair. Apart from the stories, each issue also contained other captivating material such as pictures of Takarazuka stars and *furoku* (supplementary gifts such as stationary, bookmarks, and card games) emblazoned with Nakahara's illustrations. The magazine was filled with Western images and motifs, and the lifestyle of healthy and lively Western girls was introduced to the audience.

Film versions of Western juvenile stories came to be important pointers in forming the girls' fiction of the 1930s. Around this time, a number of Western films based on famous girls' stories were released in Japan,[5] including *Little Women* (Japanese title, *Wakakusa monogatari* [titled by Yoshiya Nobuko]),[6] *Anne of Green Gables* (Japanese title, *Beni suzume*),[7] and *Heidi* (Japanese title, *Haiji*).[8] These films, introducing Western values of home and family in contrast to the traditional Japanese *ie* system, helped modernize Japanese girls' stories. Yoshiya Nobuko's *Shimake no kodomobeya* (Children's Room of the Shima Family) published in *Shōjo no tomo* from January to October 1936 is clearly inspired by *Little Women*.[9] The story revolves around the four children of the Shima family. Mihoko, a tomboy, is the oldest sister, and she shows a talent for writing. The second sister, Kikuko, a gentle and kind girl, is good at domestic work. The brother, Tōru, is cheerful and friendly, and the youngest child, Masuko, exhibits a comic wit. Although the family is poor, they love each other and live cheerfully. In the story, just as in *Little Women*, their father (in this case a painter preparing for his exhibition in a different town) becomes ill and the mother goes to nurse him. The four children are left alone in the house. They collaborate with each other to protect their home during their parents' absence. *Shimake no kodomobeya* is a heartwarming home drama, written in a casual style. As the idea of *kodomobeya* (children's room) suggests, Yoshiya regards the sphere of children as a modern and independent space free from parental control.

The contribution of another emerging writer, Yuri Seiko (1911–1943), to the Westernization of girls' fiction during this era is hard to ignore. She started by submitting compositions to *Shōjo no tomo*, and her talent was recognized by Uchiyama Motoi.[10] Her best-known work, *Chibikun monogatari* (Story of Chibi), published in *Shōjo no tomo* from 1934 to 1936, is also about the everyday lives of children in a warm modern family. Yuri's work was characterized by colloquial writing and a Western atmosphere. Her *Modan shōkōjo* (Modern Little Princess) is a parody of *A Little Princess*. Fukuda Ichiyo considers that the epistolary style employed in the story reflects the influence of *Daddy-Long-Legs* (known as *Ashinaga ojisan*[11] in Japan).[12]

Another aspect of the magazine at this time, which would prove very important, was the gradual adjustment of the nature of the *shōjo* world it painted from a dreamy realm to a more realistic one. This recalibration would shortly be appropriated by the government, as we will soon see. Both story content and editorial policy reflected this shift. Kawabata Yasunari's *Otome no minato* (Maiden's Harbor; June 1937–March 1938)[13] illustrates the S relationship of two schoolgirls, Michiko and Yōko, and the difficult experiences that each encounters in life (in Michiko's case, a problematic friendship, and in Yōko's case, financial trouble). It describes how they encourage each other to overcome their hardships. Yōko's work at an orphanage converts their S relationship into love for children, and in the end causes them to shift their eyes to the world outside school. They "get out of the dreamy world and plunge into the realistic world."[14] Unlike earlier girls' stories, which had placed great emphasis on introvertive romanticism, it sends a positive educational message to the audience.

One of editor in chief Uchiyama Motoi's educational goals was nurturing young readers' "independence and individual thinking."[15] Like Numata Rippō, the editor of *Shōjo sekai*, Uchiyama valued communication between the audience and himself. In a readers' column called "*Tomochan kurabu*" (Dear Friends Club), Uchiyama showed love and care and tried to listen to what each reader had in mind. As Uchiyama Shizue (a research staff member at the Yayoi museum) describes,

All of the letters were addressed to Uchiyama Motoi. Readers called him Uchiyama sensei and trusted him as a person who understood their problems and guided them. Uchiyama read all the submissions, which was a tremendous amount, and answered them in the magazine. In short, a "human to human" relationship was established in the readers' column of *Shōjo no tomo*.[16]

The readers' section was no longer a narcissistic space where schoolgirls exchanged emotions, but had developed into a fun community in which readers talked about their lives at home and school. Instead of regarding his audience as "pre-mature women-to-be," Uchiyama respected his readers as *shōjo* without trivializing them. Uchiyama Motoi was a driving force of *Shōjo no tomo* magazine in the 1930s.

Government Media Restrictions and Girls' Stories

Looking back at the magazines of that time, one reader recollects thus: "*Shōjo no tomo* enticed me with its fantasy and dreamy air.... At that time, Japan was proceeding to war after the Manchurian Incident, and school girls were not free.... *Shōjo*, *otome*, and romanticism only existed in this magazine."[17] However, war soon started to cast a dark shadow across the magazine pages. In 1938, *Jidō yomimono kaizen ni kansuru shidō yōkō* (The Guide for the Improvement and Purification of Stories for Children) was distributed.[18] It condemned commercialism and prohibited excessive self-promotion within magazines and vulgarity in illustrations, stories and comics, and so on. It instead encouraged children's education, instructing publishers to teach children above age ten the importance of cultivating the Japanese spirit, specifying the qualities of "religiousness, loyalty, service, honesty, faithfulness, humility, courage, and affection."[19] Publishers and editors were assembled by Japan's Home Ministry and were instructed on the content of the guide. Magazine editors had to adjust their magazine policies in order to meet governmental guidelines and expectations. The Archive Division, which was in charge of press censorship, checked publications and drew lines over any text that was considered to be problematic. *Shōjo no tomo* was carefully examined by the authorities. Beautiful prints of Takarazuka actors disappeared from the magazine, and the fancy pen names that readers conventionally used in their letters were condemned.[20] In response to the government's implementation of the new education policy, *Nihon jidō bunka kyōkai* (The Association of Japanese Juvenile Culture) revised its name into *Nihon shōkokumin bunka kyōkai*, (The Association of Japanese Citizens of the Rising Generation), redefining children's stories (including girls' stories) as a kind of literature "read by young children who will become loyal Japanese citizens in the future."[21]

1940 was the most trying year for *Shōjo no tomo*. The censorship division of the government ordered Uchiyama Motoi to eliminate Nakahara's pictures from the publication;[22] the girls Nakahara drew did not portray the image of girls that the government wanted to promote. Their skinny and fragile *shōjo* bodies looked incapable of production or reproduction, and were declared unfit for the time. Uchiyama was troubled by the government coercion and its restrictions on speech.[23] However, for Uchiyama (and other editors of the time), it was impossible to speak out against the war. If they "wanted to resist the war, they needed to understand that they risked their own lives."[24] Uchiyama reluctantly made the decision to remove Nakahara's illustrations from the magazine. With this change, the representative image of *shōjo* was drastically altered. Miyamoto Saburō,[25] who served as a war artist in South East Asia, was put in charge of cover illustrations. The *shōjo* that Miyamoto drew were girls with realistic bodies. Also, they neither had permed hair (which symbolized modernity) nor wore Western dress.

Uchiyama told the readers of his decision to remove Nakahara's pictures.

> Nakahara-san's pictures are now gone from *Shōjo no tomo*. I am sure that many readers are feeling sad and disappointed by our decision.... His pictures are beautiful and his artistic skills are excellent; however... the pictures of girls he drew do not look healthy or strong enough.... Now, we Japanese have to proceed to our goal. The goal, as you know, is the completion of our sacred war. We Japanese have to be healthy.... Nakahara-san's pictures will disappear for a while.[26]

The girls that Nakahara drew represented adolescent fantasies. What the government needed at that time were strong young women who would eventually join the system of "production" by becoming mothers in the future.

While there were letters that supported Uchiyama's decision in the September issue,[27] many others expressed their sadness and disappointment. One girl wrote that "I grew up with the atmosphere of *Shōjo no tomo*. Now I feel like my hometown has disappeared."[28] This reader clearly expresses that *Shōjo no tomo* was her home, or cultural center, and had provided her with comfort and protection. Uchiyama replied that "if a *shōjo*'s dream is something that weakens girls, it has to be given up."[29] In the editor's note, he further stated,

> The readers seem to take the idea of a dream as something fragile.... True dreams will be born in reality and have to give us the power to cultivate

healthy and strong lives. We tend to mix up real dreams with illusionary dreams. The influence of illusionary dreams is like opium.[30]

Uchiyama does not reject the idea of dreams themselves, but condemns dreams of unrealistic beauty. Ironically, however, the taste of "opium" was what had attracted schoolgirls and made the magazine so successful in the first place.

Imada Erika postulates that the publication of readers' negative reactions may have been Uchiyama's covert articulation of resistance to the government.[31] Using the letters of "immature" schoolgirls, Uchiyama managed to give his audience members an opportunity to express their voices in society and show how they felt

Figure 5.1. Cover illustration of the June 1940 issue of *Shōjo no tomo* by Nakahara Jun'ichi. *Shōjo no tomo* 33, no. 6 (1940). © Junichi Nakahara/Himawariya.

about the deprivation they experienced. The subtle resistance against authority indicated by these letters and the tension between the audience (and editor) and the government is intriguing evidence of the rebellious aspect of girls' culture.

After Nakahara left the magazine, the atmosphere of *Shōjo no tomo* quickly changed. Phrases like "*gakkō mo ouchi mo kessenjō*" (Both School and Home as Battle Fields), "*tōtoki nihon utsukushiki nihon*" (Noble Japan, Beautiful Japan), and "*watashitachi mo zōsan senshi*" (We Too Are Soldiers Working to Increase Production) started to appear on the front covers to push people's motivation for the war efforts forward. The term, *zōsan senshi* ("soldier" to increase production), in particular, frequently appeared on girls' magazines. Through articles and pictures,

Figure 5.2. Cover illustration of the July 1940 issue of *Shōjo no tomo* by Miyamoto Saburō. *Shōjo no tomo* 33, no. 7 (1940). © Mineko Miyamoto 2018/JAA1800019.

girl readers were taught about their new wartime role as factory workers (the enthusiasm and ambition of young female factory workers to meet production targets are depicted in *Ichiban utsukushiku* [The Most Beautiful], a propaganda film directed by Kurosawa Akira. This film was released in 1944). In *Shōjo no tomo* there were also articles explaining the situation in Manchukuo (or Manshūkoku), the supposed independent state consisting of five ethnic groups—Japanese, Chinese, Korean, Manchurian, and Mongolian—which was created by Imperial Japan in 1932 (in fact, Manchukuo was under the rigid control of the Japanese as part of the expansion of their power into Asia).[32] The idea of *gozoku kyōwa* (the cooperation of five ethnic groups) and the concept of Japanese leadership in Asia filled the magazine's pages. Writers had no choice but to adapt to this change.[33]

Yoshiya's Wartime Message

Yoshiya Nobuko continued to be active during this period, her stance gradually evolving. Her prolific wartime activities included writing girls' stories for *Shōjo no tomo* and *Shōjo kurabu*, and stories for housewives in *Shufu no tomo* (Housewives' Friend), in addition to submitting reports from the war zone. In 1937, she was sent to China as a special correspondent of *Shufu no tomo* magazine.[34] This contribution was recognized by the government, and in 1938, she was given the respected position of *jūgun sakka* (campaign writer), as a member of the *pen butai* (pen corps). Twenty-two literary figures[35] were chosen for the pen corps, a year after the Sino-Japanese War broke out. The goal of this organization was to accompany the Japanese military to China and write war *jūgunki* (reports on accompanying the military) from a personal perspective.[36] Travel costs were covered by the government, and if a writer was killed during their assignment, they would be consecrated at the Yasukuni shrine.[37] Through her participation, Yoshiya gained respect and recognition as a "mature writer," and began to imbue girls' magazines with the color of war. In 1940, in celebration of the 2,600th year of Imperial reign, she wrote this message to the readers of *Shōjo no tomo*: "We Japanese have a long traditional history of 2,600 years. We are now entering a new century.... Our nation is fighting for the strong unity of Asians. For this dream, we have to endure difficulties."[38] Her girls' stories expressed strong patriotic inclinations.[39]

But Yoshiya did not abandon her personal motivations for writing. The January 1938 issue of *Shōjo no tomo* published a dialogue between Uchiyama Motoi and Yoshiya Nobuko. Yoshiya complained that "girls' stories are often despised.... People tend to think that sentimentality is all there is to girls' stories."[40] She further expressed her frustration that "[w]omen are after all looked down upon by men.... I have been laughed at, because I am a popular writer who originated in girls' literature. Even when I write stories for adults, people still laugh at me and take my stories as no better than children's stories."[41] Uchiyama sympathized with Yoshiya, agreeing that "the world of girls' stories needs to be appreciated more."[42] Her original motive for participating in wartime activities was to add momentum to the promotion of her own ideas. The government's eagerness to motivate women to contribute to the war effort provided a perfect avenue for Yoshiya, as well as feminists such as Hiratsuka Raichō, Takamure Itsue, and Ichikawa Fusae, to extol the power of women.

Yoshiya's persistence in advocating her own beliefs created a mixed message in some of her stories during the war. "Hitotsubu no mugi tomo naran" (To Become a Kernel of Wheat), published in *Shōjo no tomo* in March 1941, is a good example of how Yoshiya continued to promote her own positive feelings toward the West in her work, regardless of whether it conformed to the government's directive. The story (the title of which is taken from the Bible) takes the format of a letter the author receives from a girl attending a missionary school founded by a well-known American missionary. The author is impressed by it and decides to share it with her readers. The schoolgirl states that she is sad that society has started to bear negative feelings toward Western culture and to regard Westerners as enemies. According to the letter, her school has started to send Western teachers back to their own countries, and has suddenly become a purely Japanese school. When her teacher leaves the country, she tells her students: "I loved Japan very much... but sad to say, because of the political problem between our two countries, we cannot continue our friendship, though we desire to.... I hope someday the relationship between our two countries will get better."[43] The schoolgirl writes how much she loved and respected her American teachers, and that although Japan is fighting against America, she will never forget their kindness and sincerity. She goes on to promise herself that she will become a schoolteacher someday, and, just as her Western teachers came to her country, she will go to China and work to establish friendship between China and Japan. She pledges to become "a kernel of wheat," stating that she would be willing to sacrifice her life to "educate" Chinese girls and teach them the importance of creating peace in Asia. Although Yoshiya puts herself into the service of Japanese colonial expansion, it is interesting that she borrows a Christian (Western) phrase to evoke bravery and selflessness in the girl's decision to help the Chinese. The story can be taken as Yoshiya's commentary on the anti-Western movement that was prevalent in society at the time. The way she straddles both Japanese colonial and pro-Western attitudes, seemingly sincerely in both cases, is fascinating. In fact, *Shōjo no tomo* published many articles that touched on the relationship between Japan and the West. Like Uchiyama Motoi, who expressed covert resistance to the government by employing readers' letters, Yoshiya used the format of a fictional letter to camouflage honest thoughts that were hard to state more directly.

Similarly, in the July 1941 issue, Yoshiya expresses her opposition to anti-West views in a conversation with a news chief from the military. The news chief states that "women tend to adore Western culture. That's because Western countries have established girls' schools in order to brainwash Japanese people with their culture.... Because of our excessive adoration of the West, we came to have the idea that the East is lower."[44] Yoshiya appears to be offended by his statement. She replies,

> You just stated that women tend to worship the West, but, reading a book on Meiji history, I see it was men who stressed that Japanese have to learn from the West. Studying overseas used to be considered an important step for men and men did anything to go abroad—even married rich girls for this purpose.... Now Japan is chasing Western teachers out of the country.... They truly loved their Japanese students and were true educators. I have seen the positive side of Westerners, so I cannot help but have admiration for the West.[45]

Yoshiya's stories always had a Western air that helped her and her audience escape the hard truth of patriarchy. To them, Western culture was part of their own culture. An attack on it meant that women's culture was also being criticized. Yoshiya's protest is in defense of herself as much as in defense of Western teachers and schoolgirls.

Yoshiya was always concerned for women and women's culture. She admired the hard work of military nurses, and recorded sad stories of the women who sacrificed their lives in the war. Her compassion also extended to Chinese women. For instance, Yoshiya was moved when she read a letter written by a Chinese mother who wanted her son to stop fighting and come home.[46] Yoshiya saw women as victims of the war and presented their misery with compassion. Yoshiya visited a Chinese girls' school in Shanghai that had been destroyed by the Japanese military.[47] Having found a scrap of paper in the debris that was filled with anti-Japanese statements by a Chinese schoolgirl, Yoshiya was sad, but at the same time she was deeply impressed by the girl's steadfast thoughts and patriotic spirit. Comparing this girl with Japanese schoolgirls, she stated: "In Japan, the topics of conversation among Japanese schoolgirls are Takarazuka and Shōchiku theatres. Chinese girls' interests, on the other hand, lie in anti-Japanese discussions. We Japanese women have been indifferent to the women in the neighboring countries of Asia."⁴⁸ Yoshiya saw heroism in this Chinese girl, and concluded her reportage by hoping that the Chinese girl would be safe and sound: "We, Japanese women, hope that someday you (the Chinese girl) will write about the friendship between Japan and China in an essay.... Until then, please be safe!"⁴⁹ Yoshiya's perspective was distinctively different from that of female fiction writer Hayashi Fumiko,⁵⁰ a fellow pen corps member, whose reports were filled with tales of Japanese soldiers' heroism. ⁵¹ Yoshiya's eyes were always directed to women and girls.

The message that Yoshiya constructed here can be called "universal sisterhood,"⁵² the concept of which is summarized in the following statement in a 1937 issue of *Shufu no tomo*:

> Ah, women—mothers—in the world who produce humans on this earth. Regardless of East or West, we, as women, beyond geographical borders, should stay hand in hand, united together in order to stop the violence and war. We should establish a peaceful world. It may take 100 years for this peace to eventuate, but we women should work towards this dream.⁵³

Yoshiya's message seems to have borrowed from the concept of "international bonds of womanhood" deliberated at the meetings of the Women's International League for Peace and Freedom (WILPF).⁵⁴ Women's collaborative power was a goal of feminists around the world at the time.

But Yoshiya has been disparaged by critics for her political naïveté. Kamiya Tadataka criticizes Yoshiya for decorating her writing with "sweet language" and obscuring reality.⁵⁵ Takasaki Ryūji is also critical of Yoshiya, claiming that her basic premise was always that Japan was the leader of Asia and her ideal of women's friendship coincided with the notion of Japan as colonizer. Indeed, it is clear that Yoshiya's ideas not only lacked a solution for class and racial differences, but her concept of "universal sisterhood" and the "friendship between Japan and China" perfectly dovetailed with the idea of the coprosperity of Pan-Asia, the government's excuse for colonial domination. Takasaki further posits that her writing derived from her "*jogakuseiteki shikō*" (schoolgirl logic),⁵⁶ stressing that she was a collaborator with the government and responsible for promoting the war. Yoshiya even stated that

> We have to defeat the germs of anti-Japanese sentiment and establish the foundation of eternal cooperation in the Japanese-Chinese relationship. The Japanese Imperial Army is devoting their lives by shedding blood in fighting in Northern and Southern China, in mountains and rivers. Japanese women, too, although we don't use weapons, should fight to convert Chinese women's mistaken views.⁵⁷

She believed simply in a sentimental culture of women and girls, and stressed binary gender oppositions of stereotypes—men versus women, soldier versus mother, and war versus peace—attempting to convey the disparity between the war messages of men's culture and women's culture by insisting on the superiority of the latter. But she ignored the existence of colonial tension within women and girls, only proclaiming women's sisterly bonds and urging them to mobilize for peace. Although Yoshiya was always primarily concerned with the plight of women and girls, this does not mean, as we have seen, that she would relinquish her belief in the occupation. While she presented herself as a pacifist, she acted, to the contrary, as a nationalist writer. Kan Satoko states that Yoshiya's belief in women's sympathy beyond nationality was probably sincere, but the sentimentalism that Yoshiya utilized in her fiction to provoke sympathy harbored danger, because it eventually functioned to mobilize Japanese women for war.[58]

Creating Patriotic *Shōjo*

Many other writers who were involved in girls' magazines fell into the same trap of promoting "peace creation" in Asia. In an essay written after the war, Morita Tama stated that she initially held an antiwar stance and had strong opposition to the government's policy, for which she was criticized by fellow writers, and that she eventually came to believe that what people cannot openly state in public "should be shared among family members and handed down from mothers' mouths to their children,"[59] hoping that the children of these mothers would one day create a peaceful world. In fact, Morita ended up serving as a war reporter with the Japanese navy and traveled to Southeast Asia in 1939.

Kawabata Yasunari, an active contributor to *Shōjo no tomo*, also experienced great conflict between his educational beliefs and the responsibility forced on him as a Japanese writer during the war. Kawabata tends to be viewed as having maintained a low profile during the war.[60] However, he ended up involved with Japanese language education in Manchukuo, where Japanese had become the official language in 1937.[61] He served as a commentator on readers' compositions in order to promote *tsuzurikata undō* (composition movement),[62] the original goal of which was to nurture children's pure spirits through writing, but his comments in a 1942 issue obviously confirm his involvement in the government's colonial scheme.

> Your writings printed in magazines will be read by people in Manchukuo and China.... As Japanese girls, I want you to improve your writing....
> In Manchukuo, I had a chance to look at children's compositions, but

theirs are so far behind.... Your good compositions should be the model for those who live outside Japan.⁶³

Kawabata's serialized girls' story, *Utsukushii tabi* (Beautiful Voyage),⁶⁴ also came to be filled with messages that praised Japanese superiority. The story, detailing the life of a blind and deaf girl and the devotion of her female teacher (inspired by the relationship between Helen Keller and Anne Sullivan), was abruptly converted into the story of a teacher who realizes her mission as a Japanese is to "improve" the level of children's education in Manchukuo and to "raise" their cultural standards. Thus, magazines were utilized as a perfect medium by which to manipulate people's mind-sets. Education was a practical means through which the government could justify their colonial expansion.

Meanwhile, *Shōjo no tomo*'s rival, *Shōjo kurabu* (published by Kōdansha), also developed into a patriotic magazine. The target audience of *Shōjo kurabu* was younger than that of *Shōjo no tomo*, which consisted approximately of the upper grades of elementary school through middle and high school.⁶⁵ *Shōjo no tomo* had an urban image, but *Shōjo kurabu* sold well outside of cities and its stories often took place in the countryside. Writers such as Kitagawa Chiyo, Tsuboi Sakae, Satō Kōroku (1874–1949; he is known for boys' stories), and so forth frequently contributed their stories to *Shōjo kurabu*. With the phrase "textbook in the left hand, *Shōjo kurabu* in the right hand" as its motto, it vigorously supported the war by teaching young readers their wartime responsibilities. A short story titled "Mihoko no shigoto" (Mihoko's Job) by Tsuda Katsuo,⁶⁶ for instance, teaches readers how to participate in the war practically with the example of a girl who works at a factory. The girl finds sublime meaning in her work, realizing that she is a *sangyō senshi* (industrial fighter), taking revenge on her enemies for the death of her older brother. Kitagawa Chiyo's⁶⁷ "Usagi o kau shōjo" (A Girl Who Raises Rabbits) shows readers how to raise rabbits and teaches how rabbit-fur coats and gloves are appreciated by Japanese soldiers.⁶⁸ Tsuboi Sakae's "Tsuyukusa" (Commelina)⁶⁹ is about a working girl who digs a *bōkūgō* (air raid shelter), hoping that she can take care of neighborhood children when the time comes. Many stories and articles provided tips for surviving food shortages and strongly encouraged cooperation within *tonarigumi*, neighborhood associations that consisted of small household units, formed as part of the national mobilization program. Tsuboi and Kitagawa, socialist writers, emphasized the value of labor. Their messages aligned with the goal of *Shōjo kurabu*, which tried to instruct its audience how to participate in the war as good *shōkokumin* (young citizens) of Imperial Japan through labor. These authors smoothly transformed into *jūgo no onna* (women behind shields).

Unlike *Shōjo kurabu* readers, however, the wartime role of *Shōjo no tomo*'s middle-class urban audience was ambiguous. Editor Uchiyama Motoi often received criticism for *Shōjo no tomo* readers' lack of contribution to society. Muraoka Hanako,[70] for instance, stated that "girls should think about their *seikatsu* [lifestyle] more seriously."[71] In response to educators' and officials' criticism of girls' education, Uchiyama had no choice but to "improve" the quality of his magazine by including didactic tales that taught frugality and the value of labor. He repeatedly emphasized the country's situation and that Japanese girls should recognize their responsibility as Japanese citizens. He often criticized his audience when they showed attachment to the old flowery culture. For instance, answering a reader's January 1941 letter that expressed sadness about the termination of *Kageki* (Opera) magazine,[72] he commented: "It is a shame that Japanese girls find dreams only in theatre magazines. Girls' dreams should not be small and low. Think about what the Japanese nation is trying to do now."[73] He denounced the culture that he himself had constructed and the image of "girl" that he had previously tried to protect. He now attempted to "elevate" it to meet social standards. He even changed *Tomochan kurabu* into *Seikatsu kyōshitsu* (Lifestyle Classroom) in November 1942: *kurabu*, a foreign word—in fact, "enemy language"—that denoted a circle in which girls played and shared interests, was changed to *kyōshitsu*, the Japanese word for classroom, a strictly educational space.

As the war dragged on, *Shōjo no tomo* hit upon a new strategy to regain the enthusiasm and collaboration of readers, who were displeased with the loss of elements of *shōjo* culture that had been taken from them. The authors and editors simply transformed the image of the Japanese girl from *yumemiru shōjo* (dreamy *shōjo*) into *aikoku shōjo* (patriotic *shōjo*), delineating a new fantasy that fit the time. The cheerfulness of young girls became a weapon for protecting the Japanese nation. This new image of the Japanese girl that *Shōjo no tomo* emphasized is summarized in this 1943 statement by Uchiyama.

> Schoolgirls are like beautiful flowers. If all the flowers disappeared from society, we would be sad. . . . Schoolgirls may not be able to work in factories or fight in the war, but the beauty of schoolgirls enlightens the soldiers on the battlefield. Girls provide them with cheerful and warm feelings.[74]

The readers of *Shōjo no tomo* were referred to as *gunkoku shōjo*. Their role was to become "flowers" of society and encourage the soldiers. With their youth, bravery, and beauty, they were viewed as spiritual fighters—as the "reserves of women on the home front," they became symbolic icons that were to brighten the sacred path of Japan. Artist Takamura Kōtarō[75] writes the following in a poem: "A *shōjo* is a great soldier.... / Born with a pure heart, / she understands why we fight.... / A *shōjo* is bright as the sun, / she will brighten people's hearts. / When a *shōjo* fights, / there will be a shining victory in our Great War."[76] Despite their earlier resistance, readers, who learned that they could also fight in their own way, embraced this reshaped fantasy girl image and their role as Japanese citizens.[77] One reader wrote,

> I feel happy that *Tomochan kurabu* is now changed to *Seikatsu kyōshitsu* and that we step forward strongly. This kind of change is what we have been anticipating. Let's dispose of our half-hearted attitude. Let's bring brightness and prosperity to Japan with the efforts of us young girls.[78]

This change provided young girls with confidence and a sense of identity as Japanese. Tanabe Seiko (1928–), postwar writer and a fan of Yoshiya Nobuko, recollecting her girlhood as a *gunkoku shōjo* in *Watashi no Osaka hyakkei* (Eight Views of My Osaka), writes how she was disappointed by the disappearance of *Shōjo no tomo*'s flowery culture, but how, at the same time, she enjoyed playing the role of a girl on the home front. For instance, she relates a dream she had about becoming a brave spy who successfully completes a mission for the government, earning the lasting respect of a handsome soldier.[79] Romance, dreams, and fantasy existed in the mind of a girl like Tanabe, even in this time of emergency. Honda Masuko describes this new orientation of girls' fantasy life toward real-world issues by stating that "the essence of *shōjo* existed in the horizon which is contiguous to the reality in which realistic girls wore *monpe* work pants, held bamboo spears, and prayed for the destruction of the West and Japan's victory."[80]

By 1944, *Shōjo no tomo* was acknowledged by the government as a *seinen zasshi* (magazine for youth), highly recommended for young readers.[81] From the government's perspective at least, *Shōjo no tomo* had become a first-rate, socially recognized girls' magazine.[82] Because *Shōjo no tomo* followed the government loyally, its contribution was cited and it received the *Jidō bunka shō* (Children's Culture Award) in the magazine category of 1941.[83] The award was a badge of honor given to the publisher for raising good Japanese citizens.

Shōjo no tomo underwent a radical transformation over the course of a decade. The influence of those who were involved in the magazine publication—Yoshiya Nobuko, Kawabata Yasunari, Uchiyama Motoi, and so on—was tremendous, but their ambitions became entangled in the labyrinth of the war situation. Uchiyama came to serve as a spokesman for the government, girls' story writers as "cheerleaders,"[84] and the audience ultimately as "cheer girls" for the state.

It is easy to conclude that writers as well as the girl audience were active participants in the war effort, but such simple dismissal risks ignoring the subtle friction and conflicts recorded in the magazine's pages. Despite pressures and suppressions by the wartime state, the fantasy tradition of *shōjo bunka* survived the war, merely changing in form.

Himawari (Sunflower)
Reimagining *Shōjo* during the Occupation Period

The long, exhausting war ended in August 1945. Uchiyama Motoi, chief editor of *Shōjo no tomo*, stated in that month's issue that we "headed to the enemy knowing that we were making a big mistake.... We chased after a beautiful ideal.... The method the Japanese people took may have been wrong, but the dream of constructing East Asian ethnic happiness was never fake."[1] Uchiyama's statement equivocates between regret for the war and continued adherence to the imperial expansionist principals for which it was fought.

In September, Douglas MacArthur, the Supreme Commander of Allied Powers (SCAP),[2] established his General Headquarters (GHQ) in Hibiya, Tokyo, beginning seven years of occupation. GHQ/SCAP commanded political, legal, educational, and cultural reforms intended to transform Japan into a peaceful and democratic country. All Japanese media was under the strict supervision of GHQ/SCAP, and every Japanese publication had to meet their standards. Publishers, which had supported the Japanese government during the war, gradually surrendered to the new world and altered their policies, becoming advocators of peace. *Shōjo kurabu* (Girls' Club), published by Kōdansha, and which had closely collaborated with the government during the war, wiped militarism from its pages and reinvented itself with the goal of becoming an enjoyable, fun, and bright magazine.[3] Uchiyama Motoi stepped down as editor of *Shōjo no tomo* and its contents now frequently advocated American ideals. America was the "architect of new Japan";[4] not only was the idea of democracy promoted, but American culture and American people's lifestyles were submitted as models for Japanese people. Democratizing Japan meant Americanizing Japan. Girls' magazines came to be filled with images of America.

New girls' magazines arrived on the scene. One such magazine was *Himawari* (Sunflower), which was founded in 1947 by Nakahara

Figure 6.1. Cover illustration of the January 1947 issue of *Himawari* by Nakahara Jun'ichi. *Himawari* 1, no. 1 (1947). © Junichi Nakahara/Himawariya.

Jun'ichi, the illustrator whose removal from *Shōjo no tomo* during the war had been mandated by the government. With Muraoka Hanako, Kawabata Yasunari, Yoshiya Nobuko, Fukiya Kōji, among others as inaugural contributors, Nakahara aimed to make a beautiful and educational magazine in the spirit of prewar *Shōjo no tomo*. While *Himawari* emphasized traditional female gender roles, it also reflected progressive American thoughts. The Western concept of home in particular was promoted, and girls' stories were utilized to spread new educational concepts. A new image of Japanese *shōjo*, modeled after American fictional heroines, was explored. However, reading the magazine carefully, one also finds the creators' bewilderment with rapidly changing society and nostalgia for the disappearing prewar aesthetic. Kawabata Yasunari's *Hana to kosuzu* (Flower and Small Bell) will provide a particularly good example of this; the image of an unfortunate *shōjo* is an expression of the author's lament for the disappearance of old Japanese culture.

Under the surveillance of GHQ/SCAP, girls' magazines struggled to negotiate Americanism and their own culture and to find new educational goals. But none of them grew or developed to create a culturally impactful *shōjo* community. *Himawari* accepted American culture, while it simultaneously aimed to re-create a magazine like the ones from before the war. Two impulses, progressiveness and nostalgia, coexisted in the magazine and sometimes contradicted each other. In the end, *Himawari* no longer functioned as a girls' community; it was a space in which adults could reflect on their own postwar selves.

Girls' Magazines, GHQ/SCAP, and the Development of New Japan

The urgent goals of GHQ/SCAP were to root out militarism and ultra-nationalism from Japanese culture and society and to teach Japanese citizens peace-oriented, democratic values.[5] In October 1945, the Civil Information and Education (CIE) section was established and proceeded to conduct reforms in the "areas of education, religion and public information."[6] To effectively "remold the minds of the Japanese,"[7] it took full advantage of popular media.

The CIE opened twenty-three libraries that provided books, periodicals, and pamphlets with which to familiarize Japanese people with American culture. The CIE decided that books were the "most efficacious media source for inculcating American democratic principles in Japanese people."[8] They established a competitive bidding system for the translation and publication of foreign copyrighted books. "By May 1948, one hundred foreign copyrighted books ... were granted commercial translation rights by the CIE,"[9] which, according to Ochi Hiromi's research, included American girls' stories such as *Little Women*, *Daddy-Long-Legs*, *Pollyanna*, *What Katy Did*, *The Long Winter*, and so on.[10] American women's magazines such as *Better Homes and Gardens*, *Good Housekeeping*, *Ladies Home Journal*, and so forth[11] were also placed in the libraries. The pages of the magazines—filled with modern appliances and trendy fashion—entertained Japanese women greatly (even though they did not understand English). Japanese women's magazines also extolled "the American housewife's ability to manage her home scientifically, maintain a companionate life with her husband, and forward democracy through volunteer activities."[12] From magazines, Japanese people learned the American lifestyle and "took in democracy and freedom."[13] Films were also utilized by the CIE, as were radio programs such as *Fujin no jikan* (Women's Time),[14] which began in October 1945. Morita Tama frequently appeared on this show. The goal of this program was to raise women's sociopolitical awareness. It introduced listeners to new women's culture, good books, and stories of great American women, and broadcasted domestic dramas. Educational films promoting Western culture—schools, politics, family, sightseeing places, and so on—toured across Japan. "Images related to peace, Western things, and happy families were presented one after another."[15] Japanese people enjoyed the cultural image and information provided by the CIE, and more importantly, they started to associate the idea of "happiness" and "affluence" with American culture.

GHQ/SCAP found the old-fashioned Japanese *ie* family system to be a source of gender discrimination and attempted to root it out; in its stead, they tried to spread the image of the Western home—a modern nuclear family in which a husband and a wife have a democratic relationship and children are equally treated as their treasures. Films and magazines demonstrated domesticity as women's space, and the image of happy housewives—who embraced their equal rights at home—was particularly emphasized. "The housewife became the archetypal figure of womanhood."[16] But as Mark McLelland mentions, although the US occupation authorities attempted to release women from "what were considered feudalistic customs, attitudes, and practices,"[17] they "were not advocating a radical feminist agenda."[18] Also, despite the new Japanese constitution, which protected liberal ideas of individualism, the law relating to family and nationality continued to show "traces of the patriarchal family system" in the form of *koseki* (household registration) which clearly records who the head of the household is.[19] *Minshushugi* (English title, *Primer of Democracy*), a textbook that the CIE compiled with the assistance of Japanese scholars, defined that Japanese women should be citizens who had a "high level of education and political participation."[20] Women were encouraged to show interest in public life, and expected to contribute to capitalist society as consumers/housewives, but their primary roles were assigned as mothers and wives.[21]

While the CIE played a positive role in spreading democracy in Japan, the Civil Censorship Detachment (CCD), in charge of cultural and media regulation, performed a more shadowy part. The CCD conducted censorship from September 1945 through September 1949, and its power "extended to every form of media and theatrical expression—newspapers, magazines, trade books as well as textbooks, radio, film and plays, including the classical repertoire."[22] Examiners (who understood both English and Japanese) translated every publication and ensured that they followed the press codes—ideas of revenge, feudal obligation, and anything reminding people of wartime society were suppressed. "All films with an apparent martial theme, including all 'samurai period dramas,'" were prohibited.[23] The CCD was particularly sensitive to wording that touched on the war. Tsuboi Sakae's "Ishiusu no uta" (Song of the Stone Mill), published in the September 1945 issue of *Shōjo kurabu*,[24] was censored when it was republished as a book. The story is about a girl who finds out that her parents were killed in the Hiroshima bombing while she was at her grandmother's outside Hiroshima. Its direct reference to the bombing was erased in the book version. Publications were categorized as "pass," "suppressed," or "hold," and problematic sections were marked in red. Censorship was systematically and meticulously conducted, but it was never openly acknowledged.[25] The title of literary critic Etō Jun's book, *Tozasareta gengo kūkan* (Closed Linguistic Space), communicates that Japanese publications during this era operated under close control.[26] Thus, Japan was guided by GHQ/SCAP to become a democratic and peaceful country, and its course was carefully railed out and controlled under the authority of the American government.

Children's education was appraised to be in need of urgent reform by GHQ/SCAP, for the Japanese educational system was viewed as "the very heart of the evils which caused the suffering and bloodshed."[27] In March 1946, the US Education Mission, consisting of twenty-seven educators,[28] arrived in Japan. They studied schools and consulted with their Japanese counterparts. The report they submitted to General MacArthur urged that the Japanese educational system should be decentralized,[29] and proposed a number of recommendations. One of them was the revision of the written-language system. Kanji (the Chinese character writing system) was viewed as an obstacle in the way of equal educational opportunity, so they suggested that Japanese consider using rōmaji (Western alphabetization of Japanese words), "a single and efficient medium of written communication."[30] The titles of girls' magazines started using rōmaji (together with the titles written in Japanese), and sections of poems and essays that included rōmaji words were created to familiarize readers with the rōmaji system. The decision for adaptation of rōmaji was entrusted to the Japanese government, which did not pursue the idea.[31]

Another recommendation submitted by the US Education Mission was a reform in the school system at the primary and secondary levels. During the war, education was compulsory for six years.[32] The new proposal advocated a coeducational system, instilling the 6-3-3 grade structure (six years in primary school and three years in junior high were compulsory) and making Japanese education available to everybody.[33] These proposals were put into practice in 1947. An essay appearing that year in the April issue of *Shōjo kurabu* explains the importance of the coeducation system.

> Sewing and domestic work were considered to be important only for girls in the past, but now boys will have to study them as a subject called *kateika* (domestic education). Subjects required for girls are also required for boys, because domesticity should be created through the co-operation of husbands and wives. The goal of co-education is to create bright homes and raise the status of women, which used to be much lower than that of men.[34]

The ideas of democracy and gender equality were new to Japanese people, whose society had been constrained by a deeply rooted hierarchical and patriarchal social structure. Girls' magazines explained the meanings of these newly imported concepts to their young audience in a series of essays.

The audience of *Shōjo no tomo* (whose ages were slightly higher than those of *Shōjo kurabu*) showed great interest in the coeducation system. Roundtable talks were frequently recorded on the pages of the magazine, in which groups of students—both boys and girls from Tokyo schools—eagerly expressed their opinions of the new system. In one of the meetings, Yoshiya Nobuko[35] served as the host and talked about the value of coeducation.

> If girls see smart, kind and nice boys in class, they will respect and trust men in the future. On the contrary, if they see that boys don't study and do nothing but bully girls, they will grow up believing that boys are silly and hateful.... While you are young, you should try to be respected by students of the other gender.... This is the important mission of co-education.[36]

Coeducation also influenced the culture of romance. During the war era, love stories of any type disappeared from girls' magazines. After the war, GHQ/SCAP tried to introduce the idea of courtship through films and literature to popularize *ren'ai kekkon* (marriage by love). In one of the roundtable talks, Yoshiya Nobuko, whose work had previously celebrated the S relationship, now treats it as a transitional period, a state of valuable heightened friendship but part of the process toward mature heterosexual love relationships.[37] In *Shōjo no tomo*, the fictional genre *jojō shōsetsu* (lyrical stories), which had been dominated by S romance, started to include boys. Catherine Yoonah Bae reports that male characters were usually very gentle and appeared only in an "imagined and romantic context."[38] Their sensitive feelings were expressed in the same manner as in stories of S romance. In a way, boys were fantasized by girls' story writers, through which young female readers tried to make "sense of the new social realities of heterosexualization."[39] Japanese parents actually tended to regard same-sex romance as safer than heterosexual romantic relationships. Readers letters to *Shōjo no tomo* show that the two modes of romance, one toward "*onē-sama*" (older sister, but in a meaning established in the prewar era, the girl of love) and the other toward "*akogare no kimi*" (the boy of love), coexisted.

Home as Girls' Space in *Himawari*

In contrast to postwar *Shōjo no tomo*, *Himawari* started with founder Nakahara Jun'ichi's vision to restore the prewar role of the editor as mentor and educator to his readership community, just as Uchiyama Motoi had been for his readers. Nakahara created the magazine to revive a beautiful and elegant girls' culture and to provide girls with "dreams and hope" once again.[40] Taking the role of editor seriously, he wrote an educational essay in every issue, in addition to providing the illustrations for the covers and for many of the stories.

In the inaugural edition, Yoshiya Nobuko expressed her excitement in an essay, sending an encouraging message to the audience.

> ... Young people in this country are exhausted after a dark and horrifying time. What the government insisted as "right" was in fact not right.... In the past, this country had the unfortunate tradition of not viewing women as independent beings. Because of this tradition, women could not do anything but follow the orders of men.... They could not even make smart judgments in their lives.... Lack of selfhood indicated the low level of women's culture.... However, younger readers, this despised era has passed.... Waves of women's freedom are approaching under the bright sun.... Wishing you happiness in the continuing futures of young maidens![41]

It's true that Yoshiya ignores her own participation in the war, but her point is that its cause was imbedded in male culture. The importance of female selfhood—*jiga*, a prevalent feminist term of the time—is emphasized here, and the statement recalls Hiratsuka Raichō's famous inaugural statement of *Seitō*, "In the Beginning Woman was the Sun." Yoshiya may have similarly been declaring the opening of a new era for girls, envisioning the creation of modern Japanese women and girls free from old-fashioned conventions.

However, *Himawari* never grew into the magazine that Yoshiya anticipated. Nakahara adhered to traditional feminine roles in the presentation of his new image of a Japanese girl. In a conversation with juvenile story writer Kitabatake Yao (1903–1982), Nakahara states: "There are important domestic skills that girls should learn, as they will take charge of domesticity in the future. If they don't have domestic skills, their lives won't be happy and cheerful...."[42] Nakahara implies that girls' future happiness can be obtained by becoming skillful and effective wives. In a roundtable discussion, poet Takeuchi Teruyo (1904–2001) states: "girls who write poems with affection will become good mothers in the future.... Instead of seeing great female poets, I would like to see lots of good mothers."[43] Takeuchi and the roundtable participants (who were all women) identified girls' futures as becoming mothers and discouraged them from choosing other occupations.

There was a new element of Western modernity in what *Himawari* advocated. The *Midashinami* (etiquette) section, consisting of recipes for Western food and ideas for making fashionable dresses and decorating rooms beautifully, not only taught readers how to conduct homemaking practically and economically but also how enjoyable domestic work was. Readers were encouraged to acknowledge domesticity as their personal domain. The concept of *katei* (Western idea of home), which had been imported into Japanese culture in the Meiji period, was now reconceptualized and reintroduced as a creative, warm, and pleasurable private realm for modern women, through the absorption of American values.

Through films and magazines, the CIE promoted the image of a happy American family that consisted of a husband, a wife, and children. However, the Japanese families in *Himawari* were often different, omitting the father. This difference may be attributed to the traditional custom of separation between male and female cultures (exemplified by the Confucian phrase, "*Danjo nanasai nishite seki o onajū sezu*" ("a male at the age of seven does not sit with a woman"). Another possible reason could be the fact that many soldiers had died in the war. *Himawari* might have refrained from depicting the father at home, knowing that many of their readers had lost their fathers. But perhaps the most likely reason for the male void in *Himawari* was its focus on motherhood. The magazine emphasized the relationships between mothers and children, specifically daughters, pushing fathers and romantic partners to the side if not omitting them altogether.

An abbreviated version of *Little Women* (translated as *Yonin no shimai* [Four Sisters]) was selected as *Himawari*'s first serialized story.[44] This version selects chapters that spotlight the four girls equally, expounding on the development of each. Unlike *Shōjo no tomo*'s active implementation of heterosexual relationships in girls' stories, *Yonin no shimai* does not feature romance between Meg and Mr. Brooke, nor does it dwell on the friendship between Jo and Laurie. It also lacks the presence of the father. Unlike the original *Little Women*, in which the story is concluded with the return of the father, this version ends with the mother's return from the hospital where her husband is being treated. The sentence at the end of the story—"There, everybody, mother is home!"[45]—emphasizes home as a female sphere with mother at the center.

In 1949, the film version of *Little Women*,[46] titled *Wakakusa monogatari*, was released in Japan. This film was regarded as a perfect *bungei eiga* (literary and artistic film) for women,[47] and the CMPE (Central Motion Picture Exchange) prominently advertised it.[48] *Himawari* enthusiastically featured *Wakakusa monogatari*.[49] In the February 1950 issue, an article titled "Eiga ni natta yonin no shimai: *Wakakusa monogatari*" (The Film Version of Little Women) introduces the movie's story with pictures from the film. After explaining the personality of each sister, the article addresses the role of the mother: "Mary Astor, who played the mother's part, successfully demonstrated how mothers should behave in order to gain respect from their daughters."[50] It neither mentions the father nor touches on his influence on his daughters' development, but emphasizes the importance of appreciating the moral and ethical integrity of one's mother. *Himawari*'s goals were to teach the lofty status of the mother and to help its readers to transition from girlhood to eventual motherhood.

Exclusion of the father from domesticity is observed in *Shōjo no tomo* as well. In the May 1950 issue, there is a *shashin monogatari*, a story consisting of a series of photos with explanations in short sentences, titled "Nihon no wakakusa kyōdai" (Japanese Little Sisters),[51] which illustrates how four Japanese sisters and their mother spend Mother's Day. Officially established in America in 1912, Mother's Day was introduced in Japan before the war by American missionaries, but in wartime Japan, it was altered to be a celebration of the birthday of the Empress on March 6.[52] Mother's Day here is re-introduced as a Western holiday. On the cover is a photo of the four girls, who wear Western clothes and ribbons in their hair, surrounding their mother with flowers and a large wrapped gift in their hands. The father is absent from the photo of the celebration of Mother's Day; peace and happiness are associated with the idea of motherhood and a modern home.

Japanese young girls eagerly embraced American culture. Japanese readers' fascination with and assimilation of American ways are noticeable in the fact that

Himawari's readers identify themselves with the heroines of Western stories. In the year that the film *Little Women* was released in Japan, *Himawari* held a *Little Women* project,[53] for which they selected four Japanese girls from the readership and had them impersonate the March sisters.[54] The girls all have curled hair with ribbons and Western costumes. The girl who plays Jo has a book in her hand and looks straight in the camera with decisive eyes. The one who plays Beth shyly holds a doll. At the end of the essay, Nakahara asks the readers which character they look like. Japanese girls' performative propensity is also witnessed in letters

Figure 6.2. This picture story explains how the Nishikawa family spent their Mother's Day. The gift is a cosmetic set. These sisters won second place in the Japanese *Little Women* competition held by a movie theater in Tokyo. The photo was taken by Yasuda Katsuhiko. "Japanese Little Women," *Shōjo no tomo* 43, no. 5 (1950). © Yasuda Katsuhiko/Yasuda Mitsuko.

submitted to the readers' section called "*Himawari saron*" (Himawari Salon). A girl from Chiba, for instance, writes: "Everybody in the Salon, Hello. I am Jo.... Nice to meet you. Beth in Wakayama, could you be friends with me?... My classmates call me Jo, because I am so boyish..."[55] A girl named "Budding of a New Leaf" similarly writes: "I watched *Wakakusa monogatari* the other day. It was wonderful.... I am a fan of Margaret O'Brien. Although I loved all the characters, I particularly liked Beth, who was performed by Margaret.... This is why I used this pen name, because Beth died while she was still a bud."[56] Jo March, Judy Abbott, Anne Shirley, Pollyanna, and so forth—cheerful, active and positive heroines who are usually orphans—brought a sense of affinity to the postwar Japanese girl audience and affected them greatly. These heroines from Western classical *shōjo meisaku* (girls' fiction masterpieces) never conflicted "with Japanese traditional gender norms."[57] And more importantly, these stories always had happy endings, sending the message that even if readers were orphans or had lost family members in the war, they could make their home into a happy and peaceful one.

Figure 6.3. Girls pose as the March sisters. Meg at the right top, Beth at the right bottom, Joe at the left top, and Amy at the left bottom. Nakahara Jun'ichi writes: "What type of girl are you? Why don't you try the hairstyle of the girl that you most resemble?" *Himawari* 4, no. 2 (1950). © Junichi Nakahara/Himawariya.

Hana to kosuzu and the End of *Himawari*

Himawari grew into the most popular girls' magazine. In 1948, an editor's column titled "*Himawari* crosses the ocean" proudly announced that it had been selected to represent Japanese magazine culture to America, and that it had been decided that it would be stored at the Library of Congress.[58] Nevertheless, this did not mean that *Himawari* wholly conformed to the cultural and educational reforms initiated by GHQ/CIE. Signs of hesitance and bewilderment can be observed in the essays and columns written by the magazine contributors. Although educator and translator Muraoka Hanako always expressed democratic thoughts in her articles, when discussing the language reform in which Japanese spelling was phonetically adapted and characters such as ゐ and ゑ that represented sounds no longer used in modern language were eliminated, she expostulated that it made Japanese people look "unintelligent."[59] Similarly, in an essay Kawabata Yasunari laments the loss of beautiful language due to language reform.

> ... there is no beauty nor firmness in the language in school textbooks. I feel sad that boys and girls have to learn Japanese by using them as models.... I wish I could work for the improvement of Japanese language education, but I no longer have energy for it.... I wish to show you [readers], and my daughter, books which contain beautiful Japanese language and sentences—which are like a spring in Japanese nature.... Please think about the language you use and read more critically today. I hope that in the future beautiful Japanese language will revive again![60]

In his postwar fiction as well, Kawabata expresses his sadness over losing Japanese culture. In particular, his *Hana to kosuzu*, accompanied with illustrations by Tamai Tokutarō,[61] serialized in *Himawari* in 1952, is colored with pessimism and can be read as his disavowal of prevailing Americanism.

Compared with his literary masterpieces, for which he was recognized with the Nobel Prize, Kawabata's girls' magazine stories may seem to pale in significance. In fact, it is known that some of Kawabata's serialized girls' stories were ghost-written; for example, *Asahi shinbun* reported in 1975 on female writer Nakazato Tsuneko's[62] involvement in Kawabata Yasunari's *Otome no minato* (Maiden's Harbor), published in *Shōjo no tomo* in 1937–1938.[63] It is possible that another writer was involved in the creation of *Hana to kosuzu*, as well.[64] However, as Ōmori Ikunosuke opines, Kawabata's stories, particularly the ones written after the war, "have similarities with his post-war stories written for a mature audience on the basic level, and they are probably not just coincidence."[65] Ōmori emphasizes the importance of including Kawabata's girls' stories in the study of his literature.

Hana to kosuzu (published in 1952) is the story of a thirteen-year-old girl, Tozaki Junko. The story starts with a scene in which Junko's childhood friend, Setsuko, comes back to her town after spending years in the countryside for safety during the war. They are both thrilled to be reunited. Setsuko enters Junko's Catholic girls' school. However, when Junko's family goes bankrupt, they have to move to a small apartment in a different town, and she starts attending a public school. Junko describes the difference in education in a letter to Setsuko.

> Since I moved to this school, I have been feeling sad, because I can never get used to the new environment. The school is co-educational, and I feel that the atmosphere is very different.... During homeroom, we exchange our opinions and criticism of society. However, this makes me feel that we are just trying to find fault with others. Maybe it is because I am not used to it.... Saint Theresia School stressed English education, so English class here seems very easy. At the new school, we also study rōmaji. However, I have never studied rōmaji, so I cannot smoothly read "Apollo" from Greek mythology written in rōmaji, which makes me feel depressed.[66]

The letter reflects postwar culture and society. New, Americanized education is criticized as something negative, dry, and awkward from a young girl's point of view.

As if in rejection of her new school environment, culture, and society, Junko starts to retreat into the world of art. Because of her family's financial trouble, Junko is adopted by a family that owns a *geisha* house. The new family does not intend to let Junko appear in front of customers, but she gradually becomes interested in the flowery environment: "Every day was as exciting as if she was a princess placed on a throne. What she saw and heard involved singing, dancing, hairstyles, and makeup. She became accustomed to the gaudy environment."[67] Junko starts to lose connection with her original family. She is symbolically exiled from "home," and enters into the world of performance art; she does not grow up into a domestic *shōjo*, the image of which *Himawari* cultivated.

Geisha are looked down on by other characters in the story. There is a scene in which Junko's letter to Setsuko is found by the teachers at the Catholic girls' school. The teachers discourage Setsuko from seeing Junko, because they fear that Junko will have a negative influence on her. Setsuko's mother, who had been nice to Junko, is also worried about her daughter and forbids her from seeing Junko. The idea of female beauty accompanying social vulnerability resonates with Kawabata's literature for mature audiences. In *Yukiguni* (Snow Country, 1937 and 1948), for instance, *geisha* Komako's social weakness and impractical occupation are the reasons why Shimamura, the hero of the story, is attracted to her. Komako's existence as a woman of fantasy temporarily separates Shimamura from his real life.[68]

"Izu no odoriko" (The Dancing Girl of Izu, 1926) also features a young, beautiful, and poor dancing girl; by interacting with her, the main character acknowledges the beauty of life and finds a cure for his emotional problems. In Kawabata's literature, dancing girls are often treated as icons of beauty, separated from society and even reality.

In *Hana to kosuzu*, Junko's social weakness and isolation from society, old friends, and even her own parents escalate. Contrastingly, Junko's beauty starts to shine. Setsuko, an ordinary girl, feels that Junko has changed and that they do not live in the same world any more. The gap between their worlds is symbolically implied in a scene in which Setsuko goes to see Junko's dance performance. The stage separates the worlds of the two girls—real and unreal. Setsuko is stunned by Junko's transformation.

> With the music of a *shamisen*, Junko appeared on the stage in a beautiful costume. With a white face, red lips, and a Japanese style wig, she was stunning. She was a mysterious dancer living in a fantasy world. She twirled her umbrella around. Suddenly her costume turned white and she revealed her true form, a white heron.... With a mysterious tune, she danced earnestly, swinging her sash on which foxfires were drawn.[69]

Junko performs a traditional dance called *Sagi musume* (Heron Girl), which is about a girl being transformed into a white heron. During the performance, the dancer stands on one leg and bends the other leg, moving her sleeves as if she were a bird flapping its wings. *Kitsunebi* (foxfire), an atmospheric ghost light that appears when foxes are nearby, is a common element of Japanese legends. If humans follow the *kitsunebi*, they might end up deeper in the darkness. The "white heron," a traditional motif in Japanese art, and "foxfires," a folkloric phenomenon, elicit Junko's female beauty, mysteriousness, and seductiveness. On the stage, Junko is a fantasy *shōjo*. She accepts the fact that she will no longer be able to have the life of an ordinary girl.

> I enjoy pretending to be an eagle, a flower fairy, a princess in mythology.... I can no longer return to the world where I used to belong because I know I will be lonely. Even if I return to ordinary society, I cannot function as an ordinary person. I would be absorbed with delivering the language of birds and expressing the mind of flowers. I was born to be this way.... In the *geisha* house, nobody says anything even if I daydream all the time. I feel very comfortable here. I just love to become imaginary figures.[70]

Junko chooses to live in the world of Japanese performance art, old cultural beauty. Junko and Setsuko are different not only in the worlds they occupy, but also in terms of the level of their physical maturity. In one of the letters Junko and Setsuko exchange, Junko confesses that she has begun menstruating (Setsuko on the contrary has not yet experienced it). Junko's beauty is now accompanied by female sexuality. However, paradoxically, she maintains her maidenhood as well. This is symbolized in the scene in which Setsuko's brother sends a specimen of butterflies to Junko.

> The package from him contained various kinds of butterflies. Each butterfly was wrapped in a paper and had a name on it. The butterflies were colorful. With colors such as black, blue, and red on the wings, they were vivid and beautiful. Junko also looked at the pressed mountain flowers, which Setsuko had given her a long time ago. Junko compared the butterflies and the flowers.... In the same box, the flowers and butterflies made her envisage the scene of the mountain where they used to belong.[71]

The specimens of butterflies and pressed flowers are beautiful but lifeless, conjuring frozen time and the preservation of beauty. In Kawabata's *Manyō shimai* (Manyō Sisters), serialized in *Himawari* in the previous year, spiritless beauty is represented by a "mummified crab," which perfectly retains its figure from life but is empty inside. These images symbolize the fact that the girl characters do not truly complete their development; combining purity, beauty, and female eroticism, they remain suspended on the cusp between *shōjo* and womanhood. In this way, the purity and beauty of female adolescence is preserved. The butterflies and flowers in the box in *Hana to kosuzu* signify that Junko is confined in the space of fantasy, a timeless sphere, and "her girl's essence becomes eternal."[72]

Junko is a *seishōjo* (sublime girl) created on Kawabata's aestheticism and nostalgia. *Seishōjo* appear in Kawabata's works such as *Mizuumi* (The Lake, 1955) and *Yama no oto* (The Sound of the Mountain, 1954), and according to Kobayashi Yoshihito, they represent Kawabata's "absolute and fantasized female image which would provide him with illusions of peace and happiness."[73] After the war, Kawabata retreated into his own nostalgic fantasy. In "Aishū" (Melancholy, 1949), Kawabata confesses: "I don't believe in the social condition and culture of the post-war time. I don't believe in reality, either."[74] The world of *shōjo* was a mirror of his fantasy, healing his wearied soul. It is ironic that Kawabata, who had served as a girls' story writer with a didactic purpose, ended up utilizing girls for the sake of his own art and desires, exalting them as icons of beautiful old Japanese culture. As if he knew that he was not writing for the sake of girls anymore, Kawabata stopped writing (or being involved in) girls' stories after *Hana to kosuzu* was published.

The finale of *Hana to kosuzu* in December 1952 coincided with the final issue of *Himawari*. The magazine had been deteriorating for some time, suffering dismal sales and the distancing of Nakahara, who had left for France in April 1951 to study Western design for a year and a half. Without the educational message of Nakahara, *Himawari* had become a mere facade of beautiful culture.[75] *Hana to kosuzu* symbolizes the weariness of the changing times. In the same year that the conclusion to *Hana to kosuzu* decorated the last issue of *Himawari*, the American occupation also ended. The termination of *Himawari* became an indication that educators and editors' "occupation" of the *shōjo* world had ended, to be replaced by the arrival of a new girls' magazine culture over which young women would take control.

Himuro Saeko's *Shōjo* Heroines from Heian to Shōwa

The physical and fiscal rehabilitation of Japan over the following decades proved very successful. The nation experienced a period of incredible financial growth in the 1960s and 1970s. By the second half of the 1980s, "Japan was involved in the biggest financial mania of this century."[1] It was a period known as the "bubble economy,"[2] which was characterized by extravagance and conspicuous consumption. This period was also called "the Age of Women." The Equal Employment Opportunity Law, which was passed in 1985, "inspired thousands of well-educated women in their twenties to attempt previously undreamed-of careers."[3] Working women were also powerful consumers, and their new prominence in society attracted media attention. The October 1986 issue of *Asahi Journal* includes an interview with girls' fiction writer Himuro Saeko (1957–2008) by journalist Chikushi Tetsuya. The title of the interview is "Genki jirushi no onnatachi" (Women Marked by Energy).[4] The fact that Himuro Saeko was chosen to represent women's culture indicates an acknowledgment of the cultural and commercial influence of girls' fiction.

This chapter will discuss girls' fiction in the context of women's culture of the 1980s. Intriguingly, Himuro Saeko provided commentary on the contemporary male-dominated culture's focus on business and money in works that take place in the ancient past. *Za chenji* (The Change, 1983) is a retelling of the literary classic *Torikaebaya monogatari* (The Changelings), which was written in the late Heian period by an unknown author. Both the original and Himuro's version are about a girl who has grown up as a boy, bravely serving as a government official in the imperial court. Himuro's version resonated with women who had started entering the workforce, traditionally a male sphere, in the 1980s. *Nante suteki ni japanesuku* (How Splendid Japanesque; intermittently 1984–1991)[5] is a romantic comedy centering on a married heroine, Ruri. This work is loosely connected to eleventh-century classic *Genji monogatari* (*The Tale of Genji*)[6]—the life story of the fabulous prince Genji, chronicling his love affairs and the tragedies that befall him after he secretly consummates a romance with his stepmother. Himuro's tomboyish heroine challenges and subverts the world of Genji and instead embodies a new idea of love and marriage, as well as a new set of women's values. Perhaps Himuro chose the conservative Heian period (794–1185) as the stage of these stories because it was a time when gender roles were clearly demarcated and women were utilized by men as their means of success and social promotion. Her heroines' outrageous modern behavior, defying cultural expectations, captivated readers of the 1980s.

Himuro is an important figure who created "a new direction in modern Japanese girls' literature."[7] She widened the definition of girls' fiction by portraying young adults and even married women as heroines. More importantly, her use of first-person narration and colloquial language drew her audience into the world of her stories, and the tone of sarcastic humor she deployed became an important trait of modern girls' fiction. After an overview of the transformation of girls' magazines between the 1960s and the 1980s, we will look at how Himuro Saeko's emergence, which corresponded to the women's age, revitalized the Japanese girls' fiction genre, galvanizing emerging mainstream writers as well.

The Emergence of *Junia Shōsetsu*

The termination of long-running girls' magazines *Shōjo no tomo* in 1955, and *Shōjo kurabu* in 1962, signaled the arrival of a new type of magazine called *junia shōsetsu* (junior fiction). The term *junia shōsetsu* was introduced in *Jogakusei no tomo* (School Girls' Friend, founded in 1950) around 1955, and came to be widely utilized after 1966, the year *Shōsetsu junia* (Fiction Junior) was founded.[8] Reflecting postwar youth culture and the normalization of coeducation at schools, the majority of junior fiction stories dealt with the relationship of teenage boys and girls, and with this change, the romance of S disappeared from the magazine pages.[9] *Junia* (junior) implied the "youth" of the new generation who were also exposed to American popular culture.

American teenage culture proliferated internationally. Films such as *Rebel without a Cause* (directed by Nicholas Ray in 1955) and *Blackboard Jungle* (directed by Richard Brooks in 1955), both of which dealt with teenage delinquency, had a great impact on Japanese youth culture. Japanese mass media showed great fascination with the idea of teenagers in the 1950s.[10] *Taiyō no kisetsu* (Season of the Sun), Akutagawa prize winning novel by Ishihara Shintarō (1932–), published in 1955, was a huge hit. The story foregrounds young people, frustrated with society, living aimlessly. It was later made into a film, which became a cultural phenomenon. The movie caused a sensation, as it dealt with violence and sex openly. The term *taiyōzoku* (Sun Tribe) was born out of this film, indicating young people who wore Hawaiian shirts and sunglasses to emulate the delinquent characters of the film. Sociologist Furuichi Noritoshi states that the marketplace discovered these baby boomers as a newly emerged consumer segment, "teenagers," in the mid-1950s.[11]

There was a proliferation of junior fiction magazines in the second half of the 1960s, which included *Shōsetsu junia* (founded in 1966), *Junia bungei* (Junior Literary Art, founded in 1967), and *Junia raifu* (Junior Life, founded in 1968). *Shōsetsu junia* was the most prominent of these publications, and the stories published in this magazine were later collected in the *Cobalt* book series, which also sold well.[12] Respected fiction writers such as Miki Sumiko (1908–1988), Satō Aiko (1923–), and Tanabe Seiko contributed their works to the magazine. Tomishima Takeo[13] is the most famous of them and played an important role in the development of the junior fiction genre.

Tomishima criticized the fakeness of the girls' stories of the older generation, calling their characters "dolls" and the stories "decoration cakes,"[14] and attempted to depict realistic teenagers. The consistent themes of his work were love and sex. He rendered complex emotions and desires of adolescent boys and girls. Tomishima thought that sexual desire is a natural force and an important part of young people's healthy development. His direct and descriptive sexual scenes were controversial. *Osanazuma* (Young Bride), a story about an eighteen-year-old high school student's marriage with a widowed father, published in *Junia bungei* in 1969, was his most sensational work.[15] The story's graphic descriptions and portrayal of a teenage girl who has sexual desires shocked the public.

In 1969 and 1970, critics and educators debated junior fiction in magazines and newspapers. Many characterized junior fiction as harmful to young readers. Fiction writer Tsumura Setsuko (1928–), who also wrote stories for *Shōsetsu junia*, commented that "scenes which are written just to stimulate young girls' sensuality make the story shallow."[16] Tomishima responded,

> What is junior fiction? ... It is wrong to think that a good literary work cannot be a good junior fiction work or vice versa.... We use the term junior fiction not because it is read by teenagers, but because it deals with the realistic issues that teenagers have. Junior fiction with high quality can be appreciated by readers in their twenties and forties.... I depict sex, because it is a concern that normal teenagers always face in their development. Avoiding this matter is not the right thing for a fiction writer.[17]

Tomishima insisted that he always wrote about real humans; his works were not for amusement, but serious and literary.

Kaneda Junko states that the conventional pattern of the stories in *Shōsetsu junia* was "male sexual desire as an obstacle in a romantic love relationship."[18] The teenage characters in the stories "might have some trouble with their sexual drives, but eventually correct themselves and pursue futures that adults consider to be ideal."[19] Many of the stories in this magazine came to be written from an adult perspective, and their ultimate goal was to instruct the girl audience on how to deal with males and their own sexual desire.

As Tomishima admitted, however, there were writers who were driven by commercialism. Stories in *Shōsetsu junia* became increasingly sexualized and scandalous as the publication grew.[20] The magazine also started to urge readers to participate through the submission of details of their own sexual experiences. Topics such as first sexual intercourse, masturbation, rape, incestuous relationships, and so on came to fill the pages.[21] It seems that some readers were annoyed by the increasingly prurient nature of the magazine's content. A sixteen-year-old reader named Saeko, for instance, expressed her discomfort in a readers' section called "Letter Box."

> The content of girls' fiction today is too sexual.... Of course, I have sexual desire and am curious about sexual stories.... But pure romantic love stories emotionally influence us more and stay with us longer.... Today's girls' stories are too overwhelming. What is written in a story might be reality, but I still want romance in the stories I read.[22]

Shōsetsu junia started to struggle, which is observed in the ever-shifting nature of the magazine's cover images over time; they started with illustrations of Western young boys and girls, shifted to *shōjo* manga illustrations, and finally utilized photo images of pop idol singers such as Matsuda Seiko and Kondō Masahiko. By this time, *shōjo* manga had spun off from girls' magazines, and although they shared their readership (and continue to do so), Tomishima Takeo states that the deterioration of *Shōsetsu junia*'s sales was partly caused by the burgeoning popularity of manga in the 1970s.[23] Just as in the case of traditional girls' magazines, a tight community of readers, artists, and editors shaped manga publications and offered a cultural space for the readers.[24] Young female *shōjo* manga artists cultivated new expressions of romantic love in their stories, and girl readers appreciated the emphasis placed on the perspective of girls like themselves.

To differentiate itself from *shōjo* manga, *Shōsetsu junia* changed its name to *Cobalt* (or *Kobaruto*) in 1982, and raised the age of its target audience to between twenty-two and twenty-five years old.[25] The editors' ambitions are inferred by the early issues' emphasis on women's careers, independence, and gender equality.[26] *Shōsetsu junia* was, thus, reborn as a young women's magazine. *Cobalt* employed many young female writers. Its inaugural issue, for instance, features an advertisement that promotes the magazine's "novels by young women which contain fresh feelings and dreams only they can express," including a photo of women writers[27] introduced as "The Cobalt Fresh Five." These young writers understood what their generation wanted to read.

Figure 7.1. Cover illustration of *Cobalt* 1, no. 1, 1982. Courtesy of Shūeisha Co., Ltd.

In 1977, Himuro Saeko submitted her "Sayōnara arurukan" (Farewell Arurukan) to the *Shōsetsu junia seishun shōsetsu shinjin shō* (Youth Fiction Newcomers' Prize) competition, receiving an honorable mention.[28] She was just twenty years old, a junior at Fuji Joshi Daigaku (Fuji Women's College) in Hokkaido, where she studied Japanese literature. Himuro started to write for *Shōsetsu junia* after college.[29] She wrote stories from a girl's point of view and her genuine and inornate writing was well received by the readers, who were around her age.

Soga Keiko, in her detailed sociological study of *Cobalt* magazine, explains the change Himuro brought to the world of junior fiction.

> (Before Himuro), Junior fiction writers represented love and sex between boys and girls as the main issues that teenagers face. However, a heterosexual relationship is not the only issue for real girls. Love and sex between boys and girls are not of absolute importance for them, and girls' selfhood and identity should be explored from diverse points of view.... Himuro Saeko brought the motif of *shōjo* to fiction and her novelty as a writer is attributed to the fact that she thematized friendship and struggles among girls.[30]

The emergence of young female writers such as Himuro Saeko, Masamoto Non (1953– : she received a prize in the competition the same year as Himuro), Kumi Saori (1959–), Tanaka Masami (1958–), and so forth suggested a change in the editorial process of girls' magazines; now, rather than imposing their own direction on the content, editors were much more responsive to readers' preferences.

Around the time *Cobalt* began publication, Himuro started calling her stories *shōjo shōsetsu* as opposed to *junia shōsetsu*.[31] Through the utilization of the term *shōjo shōsetsu*, Himuro tried to revive the girls' story genre and to liberate girls' stories from the carnal fiction written by older writers of the time. The new age of girls' fiction had begun with *Cobalt*.

Age of Women

After the Japanese government passed the Equal Employment Opportunity Law,[32] the number of women attending universities and junior colleges grew and young women embraced the increased opportunity to enter the workforce. Many companies instituted a two-track system for women—a managerial promotion track and a less-pressured general employee track. However, practically speaking, few were hired for the managerial promotion track. The vast majority, who were hired for the general track, were called Office Ladies (OL).³³ Karen Kelsky explains that "The OL is ideally between the ages of twenty and thirty, the graduate of a two-year junior college, unmarried, and merely passing time in the company until she receives a suitable marriage proposal."³⁴ Also, the Equal Employment Opportunity Law had pitfalls; it forbade gender discrimination in "recruitment, hiring, training, and retirement,"³⁵ but the law prescribed no sanctions or punishment for violators. In short, the law "only asked companies to grant women an opportunity not a guarantee of employment."³⁶ There were no laws that particularly protected working mothers. Women, therefore, faced two choices—career or marriage. A large number of working women ended up quitting their jobs.

Agunesu ronsō (The Agnes Debate) ³⁷ of 1987 brought to the forefront a serious problem confronting working women. The singer and essayist Agnes Chan's decision to bring her infant son to a TV studio started a national conversation on working mothers' social status and their responsibilities while on the job. Fiction writer Hayashi Mariko³⁸ and certain female intellectuals considered that Chan's actions betrayed her lack of commitment to her career; to them the workplace was a mature adult's "serious" sphere into which domestic matters should not be brought.³⁹ Hayashi and others believed that success as a career woman required one to work like a man. They expected women to become *kigyō senshi* (corporate warriors), devoting their time to the "workplace and work-related activities,"⁴⁰ if they wished to become successful. The debate unveiled the disaccord among feminists regarding how women should be viewed and treated in the traditionally male-oriented work sphere. Women's gender and social roles needed to be reconsidered. With the participation of notable feminist scholars such as Ueno Chizuko, who supported Chan, the matter was featured in popular magazines, and feminism became a conversation point beyond academia for ordinary women and housewives.

When she was asked about the Agnes Debate by feminist critic Ogura Chikako, Himuro supported Agnes, stating: "to be honest, I felt sympathetic to Agnes. Frankly, what Hayashi-san and Nakano Midori-san are saying seemed to be a kind of allergic reaction of people who don't have kids around, which I understand to be a common reaction."⁴¹ Himuro Saeko never became deeply involved in any feminist discourse, because she did not believe in waving the banner of feminism.⁴² Himuro disliked the aggressive tone taken by some feminists as well.⁴³ However, this is not to say that Himuro was indifferent to contemporary feminist concerns. Using conversational language, she explored gender, marriage, and social systems in her works.

Za chenji: Performing Gender

The Heian story *Torikaebaya monogatari*, a sad and tragic tale of a woman, was reimagined by Himuro as *Za chenji*, a lighthearted story of a powerful and vigorous girl.[44] The story takes place in the mid-Heian period. Gondainagon (Counselor of the first rank) has two wives—with the wife in the Eastern pavilion, he has a boy, and with the wife in the Western pavilion, he has a girl. These two children, born around the same time, are both beautiful and resemble each other; their personalities, however, are completely opposite. The younger brother is shy and introverted. Kira, the older sister,[45] on the other hand, is active and outgoing and shows talent for archery, football, and reading Chinese poetry, which were at that time all considered to be male cultural activities. She wears boys' attire and behaves like a boy. Kira states: "I am physically a girl, but I am mentally a boy."[46]

Socially constructed gender, according to gender theorist Judith Butler, is performative, a result of reiterated act.[47] As a child, before entering the social world, one's gender is not yet fixed, and it is natural that a girl may incline to boyish behavior. In reference to the *shōjo* manga version of *Za chenji*, manga critic Fujimoto Yukari states that

> [in *shōjo* manga] male clothing is the form taken in the temporary stage of life that precedes the one in which the girl becomes "female." . . . To put it another way, men's clothing is the expression of the girl's denial that she is a sexual being. What we need to understand . . . is that, for a woman, the only time "being a woman" becomes an issue is when she is loved by a man; until that time, she is conceived as a creature for whom it makes no difference whether she is man or woman, and who can become either one.[48]

The story includes the symbolic coming-of-age ceremonies of the era that marked children's entrance into the world of adults: *genpuku* for boys and *mogi* for girls. Instead of waiting for society to assign her as a woman, Kira decides to undergo the *genpuku* ceremony, while her brother goes through the *mogi* ceremony.[49] Kira, through this official ceremony, chooses male gender identity by her own will and enters the male sphere as a social member.

The heroine in the original *Torikaebaya monogatari* never "chooses" the male gender willfully. Her intellectual curiosity and talent simply push her into the male sphere. Without abandoning her female gender, the original heroine is portrayed as androgynous. In the Heian period, the idea of masculinity had a different standard from now and masculinity often incorporated femininity. As Kuwabara Hiroshi expresses, "Genji's (the hero in *Genji monogatari*) beauty was celebrated as being woman-like."⁵⁰ "The nature of gender itself was conceived more flexibly" back then.⁵¹ However, in the 1980s cultural framework within which Himuro writes her version, Kira's choice of male gender over female gender in *Za chenji* is portrayed as a more active and rebellious choice.

After the *genpuku* ceremony, Kira, in male garb, starts working at an imperial court (nobody but her family knows that she is actually a woman). The talented Kira is quickly promoted to the rank of *chūnagon*, middle counselor. With her intelligence and sense of justice, she starts to gain people's respect and comes to be trusted by the emperor. Kira functions as a critical observer of the male culture. Her eyes witness the ambition, jealousy, and malicious desires of male aristocrats who, behind their refined atmosphere, hold strong aspirations for power. Kira's honesty and moral purity stand out in the court.

Her male disguise sometimes causes Kira difficulty. For instance, an ambitious minister wants Kira to take his daughter, San-no-hime, as her wife. To avoid having to reveal her true gender, Kira refuses the offer at first. However, having learned that San-no-hime is treated as a tool for her father's social ambition, Kira is enraged and eventually weds San-no-hime simply to protect the young girl. Kira marries a woman out of a sense of justice and sympathy. Kira is sixteen years old and her wife is fifteen; luckily San-no-hime does not know anything about marriage consummation, so their marriage does not involve sex.

However, the flamboyant Chūjō, a friend of Kira, is enchanted by San-no-hime's innocent beauty, and ends up impregnating her. Kira's reaction is expressed thus:

> "God never grants a baby to a female couple, so the fact that she is pregnant means that San-no-hime consummated with a man in secret. Wait, I am like Genji, betrayed by Onna-san-no-miya [Genji's wife] and Kashiwagi [Genji's nephew]. I am a cuckold!"⁵²

Himuro expresses Kira's confused state of mind humorously. Clearly this is a parody of the Genji episode. Genji's bewilderment is foregrounded in *Genji monogatari*, and his jealousy, sadness and fury eventually cause Kashiwagi's death. This incident calls into question Genji's heroic integrity. Kira, however, faces this situation with humor and takes no umbrage.

Himuro adds some romantic elements to the story. Kira turns out to be the girl for whom the emperor had been long searching: years earlier, the emperor had encountered young Kira bathing in a river before *genpuku*, and had given her a purple rosary. Kataoka Asami states that this function includes Kira into the "*murasaki no yukari*,"⁵³ the "purple linkage" of Genji's women whose names are connected through the color purple (like Genji's mother Lady Kiritsubo ["kiri" being the Japanese word for "paulownia," a purple flower], his stepmother Fujitsubo ["fuji" meaning "wisteria," another flower often colored purple], and his wife Murasaki [the Japanese word for "purple"]). While these women are central figures in *Genji monogatari*, they are passive victims of Heian court culture and all come to tragic ends. However, Kira is far from passive or tragic; therefore, I would argue that rather than defining Kira as a member of *murasaki no yukari*, Himuro is parodying this character type just as she is parodying Heian stories in general.

In both stories, the heroines are attacked by Chūjō; Kira manages to fight off his advances, but the original heroine[54] is raped and impregnated. After that, it becomes obvious that she transforms into a woman physically and mentally. Her pregnancy announces the awakening of her own female body and her submission to male power and order. She starts to express her love for Chūjō, the man who raped her, and to disclose her jealous feelings toward her wife,[55] who has also been impregnated by him. In the original story, all the negative feelings of jealousy, anger, and envy are associated with women, because the Buddhist notion of the inferiority of women is an undercurrent of the story.[56] Having acquired female gender, the heroine of *Torikaebaya monogatari* is "deprived of the space where she can display her talents and abilities."[57] Her development as a human is "shuttered in patriarchal society."[58] The heroine in the original tale, therefore, is characterized as a sad woman, despite her social advancement through her eventual marriage with the emperor.

Kira, however, does not lose her lively spirit, nor does she succumb to the male cultural order. Kira decides to exchange genders with her brother, she becoming a female and he becoming male, and takes over her brother's position as a servant of the princess. Kira's acceptance of the emperor's eventual marriage proposal cements her identity as a woman. However, it does not mean that she accepts the culturally defined woman's role or submits to male authority. The end of the story shows Kira's playful attitude toward the ideas of marriage and reproduction and her manipulation of the emperor's romantic feeling toward her, as she broadly performs the role of typical Heian aristocratic woman.

> "Male child? I will consult with Buddha and the Shinto God, and ask them to grant us a jewel-like healthy baby soon," Kira says elegantly. The emperor smiles and is moved by the innocent comment of his wife, Kira. Sayuri [Kira's trusted servant] sitting quietly on the side cannot hold back her laughter and collapses in giggles.[59]

Figure 7.2. Illustration from the second episode of *Nante suteki ni japanesuku*, published in *Cobalt* (1, no. 2 [1982]), by *shōjo* manga artist Tsuchida Yoshiko. The first episode of *Nante suteki ni japanesuku* was published in *Shōsetsu junia* (April 1981). After these issues, the story was published in book form. Courtesy of Shūeisha Co., Ltd.

As her name Kira, meaning "thin silk textile," as well as superficial layer, suggests, gender is simply an arbitrary costume she wears as the occasion suits her. Although she is now in a heavy twelve-layered kimono now, underneath the clothes, she maintains her own subjectivity, exercises her own power, and controls her life.

The spirit of Kira is bequeathed to Ruri in *Nante suteki ni japanesuku*; Himuro's next heroine does not attempt to compete with men in the male sphere, but proves that women can be influential even from within the confines of their traditional domestic domain.

Nante suteki ni japanesuku: Feminization of Heian Heroes

In Himuro's next story, she addresses problems of materialism and status that were especially pertinent during the bubble era of the 1980s. Hayashi Mariko's collection of essays, *Runrun o katte ouchi ni kaerō* (Buy Happiness and Go Home), which made her an instant celebrity, projects the vitality of young women in the rising economy of the era. Hayashi, who began as a copywriter, encourages readers to be true to their desires.

> People think that advertising copywriter is a good occupation, so many young girls come up to me saying "I love to write," or "I am interested in the advertising business." But they never say "I want to become famous," "I want to work in a glamorous world," or "I want money." Surely they must have more in mind. . . . Having money is a great feeling! . . . Saying "I love money" is like saying "I love having sex." It is a courageous thing to say.[60]

However, Himuro Saeko's stories infer an attitude in opposition not only to Hayashi's, but to the general cultural zeitgeist of the time. In the late 1980s, many magazines targeting working women as powerful consumers were published. *Hanako* (founded in 1988) was one such publication; every issue featured luxurious clothing, bags, and articles about overseas travel destinations and trendy restaurants in Tokyo. The TV genre "trendy drama"[61] colluded with this economic commotion, playing an important role in defining the image of modern urban women. The target audience was "female and in their 20s,"[62] and the programs featured fashionable and beautiful female characters who spoke multiple languages, wore brand name clothes, and worked at first-rate companies. Mass media fanned women's ambitions not only in the areas of career and money, but also marriage status. Given their increased options for independence, women were able to evaluate the criteria for a prospective husband's potential for increasing their social status with a somewhat cynical detachment. For example, the popular concept of the *sankō* (three highs) described the desirability of "high education, high income, and physical height" in a mate. Marketing writer Ushikubo Megumi maintains that the romantic ideology that defines marriage as the ultimate result of intense love collapsed in the 1980s.[63] Many young people tended to separate marriage from romantic love and felt that "the conditions for the marriage partner and those for romantic partners were different." [64] Social and financial stability were the primary criteria for choosing a husband. Himuro's heroines, however, stand in opposition to this value structure, eschewing materialism and emphasizing the value of emotion and love in marriage.

When Himuro Saeko was writing *Nante suteki ni japanesuku*, she was in her late twenties.[65] Despite her success, Himuro felt that she was never treated as *ippashi no onna* (mature independent woman). As she writes in her essays, because she was young, a woman and single, some male editors failed to show Himuro much respect. In 1980s society, the belief that a woman's maturity as a social being could only be achieved after marriage still existed. Her mother was a strong believer in this idea.[66] She held that marriage was a woman's responsibility and that it was more important for women than career pursuit. She constantly pressured Himuro to find someone to marry. Himuro's mother even appeared on a local radio show in Hokkaido, consulting a fortune-teller regarding her daughter's indifference to marriage. The mother used Himuro's real name, Usui Saeko, but the radio host and the listeners immediately understood that she was talking about Himuro Saeko.[67]

Himuro states that the original motive to write *Nante suteki ni japanesuku* was "to write something that would make her readers, who are vexed by the pressure of marriage, feel good."[68] The heroine of *Nante suteki ni japanesuku* is married, but her marriage is unconventional both by Heian and 1980s standards. Himuro does not oppose marriage, but re-creates it into something not colored by the norms of bubble culture but into something that is more hopeful and exciting for girls and young women.

Ruri, the name of the heroine in *Nante suteki ni japanesuku*, alludes to *Genji monogatari*. Ruri[69] is the childhood name of Tamakazura, Genji's adopted daughter. Tamakazura is a strong woman who resists Genji's romantic pursuit and eventually settles in marriage with General Higekuro, according to her own will. The episodes involving Tamakazura communicate the egoism of the aging Genji. Naming the heroine Ruri can be understood to indicate Himuro's antithesis to the idea of romance in the world of *Genji monogatari*.

Nante suteki ni japanesuku starts with the introduction of Ruri, the sixteen-year-old daughter of the counselor of the first rank. She is known as an eccentric girl who behaves in an unfeminine manner and has a foul mouth. Two court ladies gossip.

> "Rurihime... used to live away from the capital when she was a child. That's why she looks rustic and unusual. She rushes through the mansion and uses dirty words. She is not a decent girl. Someone said that she is possessed."... "How awful! I hate unsophisticated women...."[70]

Listening to the women's conversation, Ruri is furious and manages "to suppress her impulse to kick the door open and to slap their faces. 'By God! Who do they think I am? I am a daughter of the family which traditionally serves as the regent to the emperor.' "[71]

Wearied by the tomboyish and hot-tempered Ruri, her parents try to find a husband for her to make her settle down. Outrageously for a young Heian woman, however, Ruri refuses to marry. She argues about marriage with her stepmother, who believes women can obtain happiness only after they find good husbands with good family backgrounds. But Ruri thinks that marriage would deprive her of her freedom.[72] She states,

> "Our marriage system is polygamy. Men are all like my father. Even shining prince Genji, the hero created by a middle aged woman named Murasaki Shikibu, is just an ordinary man; what he does is hunt women. Women are only supposed to wait [for their husbands' visitation] and endure. To hell with that!"[73]

In the cloak of the heroine's immaturity and her unusualness as a Heian woman, Himuro not only calls Murasaki Shikibu "*obasan*" (middle-aged woman) but also criticizes Prince Genji, the most famous hero in Japanese literary history. She finds fault with the notion that marriage is a woman's primary responsibility and disparages Heian literature, which only includes the beautiful aspects of court culture while ignoring the plight of women who were deprived of freedom and independence and utilized as objects for familial prosperity.

Most of the female characters in *Nante suteki ni japanesuku* are strong and powerful. When women see other women in jeopardy, they scheme to save them using a sisterly collective power literally behind the curtains. But nobody can beat Ruri's energy. Curious and outgoing, Ruri steps out from behind the scenes and becomes involved in numerous imperial intrigues.

Early in the story, Ruri learns about an assassination plot against Prince Takao planned by a political opponent; she saves the prince, putting herself at risk. Impressed, Prince Takao (although he already has consorts) courts Ruri. Marriage with the prince or someone of prestigious social status is normally the highest achievement in romance stories. However, Ruri is different from princesses who aspire to have *tamanokoshi*, a Cinderella-like marriage with a wealthy man. Ruri is irritated by the prince's egotistic approach, stating,

> "People like my father... who belong to the political world, all succumb to the emperor, the absolute power. But this kind of power does not work for women. Women like strong men, but having political power and being strong are two different things."[74]

Ruri turns down the prince's proposal. The man whom she eventually chooses is Takaakira, her childhood friend who is one year younger than her.

The name Takaakira is another wink at *Genji monogatari*; Minamoto no Takaakira (914–983), emperor Daigo's tenth son, is believed to have been one of the models for Genji.[75] Takaakira woos the woman he loves, Ruri, and eventually they marry. Takaakira is no playboy, and his courtship of Ruri is clumsy and humorous. Despite the allusion to Genji in his name, Takaakira does not have Genji's sophistication, glamour or seductive appeal. Rather, his heroic quality is his devotion to and honesty with Ruri, in addition to his loyalty to the emperor. Himuro, in fact, states that Genji "is not attractive as a human.... He is a perfect but unrealistic man."[76] Takaakira is a humane character of whom girl readers of the 1980s would approve as the partner of their *shōjo* heroine.

Despite her initial refusal, once she is married, Ruri is excited about the idea of marriage. Her excitement is expressed comically: "I am a married woman! 'A married woman' sounds so gorgeous. Now I am a beautiful lady who is beyond the reach of men.... I am like Aoi, Genji's wife. I always wanted to play the role of Aoi."[77] For Ruri, marriage is play. She does not care about the responsibilities attached to the system of marriage, nor does she accept the behavioral codes that married women should understand. There is a scene in which she utilizes a temple visitation ritual called *kodakara kigan* (praying for pregnancy) as part of a scheme to protect herself from a suspicious man who has been following her around. While her husband Takaakira, who does not know the scheme, is elated by her apparent interest in conceiving a child, Ruri has no such desire. Still young, she wants to have more fun and be free from domestic responsibilities for a while.

Ruri is not interested in public matters, familial prosperity, or even her husband's *shusse* (social advancement). Ruri treasures *jō* (sympathy and compassion), a powerful and influential value. The story describes two similar political incidents that involve two male traitors, Yoshino-no-kimi (the boy from Yoshino Mountain), who is Ruri's first love, and Sochi-no-miya (Governor General), the emperor's uncle and the empress's first love. Despite their misguided actions, these two men are characterized as sympathetic men who suffer from unrequited love. It is traditionally women who express overwhelming emotions of jealousy, anger, and uncontrollable love in Japanese literature, exemplified by Lady Rokujō in *Genji monogatari*. However, Himuro subverts the literary gender role, and assigns these emotional traits to Yoshino-no-kimi and Sochi-no-miya, in contrast to the salvaging power of *jō* exhibited by Ruri. Although Himuro's feminization of these characters imbues them with emotional weakness, the fact that they value emotion over societal power includes them in the compassionate community of girls.

Yoshino-no-kimi is one of the emperor's sons. However, due to his mother's modest background, she could not find a place in the imperial court and so they fled to the mountains, where Yoshino-no-kimi found a friend, young Ruri. As children, they promised to stay together forever, but eventually were separated. After many years, Ruri reunites with Yoshino-no-kimi, but he has changed into a coldblooded man. He no longer shows any affection toward Ruri. Ruri soon learns the truth; in order to proudly court Ruri as a prince, Yoshino-no-kimi had attempted to gain the acknowledgment of his father, the emperor, but was rejected by him. With desperation, anger, and sadness, Yoshino-no-kimi enters into an imperial assassination plot.

Sochi-no-miya is another tragic figure who has spent a lonely childhood away from the imperial court. The woman he loves is called Lady Kiritsubo, his childhood friend, who is now the empress, having married Sochi-no-miya's nephew, the new emperor. Unable to suppress their love, Sochi-no-miya and Lady Kiritsubo commit adultery and have a baby boy.

This forbidden relationship resembles that of Genji and his stepmother Fujitsubo; their son eventually becomes the emperor. But in Himuro's story, in addition to his wish to protect his lover, Sochi-no-miya hopes that his son will avoid politics and enter the priesthood and so attempts to prevent the discovery of his true parentage. It is not political ambition but affection for his lover and son that drives him to commit crimes, including attempted assassination.

In both cases, Ruri tries to stop the plots in order to save the emperor, endangering her life. But when she learns the sad stories behind the conspirators' actions, Ruri is moved. With the assistance of Takaakira, who risks his social position, Ruri eventually helps both Yoshino-no-kimi and Sochi-no-miya escape from the capital (in the case of Sochi-no-miya, together with his lover and son).

The episodes of Yoshino-no-kimi and Sochi-no-miya follow the same pattern—their desperation in love drives them to commit evil actions. They are both tragic figures, socially marginal characters who cannot find a place where they belong. Despite their evil actions, girl readers are attracted to these characters because of their faithfulness to their love.

Nante suteki ni japanesuku is a modern take on *Genji monogatari*. The world of Genji is examined and critiqued from the perspective of 1980s girls, and Genji's tale is subverted and made into a modern girls' fiction. Himuro re-creates the grand tale about the shining hero Genji and his vulnerable women into a new tale about the brave heroine Ruri who casts light on romantically pure and emotionally vulnerable men. *Jō*, sympathy and compassion, is asserted as a cultural value in opposition to economic and social advancement, values emphasized by society in both the Heian era and the 1980s. Himuro associates the former with girls' culture and the latter with male-oriented culture.[79] By having Ruri save men and include them into female culture, Himuro attempts to show the power of girls' values. Ruri's honesty and warm, casual personality, moreover, draw others, including the emperor, to her side, the world of *shōjo*. *Nante suteki ni japanesuku* presents a new prototype: a tomboyish and righteous married heroine animated by *shōjo* spirit who exerts a positive influence on those around her.

Himuro's *Shōjo* Literature

Himuro Saeko stated that the woman's age of the 1980s existed "in tandem with the girls' age," in which girls "hand in hand with women"[80] fought against male-centered conventions. *Shōjo shōsetsu* proliferated during this period. Unlike the junior fiction of the previous era, the girls' fiction that Himuro and her cohorts created never objectified female heroines as sexual beings, but focused on harmonious relationships between boys and girls with the same cultural values.

Yamashita Etsuko's study of the "women's age," however, contends that this phrase was invented as a strategy to nurture the female economic market; in other words, business and mass media viewed women as valuable consumers rather than as people with professional ambitions.[80] Himuro felt that her girls' fiction also became commodified, and that the girls' fiction industry was becoming increasingly profit oriented.[82] She confessed that, by around 1986 or 1987, she was vexed by being called a *shōjo shōsetsuka* (girls' fiction writer):[83]

> The image of *shōjo shōsetsu* that publishers and mass media have is a school love comedy typically seen in *shōjo* manga.... The stories are all about love relationships with boys filled with monologues.... Girls' fiction and *shōjo* writers were under heavy influence of publishers and editors...[84]

Himuro wrote empowering girls' fiction that taught *shōjo* values she felt readers of the 1980s should hold. But girls' fiction writers came to be treated as cogs in the publishing business machine.

Tomoko Aoyama and Barbara Hartley write that, although "[t]he literary establishment was prepared to concede 'serious writer' status to selected women such as Miyamoto Yuriko, Sata Ineko, Hirabayashi Taiko, and Enchi Fumiko," "[l]iterary girls"—young authors who deal with the topic of girls—"have often been constructed as light weight, narcissistic, consumer-oriented and lacking in social substance."[85] Himuro and her works in particular have long been undervalued. Yanabu Akira states that "amongst the girls' story writers, Himuro Saeko is the most talented."[86] Himuro herself never viewed her girls' fiction to be inferior to mainstream literature. Answering the question "why don't you write stories for adults," she stated, "I never write stories thinking that they are for children."[87]

It is a satisfying coincidence that in 1987, the year that Himuro's *Nante suteki ni japanesuku* became popular in the world of girls' fiction, the twenty-three-year-old Yoshimoto Banana (1964–) received the Kaien shinjin bungaku shō (Kaien Newcomers' Literary Prize) for her *Kicchin* (Kitchen). Critics found that the writing of this work, "reminiscent to a teenager's diary, evokes what is commonly if curiously termed the 'unique world' of Japanese schoolgirls."[88] Some were bewildered by her nontraditional writing style, but many viewed her manga-like expressions, usage of katakana words, and inclusion of an afterward as representing unique innovations. Literary critic Saitō Minako accurately points out that these features have in fact long existed in *Cobalt* literature.[89] Now, *Kicchin* is regarded a modern classic. Yoshimoto Banana's success should equate to *Cobalt* writers' acknowledgment by the *bundan*, literary circle.

Cobalt continued to develop by extending the overarching girls' story genre to include *yuri* (girls' love), BL (boys' love), science fiction, fantasy, and so on.[90] Editors of *Cobalt* devoted energy toward discovering talented young writers and encouraged readers to submit their work to the magazine.[91] Many young writers who emerged from *Cobalt* culture also flowed into the mainstream literary world, including the Naoki prize recipients Yamamoto Fumio (1962–), Kakuta Mitsuyo (1967–), and Yuikawa Kei (1955–), to name a few. Among the diverse subjects these authors address are their feelings of marginality within women's culture, the difficulty of continuing female friendships, troubled relationships with mothers, and so forth.[92] One connection that these authors share is that they tend to thematize the confused feelings that women experience in the post-*shōjo* stage of their lives. These female writers are creating a new trend in Japanese women's literature.

CHAPTER EIGHT

Tanabe Seiko and the Age of *Shōjo*

In the world of bubble-era Japanese literature, there appeared a memorable female heroine endowed with energy and power equal to that of the youthful Ruri in *Nante suteki ni japanesuku*. However, this heroine was a seventy-six-year-old woman named Yamamoto Utako, the main character of the *Ubazakari* (Blossoming Old Woman) series (1981–1993) written by Tanabe Seiko. It is known that Tanabe grew up reading *Shōjo no tomo* and was a fan of Yoshiya Nobuko; her deep respect and admiration for the author is expressed in her biography of Yoshiya, *Yume haruka Yoshiya Nobuko* (Far Away Dream, Yoshiya Nobuko).[1] Girls' magazine culture not only inspired her to pursue writing as her future career, but also taught her the power that stories held over readers.

This chapter will first look at Tanabe Seiko's autobiographical account of her childhood, investigating the meaning girls' magazine culture, especially girls' fantasy, had in her life. Through the examination of her *Ubazakari* series, it will then survey Tanabe's utilization of fantasy and humor to amplify the impact of her message regarding the reality of aging society. There is a connection between the idea of *shōjo* and *rōjo* (elderly women), which she illuminates; with no productive or reproductive obligations, they both tend to be viewed as marginal beings in society. Marginality, however, does not equate to weakness for Tanabe's characters, but grants them freedom to point out social wrong. Having immersed herself in girls' culture, Tanabe acquired *shōjo* spirit, the idea that a marginal voice can be a literary tactic. She wrote girls' fiction for magazines like *Shōsetsu junia*, but the majority of Tanabe's works are published in literary magazines such as *Shōsetsu gendai* (Contemporary Fiction), *Ōru yomimono* (All Readings), *Shōsetsu shinchō* (New Tide Fiction), and so on, aimed at mature adults, both male and female. We can perceive in her literary foundations aspects of the girls' culture from which she emerged. Tanabe can be placed in the genealogy of "*shōjo* writers," her works sharing literary and cultural underpinning with those by her *shōjo* literary predecessors.

Figure 8.1. Cover page of Tanabe Seiko's *Ubazakari* (Shinchōsha, Shinchō bunko, 2009). Courtesy of Shinchōsha.

Tanabe Seiko as a "Scribbling Girl"

Tanabe's wartime autobiographical account, *Hoshigarimasen katsumadewa* (Until We Win, We Won't Ask for Anything, 2009) explains how deeply she was enthralled by *Shōjo no tomo* when she was a child.

> I am thirteen years old, second year in girls' school.... I am fascinated by the world of Yoshiya Nobuko's stories. I should say that I am crazy about her works. Because I love Nakahara Jun'ichi's illustrations, I had decided to subscribe to *Shōjo no tomo*, instead of *Shōjo kurabu*.... A beautiful dreamy girl with big eyes and long arms and legs as depicted by Nakahara is my dream.... The adventure stories of Yamanaka Minetarō also fascinate me.... His stories make me feel like I am a brave *shōjo* spy.[2]

Born in Osaka in 1928, the daughter of owners of a photo studio, Tanabe Seiko grew up into a typical schoolgirl who indulged herself in her *shōjo* imagination. She was a frequent contributor of compositions and poetry to *Shōjo no tomo*. One of her submissions, titled "Sara" (Plates), was selected for publication in the July 1943 issue. Her composition is about the beauty and unique characteristics she finds in the plates she uses every day: "If we don't look at them closely we don't find their beauty, but if we try to examine them carefully and touch them quietly, we will find inexplicable beauty in them and feel some nostalgia."[3] Kawabata Yasunari, a standard-bearer of the composition movement *tsuzurikata undō*, who served as a commentator for the composition section for the magazine, complimented Tanabe's writing, stating that it captures the important essence of children's composition.

When she was in girls' school, she created handwritten literary magazines with her friends. The magazines faithfully followed the format of a conventional girls' magazine, including a foreword essay, Bible teachings, *shōjo* tales, classical poetry, letters, and an editorial column. She was in charge of the cover illustration, too. Like Yoshiya Nobuko, Kitagawa Chiyo, and Morita Tama who, as girls decades earlier submitted their compositions to *Shōjo Sekai*, Tanabe was a next-generation "scribbling girl" who aspired to be a writer.

However, Tanabe's girlhood was soon darkened by the war. The government forced the removal of her favorite illustrator, Nakahara Jun'ichi, from *Shōjo no tomo* in 1940. Tanabe was among the readers who felt aggrieved. However, it did not take much time for her to adjust to the changing times. Like the majority of girls' magazine readers, she embraced the new role of a *gunkoku shōjo*, which was fervently promoted by the government. Tanabe writes,

> I became accustomed to terms such as *gyokusui* (death for honor) and *zenmetsu* (total eradication), and came to believe that someday we, Japanese citizens, would fight against the enemy and die together.... Reading the tales of brave *tokkōtai* (suicide attack units), I thought that dying for the Yamato race was the most honorable way of ending one's life. If the battle front approached to our land, I was going to die for the country and to defend the nation, taking a bamboo spear with me.[4]

Tanabe confesses that the idea of a brave *shōjo* fighter fascinated her. However, it did not mean that she abandoned the world of Yoshiya's stories, beautiful *shōjo* fantasy. Her autobiography suggests that the image of a *gunkoku shōjo* simply served as a substitute for a sentimental *shōjo*. Tanabe still lived in a fantasy, performing the new version of *shōjo*—a self-sacrificing military girl—which prevailed in wartime girls' fiction.

Tanabe experienced an air raid in Osaka and suffered food deprivation as the war worsened. She came to a realization after the war: "I used to believe that one finds happiness in devoting oneself to the emperor. But now I realize that I was just lying to myself.... During the war,... I was covering up my true feelings."[5] Through her recollection of her childhood and her war experiences, Tanabe teaches her audience of both the beauty and the danger of living in fantasy alone—that while it is important to dream to enrich one's life, it is also important to understand that fantasy can blind people from truth.

After working as a radio script writer upon graduating from Shōin Joshi Senmon Gakkō (later Shōin Women's College),[6] she made her debut as a fiction writer in 1958. In 1964, she received the *Akutagawa shō* (Akutagawa Prize) for her *Senchimentaru jānī* (Sentimental Journey), the story of a thirty-seven-year-old single woman and her failed love relationships as narrated by her younger male colleague. Many of Tanabe's stories deal with unmarried working women in their thirties. The women that Tanabe portrays are energetic, sexual, and ambitious, and do not abandon their careers for men. Kan Satoko states that unmarried women above the average marriage age used to be viewed negatively and were referred to as *ikiokure* (old maid) or *ōrudo misu* (old miss). But Tanabe's stories portray these characters as being attractive and charming.[7] Her works are categorized as *chūkan shosetsu* (midway fiction), a genre that emerged after the war, which possesses both *jun bungaku* (pure literature) and popular literary qualities. While she writes for an audience that includes both men and women, Tanabe challenges stereotypes of women. Tanabe's work is filled with humor and optimism, and is not limited to fiction. After marrying a private practicing doctor in 1966, she published a series of essays that humorously chronicle her married life. Saitō Minako explains that the 1960s and 1970s saw the establishment and recognition of the comedy essay genre, represented by works by the male writers Kita Morio (1927–2011) and Endō Shūsaku (1923–1996). Tanabe represented this trend as well, but extended humor even to a classical masterpiece such as *Genji monogatari*. Aside from her success as a fiction writer and essayist, she is known as an expert on classical Japanese literature, and has published modern translations of several literary works, including *Genji monogatari*. However, she also penned *Shihon genji monogatari* (My Original Tale of Genji), a parody in which Genji is portrayed from his servant's point of view as an earthy man who indulges in the pleasures of food and women. The servant exposes Genji's daily life and expresses his honest feelings about the characters and famous incidents in the story. For instance, Lady Rokujō, Genji's older lover, is called "Rokujō *no obahan*" (Rokujō, the middle-aged woman), and described as sarcastic and complaining, a portrayal that is far from the original Rokujō's elegance and sophistication.[8] The adolescent Murasaki, Genji's future wife, is a *shōjo* who is disgusted by Genji's desire for her to become more sexually charming and treats him harshly. Her cold attitude and sharp words emotionally devastate him.[9] Tanabe re-creates the world of Genji with her *honne* (true feelings). The way Tanabe utilizes humor as a means of literary criticism reminds us of Himuro Saeko, who similarly played with *Genji monogatari* in the 1980s.

Tanabe's characters encompass modern heroines and ancient ones, and also include a wide range of ages. Around this time, the media began focusing on aging and the elderly. *Kōkotsu no hito* (A Man in a Trance), written by Ariyoshi Sawako[10] in 1972, was one of the first literary works to spotlight the realistic issues of aging. The story, which contains scenes of *netakiri rōjin* (bed-ridden elderly) and *boke rōjin* (senile old people), signaled Japan's entrance to an aging society.[11] The subject continued to be addressed in mass media through the 1980s. Kan Satoko rightfully declares, however, that journalists focused on male aging and that even now, "women have been excluded from the category of old people."[12]

However, modern female Japanese writers often deal with the topic of women's aging in literature, in particular exploring the loss of youth, beauty, and sexuality. The characters' cultural otherness and social marginality, which are often compared to the isolation of Japanese folkloric mountain witches or other wild supernatural women, have contributed to dark and subversive texts in works by such authors as Enchi Fumiko, Okamoto Kanoko (1889–1939), and Ōba Minako (1930–2007).[13]

In contrast, Tanabe Seiko's works are always optimistic and deal with ordinary life. In 1979, when Tanabe was fifty-one, she wrote "Ubazakari," a story about the lives of elderly people centering on heroine Yamamoto Utako, which was published in *Shōsetsu shinchō*. The story was very well received and Tanabe was asked to continue it as a serial. Her "Ubazakari" episodes were later compiled in book form: *Ubazakari* (Blossoming Old Woman, 1981), *Ubatokimeki* (Old Woman's Fluttering Heart, 1984), *Ubaukare* (Joyful Old Woman, 1987), and *Ubagatte* (Selfish Old Woman, 1993). The *Ubazakari* series was also adapted as a TV drama in 1986–1988,[14] and Utako's powerful personality attracted new fans.

Tanabe's goal was to foreground the aspects of the lives of elderly women that are seldom featured in mass media. While acknowledging the problems of old age, Tanabe's stories have a cheerful tone and allow for the possibility of the elderly to remain active participants in society rather than being excluded and isolated.

Aged Women's Reality in the *Ubazakari* Series

Tanabe's elderly *Ubazakari* heroine Utako is finally enjoying freedom in the twilight of her busy life. Her husband, the owner of a textile company in Osaka, has long since passed away. Now, having handed the business over to her eldest son, the retired Utako lives in a luxurious apartment in Kobe. She teaches calligraphy a few times a week, takes English conversation lessons, travels overseas and enjoys the Takarazuka revue, of which she has long been a fervent admirer. Holding "*kiyoku tadashiku utsukushiku*" (Pure, Proper, and Beautiful)—the Takarazuka music school's slogan—as her motto, she lives gracefully and elegantly. Despite her refined atmosphere, however, she has a hot temper and a sharp tongue, and, like Ruri, she is humorously headstrong.

In the beginning of the series, Tanabe introduces Utako as if she were the heroine of a Western romance novel.

> Sitting on a firm chair which appears to have been made in England, I elegantly eat my breakfast . . . looking out at the sea from the window. I enjoy English tea, toast, eggs sunnyside up, and grapefruit. I cut the toast in half and eat it with either butter or marmalade. When I spread the jam, it has to be a gooseberry jam from Asama Mountain. . . . I handle my delicate plates with my clean nails. I don't apply nail polish, as it will be bad for my nails. I just use olive oil and polish them with deer skin. I read the newspaper in my lavender colored lounge wear which is made of soft silk.[15]

In the story, however, her quiet and elegant moment of breakfast time is suddenly intruded on by a young policeman, who rings the bell to make sure that she is safe and not lonely. From the other side of the door, he says in a soft and sweet voice:

"*Obāchan* [granny], please open the door for me."[16] Utako is unhappy about his sudden visit. The fact that he calls her "*obāchan*" upsets her the most. She complains in her mind: "Don't treat me like a child. And don't expect that I will open the door simply because you are a young cop! . . . Even though I am seventy-six years old, I am still a woman. Who knows, you might be sexually enchanted by me."[17] Utako's anger and outrageous comments are accentuated by her humorous use of the Osaka dialect. She refuses to be treated as the stereotype of a cute and vulnerable elderly Japanese woman. She believes that it is important to educate men to look at the individual and to come up with the appropriate way to address each person. Utako thinks that "elderly woman" is a social and cultural category made to disempower women. Therefore, she always "puts on trendy clothes and makes herself look neat and fashionable."[18] Fashion is her armor, a sign of her resistance against stereotype.

Utako repeatedly states that only at the age of sixty did she finally achieve freedom. She says: "I thank the war. Without the war, I would have been bonded by the old conventions. . . . The war was horrible, but it demolished bad old things."[19] She explains how she used to be bound by the tradition of *ie* and the customs of Senba (the traditional commercial center in Osaka). As the wife of the son of a business owner, she had many roles that she had to fulfill: dutiful daughter-in-law, wife in a merchant family, and mother of three sons. Her life was solely devoted to the prosperity of her family and the protection of the family business. Utako calls her late husband *akantare* (an Osaka expression, meaning "idiot"), emphasizing how much he needed and relied on her; when the enterprise was on the verge of failure during the war, Utako worked hard to revive it and pushed it forward. Now, the occupation has swept the *ie* system away, her husband has died and Utako feels liberated. She is free from domestic obligations; she no longer prioritizes her role as a mother, as her sons have become independent. She is also free from her own culturally defined "female body"; she is no longer bothered by female physical matters such as menstruation, reproduction, and menopause. In society and culture, the lack of reproductive capability in women (and of financial productivity in men) are viewed as weaknesses, and elderly people suffer from the stigma that they lack social utility and require care from their children and society. However, Utako views old age positively and lives as she pleases. She states that she has finally achieved a "golden age."[20]

Utako's role throughout the series is to listen to her friends and observe the unfairness of modern society, which oppresses elderly women. Readers soon realize that not all the women in her social group can live as freely as Utako does. Although her friends seem to be living enjoyable and cheerful lives, they cannot escape from their domestic responsibilities and roles. Wakita Tsune, for instance, is the wife of a controlling man who considers a wife's primary job to be taking care of her husband. She even needs his permission to take calligraphy lessons from Utako. After having put up with her husband's selfish behavior for a long time, Tsune starts to contemplate divorce. However, one day her husband collapses from a cerebral hemorrhage and becomes paralyzed. Seventy-three-year-old Tsune devotes herself to his care; she feeds him, cleans him, and helps change his clothes every day, in addition to her own domestic chores. She even quits the calligraphy lessons that she loved so much. Tsune, in a letter addressed to Utako, states: "Men have time to retire, but why are women never able to retire from work?"[21]

Although *netakiri* (bed-ridden) elderly people are generally viewed sympathetically, Tanabe does not spotlight the plight of the paralyzed man. Her focus is on the predicament of the wife who is the caregiver. Although done humorously, Tanabe projects a cruel world in which women suffer doubly during their husbands' postretirement years. Kasuga Kisuyo states that the Japanese family system, which traditionally assigned a son's wife to be the caretaker of his parents, has substantially collapsed; now, a new type of family structure—which values affection over obligation—has become the mainstream.[22] It has now become the aged wife's job, rather than her daughter-in-law's, to serve the role of caretaker of her husband. Women of older generations are trapped between the conventions of traditional family and the idea of modern family. Modern notions of family and home actually increase the burden on elderly Japanese women. In the story, the invisibility of the wives' suffering and sacrifice is stressed when Tsune suddenly passes away. Although her son praises Tsune by remarking how devoted she was to her family and how loving a mother and wife she was, he does not understand her true feelings and the physical and emotional burdens that she endured behind her good, devoted mother-image.

Mrs. Hasegawa is another example. Whenever she practices her hobby karaoke in front of her friends, she always wears "a dress which is like a parachute"[23] and immerses herself in her music. Like "a giant whale, her body stretches upward and swings right and left, as her fat arms wave in tune with her singing."[24] She has been practicing her favorite song for two months in preparation for the upcoming community karaoke contest. She sings as if in a trance.

A week before the contest, however, Mrs. Hasegawa calls Utako in tears saying that her husband has gotten sick and has forbidden her from attending the event so that she can stay home to take care of him. He has cut into pieces the shiny dress that she was going to wear to the contest. It is ironic that the song that she has been diligently practicing is "Futari zake" (Couple's Wine),[25] an *enka* (sentimental ballad) about the love and care of a husband for his wife; for Mrs. Hasegawa this image of a perfect married couple only exists in the world of karaoke.

Having witnessed this merciless episode, Utako proclaims: "I cannot tolerate this anymore!... Why do women always have to be *kannons* [merciful goddesses]? Our roles as goddesses should include time for retirement."[26] She suggests Ms. Hasegawa threaten her paralyzed husband by telling him a newspaper story about an American couple; a corpulent wife jumped on top of her husband during a fight and accidentally smothered him to death. Utako cheers Mrs. Hasegawa up: "... Don't be afraid of your husband. He cannot even move by himself."[27] They laugh, further agreeing that the male character in the song is just an illusion.

Utako's biting language excoriates the unfairness of society. Touching on the tradition of female submission, Utako insists that the old Confucius proverb "*onna sangai ni ie nashi*," meaning a woman has no home of her own in the three worlds—spending the past as a daughter, present as a wife, and future as a mother of a son—is nothing but a means for men to control women.

> To hell with the teaching of women's submission! It is a vicious male plot to deprive women of wealth and pride. Men have succeeded in doing it. But now, women have information. Increasing numbers of women don't succumb to social pressure and they say "to hell with society."[28]

The story's humor increases in step with Utako's outrage. Humor is a means to expose Tanabe's and Japanese elderly women's *honne*.

Tanabe Seiko and the Age of Women

The *Ubazakari* series was published during the Age of Women. Utako's messages address women's issues and show aspects of feminism, but the political impact is mitigated with humor. Saitō Minako states: "most people probably did not realize it, but Tanabe is a '*ribu na onna*' [a woman who shares similar values with women's lib activists]."[29] Tanabe's feminism, peppered with humor and wit, is observed not only in the stories, but also in some of their titles. For instance, Tanabe combined two words, "*uba*" (old female) and "*zakari*" (blossoming), subverting the conventional use of "blossoming" in connection with young women (*musume zakari* [blossoming maiden]). The title "Jijisute no tsuki" (the Moon to Watch on the Day to Abandon Elderly Men) parodies the term "*ubasute*" (abandoning elderly women), a horrific old custom of Northern villages in which younger villagers left their aged mothers in the mountains in times of famine in order for the rest of the family to survive.[30] The clever titles make readers realize how many ideas associated with elderly women are negative, condescending, and biased. Tanabe's wordplay recalls that of Yoshiya Nobuko, who similarly made political points by playfully titling her works in a provocative manner; *Otto no teisō* (Husband's Chastity) and *Onna no kaikyū* (Women's Class) serve as good examples.

Tanabe's feminist consciousness, specifically as it applies to ageism, is clear in the following statement:

> When "Ubazakari" was first published in 1979, it was rare to see fashionable aged women. But in the past decade or so, women's attitude toward old age has changed.... Today women of age seventy are active. Elderly women are fashionable. Society has changed quickly.... "Even though I am old, I need to be fashionable!" This kind of woman's voice has spread throughout the culture. This is one of the signs of women's liberation.[31]

Surely, women's mind-set toward and public views on aging have changed. In 1991, lively one-hundred-year-old twins, Narita Kin and Ganie Gin, appeared in a TV commercial and became instant celebrities. They even released a CD titled *Kin-chan to Gin-chan* (Kin and Gin; *chan* is an affectionate suffix added to names), and public fascination with the beloved twins spread throughout Japan.[32] Today, aged women are more physically and mentally active than ever.

Nevertheless, Īda Yūko expresses uneasiness in discussing Tanabe's works in the context of feminism, because they contain many aspects that do not follow the theory of feminist argument. As she states, "I am not saying that Tanabe's literature and feminism contradict each other. They slightly overlap but are looking in different directions."[33] Īda clarifies, "Tanabe Seiko does not attempt to foster social change, but depicts women who become empowered while adjusting themselves to reality," without rejecting gender and patriarchal normativity.[34] She makes a good point. Although Utako criticizes her late husband and her mother-in-law now that she is retired after handing the family business to her son, she patiently complied with and endured patriarchal family tradition for years in her younger days.

Indeed, although the humor in her fiction is an effective vehicle for imparting subversive ideas, her stories have not been written for the sole purpose of feminism. They are written to entertain an audience, which looks both for fantasy and for outlets for the frustrations of mundane reality. Conformity and resistance, reality and fantasy, coexist in Tanabe's story. Tanabe herself states that Utako is not realistic, confessing that she simply wanted to write a story about "*ahorashiki rōnen*" (aging in a comical, carefree manner).[35] For aged women to live powerfully, financial security, familial support, and good health are essential. Utako has enough money to live in an expensive apartment. Her freedom is constructed on the health and wealth with which she is blessed. Utako's life is a fantasy for the readers.

Unlike the fantasy of an adolescent girl seeking to avoid her entrance into the world of domestic womanhood, *Ubazakari* is escapist fantasy for women who have already arrived there. However, reading the stories does not necessarily represent a mere temporary, passive retreat from real life. Janice Radway, the author of *Reading Romance*, appraises reader response to Western romance novels—popular fiction which, like Tanabe's *Ubazakari* stories, are female centered and receive little serious critical attention. Focusing on the value of the reader's contribution to the reading experience, Radway states,

> It is the *act* or *event* of romance reading that permits the... woman to reject those extremely taxing duties and expectations she normally shoulders with equanimity. In picking up her book, she asserts her independence from her role, affirms that she has a right to be self-interested for a while, and declares that she deserves pleasure as much as anyone else. [36]

Readers' decision to read the *Ubazakari* series is their modest resistance to their own social restraints. Readers, further, interpret the stories, scrutinize them, and take from them what is useful to their real lives.

Her autobiography details how Tanabe, as a young reader, was emotionally saved in her most difficult time by fantasy fiction. She imbues her work with some of the dreamy spirit of those old stories, blending them now with social awareness. The product of the *shōjo* values and aesthetic that nurtured Tanabe, Utako fights against social inequality and voices her *honne* on behalf of her friends, as well as her fans. Tanabe continues to encourage her readers regardless of their age with her powerful heroines, inviting them to the world of her fiction and *shōjo* culture.

EPILOGUE

In the summer of 2017, more than twenty Japanese women visited Vassar College in Poughkeepsie, New York, where I teach. They were on a tour organized by award-winning fiction writer Matsumoto Yūko,[1] known also for her annotated translation of *Anne of Green Gables*. They came to Vassar to see the college from which Jean Webster, the author of *Daddy-Long-Legs*, graduated. These women also visited the house of Louisa May Alcott, the author of *Little Women*, in Concord, Massachusetts. Why do classic Western girls' stories written over a century ago still fascinate Japanese women to the degree that some even participated in this girls' fiction pilgrimage, traveling all the way to America?

This tour was a journey for these women to their cultural origin. The first book that they were given to read was likely a Western juvenile classic. They probably read such stories multiple times, as they were always accessible at school and at home. Such works as *Heidi*, *Anne of Green Gables*, *Little Women*, *A Little Princess*, *Pollyanna*, and *Daddy-Long-Legs* were also adapted into TV animation series,[2] and many women grew up watching them. These stories have also inspired *shōjo* manga. Igarashi Yumiko's *Kyandī kyandī* (Candy Candy, story by Mizuki Kyōko),[3] which was a big hit among young girls in the late 1970s, is a good example. It is the coming of age story of an American orphan who maintains a cheerful attitude even under difficult circumstances with the support of her friends and wealthy cousins. The premise and plot seem to be borrowed from Louisa May Alcott's *Eight Cousins* and *Rose in Bloom*, with a dash of *Daddy-Long-Legs*. Western girls' stories have been part of Japanese women's cultural foundation for many generations.

Generally speaking, Japanese girls' fiction is understood as consisting of stories whose target audience is girls or young women, with characters around the same age as the readers. However, my approach—reading stories in the context of cultural history—maintains that girls' fiction cannot be easily summarized by a single definition, because its themes, goals, and readership diversified as this genre grew.

Shōjo shōsetsu started as a hybrid of Western girls' literary tradition and Japanese culture. When Western girls' stories were introduced in Japan during the Meiji era, they were modified and arranged by Japanese authors to correspond to cultural conditions and avidly read by their audience, and they spurred new writers in the creation of their own stories. Girls' magazines played an important role in this development and refinement of a new literary genre. The magazines also helped spread, evolve, and enrich the term *shōjo*, which was originally a mere social category. Through magazine stories and illustrations, readers came to acknowledge themselves as *shōjo*, a new cultural identity.

Shōjo has become a powerful and independent cultural force. Throughout modern history, it has evolved into an agent that represents those who are dissatisfied with social norms, bestowing the opportunity to express oneself. I would term this force, which winds through the stories and the authors who wrote them, the readers they enthralled and the attitude and way of thinking they engendered, the "way of *shōjo*." This idea is neither merely a historical process nor a temporary haven in the cultural life of a growing girl. Simply put, it is the power of marginality. Delivered from a position of cultural weakness, messages of resistance against disagreeable cultural conditions are cloaked in fantasy, sentimentalism, humor, and sarcasm. The way of *shōjo* has emerged from the cyclical interaction of authors, editors, and readers within the magazine community.

This book has detailed the transformation of Japanese girls' fiction. The trajectory of this genre can be roughly divided into five phases; the adaptation of Western stories in the Meiji period, the emergence of original "scribbling girl" writers in the first half of the 1910s, the development of girls' fiction and literature in the late 1910s to the 1930s, girls' stories during the war and occupation era, and empowered postwar girls' fiction. Girls' magazine culture has always served as nurturing soil in which new generations of writers grow.

Authors such as Yoshiya Nobuko, Kitagawa Chiyo, and Morita Tama, all of whom emerged from girls' magazine culture, understood the influential power of this community, and utilized their stories to declare their aesthetics, philosophies, and political beliefs—each put forward their own version of the way of *shōjo*. The characters they portrayed were naive, dreamy, rebellious, and aloof, but their "immature" qualities and social marginality gave authors power to express their thoughts without worrying about the reaction of authority. In short, the concept of *shōjo* served as a literary tactic. These authors remained connected with girls' magazines throughout their lives. Even after Yoshiya shifted toward a wider and more mature audience, her work still maintained artistic and narrative qualities commonly observed in girls' fiction, the characters in the stories challenging patriarchal society with a *shōjo*-like attitude. Her readers and fans continued, as trusting accomplices, to support her.

The way of *shōjo* took hold and prospered within the community of readers. The stories in wartime magazines were vulnerable to control by the state. But authors and readers managed to find ways to protect their *shōjo* values, which were then inherited to postwar girls' fiction. With a push from the feminist movement and the skyrocketing economy of the 1980s, girls' fiction was further vitalized, becoming bold and free. Writers such as Himuro Saeko even re-created classical Japanese literature into works with characters fit for the 1980s audience, celebrating the new strength young women held in society, but with a note of caution to focus on pure values rather than material excess and power.

One may wonder how this study of girls' fiction relates to the larger picture of Japanese girls' culture. One very important incursion of the way of *shōjo* into popular culture is clearly witnessed in *shōjo* manga, which describe girls and young women's pursuit of ideal love, ambition for career goals, search for justice, and more, and often take place in the realm of fantasy. *Shōjo* fantasy empowers authors and their audiences to explore the refutation of cultural realities. Art educator Masami Toku states that "[s]ince World War II, the role and the value of shojo manga have become significant in Japan, reflecting girls' and women's desires and dreams. In its subjects and expressions, manga reflects female aesthetics and fulfills female dreams."[4]

Jennifer Prough explains that "[i]n recent years international venues have been embracing manga and anime at the level of pop culture and high culture, commercial goods, and art."[5] *Girl Speak: Shōjo Manga and Women's Prints from the Turner*[6] was a unique exhibition held in 2013. *Shōjo* manga art pieces and Western prints were displayed together to illuminate women artists' imaginations and their cultural and historical similarities. Toku Masami's world-traveling art exhibition, *World of Shōjo manga!: Mirrors of Girls' Desires*,[7] showed artwork of twelve *shōjo* manga artists.[8] This exhibition launched in 2013, and I was fortunate enough to be involved with it when it came to Vassar College in October 2014. Close to sixty works of art from seventy years of *shōjo* manga history were displayed, portraying characters of all genders and ages. They were all drawn in the *shōjo* manga style, and depicted stories ranging from classics such as *The Tale of Genji* to modern works. Meg, Jo, Beth, and Amy of *Little Women*[9] were included in the circle of *shōjo*, side by side with Midori, the adolescent heroine of Higuchi Ichiyō's *Takekurabe*,[10] a well-known Meiji-era story. Many American attendees with whom I spoke were fascinated with the diverse representations of *shōjo*, and told me that the exhibition broke their preconception that *shōjo* manga are always stories about *kawaii* (cute) characters written for little girls.

The way of *shōjo* has propagated throughout culture well beyond its original boundaries. In the fine arts, for example, contemporary visual artist Yanagi Miwa creates powerful and imaginative images of women combining aspects of youth (*shōjo*) and old age (*rōjo*).[11] *Shōjo*-inspired Lolita fashion with its frilly Victorian accoutrements enchants women in and outside Japan, because it "makes them feel beautiful"; they "dress for their own happiness, not for the approval of the opposite sex."[12] Even the Japanese government, which in the past had tried to control the force of *shōjo* culture, now rides on the trend. The foreign ministry selected three female "ambassadors of cute" in 2009 and sent them around the world to introduce Japanese pop culture.[13] *Shōjo* culture has now become "the mediator of Japanese culture"[14] globally.

Stepping back, we see the way of *shōjo* originally made manifest by Jo March/Shindō Takashi, who managed to find a way to become a writer, despite her conservative cultural environment. The seeds planted by Western literary predecessors grew independent, blossomed, and mutated in Japan's soil as future writers and readers learned the importance of being truthful to their own desires and the value of being a *shōjo*.

We will see how Japanese *shōjo* culture further grows and transforms through interactions with other cultures. The way of *shōjo*, cultivated in the age of *shōjo*, continues to entice people beyond age, gender, and nationality.

NOTES

Introduction

Author note: All translations are mine, unless otherwise indicated.

1. See Saitō, ed., *L bungaku kanzen dokuhon* (Tokyo: Magajin Hausu, 2002).
2. Wakamatsu Shizuko (1864–1894) was a translator born in Fukushima. After studying at Ferris Academy (the first missionary school for Japanese girls), she became an English teacher. In 1889, she married Iwamoto Yoshiharu (1863–1942), a Christian educator and founder of *Jogaku zasshi*. Shizuko's translations of Western stories and poems were published in this magazine. She translated such works as *Little Lord Fauntleroy* ("Shōkōshi," published in *Jogaku zasshi* between 1890 and 1892) and *A Little Princess* ("Seirā kurū no hanashi," published in *Shōnen'en* ([Youth Garden] in 1893).
3. *Jogaku zasshi* (1885–1904) was "Japan's first mass-circulation periodical designed for women" (Michael C. Brownstein, "*Jogaku zasshi* and the Founding of *Bungakukai*," 319). It supported feminine ideals based on Christianity.
4. Kume Yoriko, "Shōjo shōsetsu no shuppatsu to hensen," in *Shōjo shōsetsu jiten*, ed. Iwabuchi Hiroko et al. (Tokyo: Tōkyōdō Shuppan, 2015), 7.
5. Yokokawa, "Shōjo shōsetsu," in *Nihon jidō bungaku daijiten*, vol. 2, *Jinmei na–wa*, ed. Osaka kokusai jidō bungakukan (Tokyo: Dainihon Tosho, 1993), 416.
6. *Shōnen* originally meant *youth*, including both boys and girls.
7. Ōtsuka Eiji, *Shōjo minzokugaku* (Ethnography of the Girl) (Tokyo: Kōbunsha, 1997), 19.
8. John Whittier Treat, "Yoshimoto Banana Writes Home: Shōjo Culture and the Nostalgic Subject," *Journal of Japanese Studies* 19, no. 2 (1993): 364.
9. Aoyama Tomoko, "The Genealogy of the 'Girl' Critic Reading Girl," in *Girl Reading Girl in Japan*, ed. Tomoko Aoyama et al. (New York: Routledge, 2009), 39.
10. Originally published by Kinokuniya Shoten in 1982. Reprinted in *Ibunka to shite no kodomo* (Tokyo: Chikuma Shobō, 1998). Part of chapter 3 is available in English translation: "The Genealogy of *Hirahira*:

Liminality and the Girl," trans. Tomoko Aoyama and Barbara Hartley, in *Girl Reading Girl in Japan*.

11. Honda, "The Genealogy of *Hirahira*," in *Girl Reading Girl in Japan*, 27.

12. Miyasako Chizuru, *Chō shōjo e* (Tokyo: Shūeisha, 1989).

13. Ibid., 204–5.

14. Ibid., 205.

15. Yokokawa Sumiko, *Shochō toiu kirifuda: Shōjo hihyō josetsu* (Tokyo: JICC Shuppankyoku, 1991), 58. In this book, Yokokawa also criticizes the ethnographer Ōtsuka Eiji's *Shōjo minzokugaku* (originally published in 1989), which focuses on 1980s girls' culture in the context of consumer society. *Shōjo minzokugaku* characterizes 1980s culture with the word, *kawaii* (cuteness), intimating that cute tiny mascots and goods that girl consumers purchased not only helped create girls' cute community, but also created a business driven by *shōjo* culture. Yokokawa states that Ōtsuka's study is not about *shōjo* but male culture or Japan as the state.

16. Takahara Eiri, *Shōjo ryōiki* (Tokyo: Kokusho Kankōkai, 1999). Part of the introduction is available in English translation: "The Consciousness of the Girl: Freedom and Arrogance," trans. Tomoko Aoyama and Barbara Hartley, in *Woman Critiqued: Translated Essays on Japanese Women's Writing*, ed. Rebecca L. Copeland (Honolulu: University of Hawai'i Press, 2006).

17. Takahara, "The Consciousness of the Girl," 192.

18. Ibid., 193.

19. Tomoko Aoyama, "The Genealogy of the 'Girl' Critic Reading Girl," in *Girl Reading Girl in Japan* 38.

20. In "The Genealogy of the 'Girl' Critic Reading Girls," Tomoko Aoyama names Honda Masuko, Yagawa Sumiko, Saitō Minako, and Kawasaki Kenko as "girl-reading" critics and discusses their approaches. See Tomoko Aoyama, "The Genealogy of the 'Girl' Critic Reading Girl," in *Girl Reading Girl in Japan*.

21. Michael Cart, *From Romance to Realism: 50 Years of Growth and Change in Young Adult Literature* (New York: Harper Collins Publishers, 1996), 4.

22. *Shōjo Sekai* (1906–1931) was published by Hakubunkan.

23. *Shōjo no tomo* (1908–1955) was published by Jitsugyō no Nihonsha.

24. *Himawari* (1947–1952) was published by Himawarisha.

25. *Cobalt* (1982–) is published by Shūeisha.

26. Some of Himuro's works were made into TV dramas and *shōjo* manga. Himuro's *Umi ga kikoeru* (English title, *Ocean Waves*) was adapted into an animated film produced by Studio Ghibli.

27. *Hanako to An* is based on the life of Muraoka Hanako, translator of *Anne of Green Gables*. The drama, directed by Nakazono Miho, aired on NHK from March 31 to September 27, 2014.

28. "Watashi no Margaret-ten," a manga exhibition tour, was held from September 2014 to May 2016. http://my-margaret.jp/.

Chapter One

1. Louisa May Alcott (1832–1888) grew up in the Transcendentalist circle in Boston and Concord, Massachusetts. Her works include *Little Women* (1868), *An Old-Fashioned Girl* (1870), *Little Men* (1871), and so on. She was an educator, abolitionist, and feminist.

2. Transcendentalism was a philosophical movement in nineteenth-century New England. Transcendentalists such as Ralph Waldo Emerson, Henry David Thoreau, Margaret Fuller, and so forth believed in the essential unity of all creation and the innate goodness of humankind.

3. See Elaine Showalter, *Sister's Choice: Tradition and Change in American Women's Writing* (New York: Oxford University Press, 1994).

4. Kawato Michiaki, "Wakamatsu Shizuko to shoki no hon'yaku jidō bungaku: Nihon ni okeru kindai jidō bungaku no shuppatsuten," in *Meiji no joryū bungaku, hon'yaku hen*, vol. 1, *Wakamatsu Shizuko shū*, ed. Kawato Michiaki, et. al. (Tokyo: Gogatsu Shobō, 2000), 274.

5. Twenty-two chapters were originally published by Roberts Brothers in 1868. The second part, which starts with the chapter "Aunt March Settles the Question," was released in 1869. *Shōfujin* is an abridged translation of the first part.

6. In the preface, it is implied that this was Kitada's first translation work. Kitada writes: "I am not worthy of the task of translating such a work, but I have managed it with the help and advice of my mentor and the support of the copyright holder" (*Shōfujin*, trans. Kitada Shūho [Tokyo: Saiunkaku, 1906], n.p.).

7. Renowned translators such as Muraoka Hanako and Matsumoto Keiko also produced Japanese versions of *Little Women*.

8. The term *ryōsai kenbo* was popularized by Kikuchi Dairoku, Minister of Education. See Haga Noboru, *Ryōsai kenboron* (Tokyo: Yūzankaku, 1990).

9. Kazue Muta, "Images of the Family in Meiji Periodicals: The Paradox Underlying the Emergence of the 'Home,'" *U.S.-Japan Women's Journal*, English Supplement 7 (1994): 58–60.

10. Sharon H. Nolte and Sally Ann Hastings, "The Meiji State's Policy toward Women, 1890–1910," in *Recreating Japanese Women, 1600–1945*, ed. Gail Lee Bernstein (Berkeley: University of California Press, 1991), 152.

11. Ibid., 173.

12. See Carroll Smith-Rosenberg, *Disorderly Conduct: Visions of Gender in Victorian America* (New York: Alfred A. Knopf, 1985).

13. Fukaya Masashi, *Ryōsai kenbo shugi no kyōiku* (Nagoya: Reimei Shobō, 1998).

14. Kume Yoriko, "Shōjo shōsetsu: Sai to kihan no gensetsu sōchi," in *Media, hyōshō, ideorogī: Meiji sanjū nendai no bunka kenkyū*, ed. Komori Yōichi et al. (Tokyo: Ozawa Shoten, 1997), 198.

15. For a detailed explanation, see Koyama Shizuko, *Ryōsai kenbo to iu kihan* (Tokyo: Keisō Shobō, 2004), 22–23.

16. Kathleen S. Uno, "Women and Changes in the Household Division of Labor," in *Recreating Japanese Women, 1600–1945*, 25.

17. Tsubouchi Shōyō (1859–1935) is known as a pioneer in the fields of modern Japanese literature, drama, children's plays, and education. He is also known as a translator of works by William Shakespeare. His contribution to the establishment of modern Japanese literature and drama is highly regarded today.

18. Aeba Kōson (1855–1922) was a fiction writer, drama critic, and scholar of Edo literature. He is also known as a translator of Edgar Allen Poe.

19. Tsubouchi and Aeba were friends and frequent contributors of articles to *Shumi* (Hobby), a periodical published by Saiunkaku, which also published *Shōfujin* (Kotani Kanako, "*Wakakusa monogatari* no Meijiki hon'yaku no shomondai: *Shōfujin* ni mirareru sakujo," *Baika jidō bungaku* 7 [1999]: 23).

20. Aeba, "Jo," *Shōfujin*, n.p.

21. Kitada, *Shōfujin*, n.p.

22. Daniel Scott Smith, "Family Limitation, Sexual Control, and Domestic Feminism in Victorian America," *Feminist Studies* 1, no's. 3–4 (1973): 53.

23. Alcott was acquainted with many feminists of her time. Her feminist views are reflected in her works. See Joy S. Kasson, introduction to *Work: A Story of Experience* (New York: Penguin, 1994), xxi.

24. Chie Nakane, *Kinship and Economic Organization in Rural Japan* (London: Athlone Press, 1967), 1–2.

25. Jordan Sand, "At Home in the Meiji Period: Inventing Japanese Domesticity," in *Mirror of Modernity: Invented Traditions of Modern Japan*, Stephen Vlastos, ed. (Berkeley: University of California Press, 1998), 192.

26. Daio, "Shasetsu," *Jogaku zasshi* 172 (1889): 387.

27. Quoted in Muta, "Images of the Family in Meiji Periodicals," 57.

28. Yōko Nishikawa, "The Changing Form of Dwellings and the Establishment of the *Katei* (Home) in Modern Japan," *U.S.-Japan Women's Journal, English Supplement* 8 (1995): 21.

29. Women's magazines and literature "frequently included portraits of particular households, detailing everything from the appointments of their interiors and daily life within them to the particulars of the family budget" (Sand, "At Home in the Meiji Period," 196).

30. Christmas was commonly celebrated in late Meiji Japan (David W. Plath, "The Japanese Popular Christmas: Coping with Modernity," *American Folklore* 76, no. 302 [1963]: 309).

31. Louisa May Alcott, *Little Women* (New York: Signet Classic, 1983), 47.

32. Rebecca Copeland, *Lost Leaves: Women Writers of Meiji Japan* (Honolulu: University of Hawai'i Press, 2000), 26.

33. Muta, "Images of the Family in Meiji Periodicals," 158, and Koyama Shizuko, *Katei no seisei to josei no kokuminka* (Tokyo: Keisō Shobō, 1999), 35.

34. When *Kōtō jogakkōrei* (the Women's Higher School Act) was issued in 1899, the "Good Wife, Wise Mother" ideal became an official basis of education for girls. According to the school curriculum, schoolgirls studied such subjects as Japanese, history, geology, mathematics, science, calligraphy, reading, music, and sports. Also, subjects such as *shūshin* (moral training), *saihō* (sewing), and *kaji* (housekeeping) were mandated (Watanabe Shūko, *Shōjozō no tanjō: Kindai nihon ni okeru shōjo kihan no keisei* [Tokyo: Shinsensha, 2007], 320).

35. Alcott, *Little Women*, 110–11. I am quoting *Little Women* here, since Kitada's translation is true to the original.

36. Kotani Kanako notes that Kitada omits or summarizes parts which sound preachy (Kotani, "*Wakakusa monogatari*," 33).

37. Alcott, *Little Women*, 207.

38. Despite the cheerful mood of the scene, critics contend that Jo's development into a woman is a disappointing metamorphosis (Sharon O'Brien, "Tomboyism and Adolescent Conflict: Three Nineteenth-Century Case Studies," in *Woman's Being, Woman's Place: Female Identity and Vocation in American History*, ed. Mary Kelly [Boston: G. K. Hall and Co., 1977], 365–66). The mother's home is eventually returned to the father. The father's approval of the daughters' completion of their journeys to womanhood portends their departure from the March household before too long.

39. *Shōfujin*, 343.

40. Ibid.

41. Toshiko Kishida, "Daughters in Boxes," trans. Rebecca Copeland and Aiko Okamoto MacPhail, in *The Modern Murasaki: Writing by Women of Meiji Japan*, ed. Rebecca L. Copeland (New York: Columbia University Press, 2006), 63.

42. *Shōfujin*, 7.

43. Ibid., 199.

44. The age range of the characters in the original *Little Women* (between twelve and seventeen) matches that of Japanese girls for whom schooling was available in the Meiji period. Perhaps this book was chosen by Japanese educators partly for this reason.

45. Watanabe, *Shōjozō no tanjō*, 79.
46. See Jane Tompkins, *Sensational Designs: The Cultural Work of American Fiction* (New York: Oxford University Press, 1985).
47. See O'Brien, "Tomboyism and Adolescent Conflict."
48. Mukōgawa Mikio, "Yōranki no shōjo shōsetsu: *Shōjokai* o chūshin ni," *Gengo hyōgen kenkyū* 12 (1996): 6.
49. Ibid., 9.
50. Kume, "Shōjo shōsetsu," 201.
51. "Shōjo no chikara," *Shōjo sekai* 4, no. 2 (1909): 100–2.
52. Asō Shōzō, "Beikoku no jogakusei," *Shōjo sekai* 2, no. 14 (1907): 37.
53. Alcott, *Little Women*, 4.
54. *Shōfujin*, 6.
55. Kitada uses 男 (and indicates the pronunciation *otoko*), signifying a mature man here.
56. Here, Kitada uses 男子 (and indicates the pronunciation *otoko*), which can mean man or boy.
57. *Shōfujin*, 69.
58. Alcott, *Little Women*, 39.
59. *Shōfujin*, 80.
60. Alcott, *Little Women*, 6.
61. Ibid.
62. *Shōfujin*, 10.
63. Ibid., 74.
64. Alcott, *Little Women*, 46.
65. Watanabe, *Shōjozō no tanjō*, 99.
66. Honda Masuko, *Jogakusei no keifu: Saishoku sareru meiji* (Tokyo: Seidosha, 1990), 22.
67. Ibid.
68. *Shōfujin*, 6
69. Nathaniel Hawthorne derogatorily stated: "America is now wholly given over to a d****d mob of scribbling women, and I should have no chance of success while the public taste is occupied with their trash" (Elaine Showalter, *Scribbling Women: Short Stories by 19th Century American Women*, ed. Elaine Showalter [New Brunswick: Rutgers University Press, 1996], xxxv).
70. Copeland, *Lost Leaves*, 37.
71. Kan Satoko, *Media no jidai: Meiji bungaku o meguru jōkyō* (Tokyo: Sōbunsha Shuppan, 2001), 193–94.
72. Copeland, *Lost Leaves*, 16.

73. Alcott, *Little Women*, 133.
74. Copeland, *Lost Leaves*, 15.
75. *Shōfujin*, 237.
76. Alcott, *Little Women*, 145.
77. A new translation of *Little Women*, titled *Yonin kyōdai* (Four Sisters), was serialized in *Shōjo gahō* between April 1917 and April 1918. The translator's name is given only as Mitsuko. This is an abridged translation of *Little Women*, part I. The translator focuses on scenes occurring in the home (episodes that concern society and romance are omitted). Perseverance, self-sacrifice, and self-discipline are emphasized throughout. In 1909, a brief biography of Louisa May Alcott had been introduced in *Shōjokai* 8, no. 3. Her self-sacrificing spirit is praised in a segment describing her work as a military nurse.

Chapter Two

1. Honda, *Ibunka to shite no kodomo*, 206.
2. Inagaki Kyōko states that there were 193 girls' schools in 1910 (Inagaki Kyōko, *Jogakkō to jogakusei: Kyōyō, tashinami, modan bunka* [Tokyo: Chūō Kōronsha, 2007], 6).
3. According to Imada Erika's research, *kyōikurei* (the Order on Education) issued in 1879 separated middle schools based on gender for the first time. Since then, the separation of boys and girls cultures has become conventional (Imada Erika, "'Shōnen' kara shōnen, shōjo e: Meiji no kodomo tōkō zasshi *Eisai shinshi* ni okeru jendā no henyō," *Kyōikugaku kenkyū* 71, no. 2 [2004]: 62–75). *Shōnen sekai* magazine, therefore, originally had an English translation of the title, "Youth's World," on the cover page (ibid., 71).
4. Imada Erika, "Shōnen zasshi ni okeru senchimentarizumu no haijo: 1930 nendai no *Nihon shōnen*, *Shōjo no tomo* tōkōran no hikaku kara," *Nihon joseigaku* 11 (2003): 86.
5. Kume, "Shōjo shōsetsu," 195–222. Also see Kume Yoriko, *Shōjo shōsetsu no seisei: Jendā poritikkusu no seiki* (Tokyo: Seikyūsha, 2013), 69–73.
6. In the 1900s, Hakubunkan started to cultivate new readers. *Yōnen sekai* (Children's World, founded in 1906) was created for younger children than the readers of boys' and girls' magazines.
7. *Différance* is a term coined by Jacques Derrida. Derrida considers that meaning is not produced in the static closure of binary opposition (for instance, masculinity is not always defined as the binary opposition to the feminine). It is achieved through the "free play of the signifier . . . : meaning is never truly present,

but is only constructed through the potentially endless process of referring to other, absent signifiers" (Toril Moi, *Sexual/Textual Politics: Feminist Literary Theory* [New York: Routledge, 1985], 105–6).

8. See Imada Erika, "Jendāka sareru kodomo: 1985–1945 nen no shōnen shōjo zasshi hyōshie bunseki kara," *Soshioroji* 48 (2003).

9. *Jogaku sekai* (School Girls' World, founded in 1901) was designed for more advanced readers. *Jogaku sekai*'s stories were mostly *katei shōsetsu* (domestic fiction), which was a popular genre in mainstream literature comprised of stories that usually dealt with women's suffering in marriage.

10. Yamaguchi Hatsuko. *Shōjo sekai* 1, no. 1 (1906): 111.

11. Iwaya Sazanami (1870–1933) wrote many children's stories, including *Koganemaru* (Koganemaru, the Dog, 1891) published by Hakubunkan.

12. Numata Rippō (1881–1936), sometimes referred to as Ryūhō, was an editor, writer, and educator. After graduating from the Kokumin Eigakusha, he worked as an editor for *Nihon no katei* (Japanese Home). In 1906, he was invited to serve as *Shōjo sekai*'s chief editor. He worked for this magazine until he became president of Shōei Girls' High School in 1921 (Tsugihashi Tatsuo, "Numata Ryūhō," in *Nihon jidō bungaku daijiten*, vol. 1, *Jinmei a–to*, ed. Osaka kokusai jidō bungakukan [Tokyo: Dainihon Tosho, 1993], 52).

13. Atomi Kakei. "Joshi no shūyō," *Shōjo sekai* 1, no. 1 (1906): 51.

14. "Shōjo no sekai," *Shōjo sekai* 3, no. 2 (1908): 42.

15. Numata Rippō, "Mannikanen," *Shōjo sekai* 3, no. 12 (1908): 22.

16. Numata Rippō, "Shōjo kyōshitsu," *Shōjo sekai* 2, no. 3 (1907): 111.

17. Kume Yoriko, "Kōsei sareru shōjo," *Kindai nihon bungaku* 68 (2003): 8.

18. Numata, "Mannikanen," 22.

19. Kume, "Shōjo shōsetsu," 200.

20. Kaiga Hentetsu, "Ame," *Shōjo sekai* 1, no. 3 (1906): 25.

21. This genre labeling started in the third volume of *Shōnen sekai* (Kume, "Shōjo shōsetsu," 202).

22. Louisa May Alcott served as a military nurse during the Civil War. *Hospital Sketches* (1863) explains her experiences.

23. Oshikawa Shunrō (1876–1914) was a juvenile fiction writer. He made his name with "Kaitei gunkan" (Undersea Warship), which he wrote in 1900 while he was a student at Tokyo Senmon Gakkō (later, Waseda University). He wrote stories for *Shōnen sekai*, and his works often contain nationalism and futuristic elements.

24. See Kume, "Shōjo shōsetsu," 215–16.

25. Oshikawa Shunrō, "Shōjo bōkentan," *Shōjo sekai* 1, no. 2 (1906): 66.

26. Numata Rippō, "Kokoro no ane," *Shōjo sekai* 4, no. 1 (1909): 34–53.

27. Japan was Taiwan's colonial occupier from 1895 to 1945.
28. Matsui Yuriko, "Yūbe no hoshi," *Shōjo sekai* 5, no. 7 (1910): 36.
29. Ibid.
30. Some critics consider that Matsui Yuriko was the predecessor of Yoshiya Nobuko, who became the most popular girls' story writer of the next generation (see Nagai Kiyoko, "Tanjō, shōjotachi no kaihōku: *Shōjo sekai* to *Shōjo dokushokai*," in *Onna to otoko no jikū: Nihon joseishi saikō*, vol. 9, *Semegiau onna to okoto kindai*, ed. Okuda Akiko [Tokyo: Fujiwara Shoten, 1995]). However, Yoshiya herself states in an interview in *Shōjo no tomo* that Izawa Miyuki, a popular writer of *Shōjo gahō*, had a direct influence on her (Yoshiya Nobuko, "Ichiryū no joryū sakka to naru niwa," *Shōjo no tomo* 42, no. 4 [1949]: 27).
31. Numata Rippō, "Aidokusha taikai no ki," *Shōjo sekai* 3, no. 4 (1908): 83–87.
32. Tokutomi Roka (1868–1927) was a fiction writer. His *Hototogisu* (The Cuckoo), published in 1900, is a melodramatic account of the tragic lives of a young married couple. The work was a commercial success and influenced women's culture.
33. Ōmachi Keigetsu (1869–1925) was an essayist and literary critic. He wrote for *Bungei kurabu* (Composition Club) and *Taiyō* (Sun). He also published *Bibun inbun hanamomiji*, a collection of poetry written in elegant and classical language, which became very popular.
34. Nakamura Tetsuya, "Shōjo shōsetsu o yomu," in *Nihon jidō bungakushi o toinaosu: Hyōgenshi no shiten kara*, ed. Nihon jidō bungakukai (Tokyo: Tōkyō Shoseki, 1995), 258–59.
35. In the same section, a composition by Kitagawa Chiyo took second place.
36. Morinaga Matsue, *Shōjo sekai* 2, no. 12 (1909): 114.
37. Numata Rippō, "Kongetsu no tōsho," *Shōjo sekai* 6, no. 12 (1911): 192.
38. The inclusion of compositions of this tone was not original to *Shōjo sekai*. As Kawamura Kunimitsu's *Otome no inori* details, it is also witnessed in *Jogaku sekai*, a magazine targeted at older readers. See Kawamura Kunimitsu, *Otome no inori: Kindai josei imēji no tanjō* (Tokyo: Kinokuniya Shoten, 1995).
39. See Benedict Anderson, *Imagined Communities: Reflections on the Origin and Spread of Nationalism* (New York: Verso, 1991).
40. See Honda, *Jogakusei no keifu*. While Honda defines girls' culture as "*shōjo*'s imaginary community," Kawamura Kunimitsu names it "*otome*'s community" in order to emphasize the term *otome* (virgin or maiden), which carries a stronger connotation of the idealistic self-image of modern school girls (Kawamura, *Otome no inori*, 111).
41. *Shōjo sekai* 6, no. 12 (1911): 58–59.

42. Other such magazines were *Shōjokai* and *Shōjo no tomo*. In *Shōjokai* magazine, Kitagawa Chiyo was compared to the literary figure Sei Shōnagon, the author of *The Pillow Book* from the eleventh century.

43. *Shōjo no tomo* (1908–1955) was one of the earliest Japanese girls' magazines published by Jitsugyō no Nihonsha.

44. Yosano Akiko (1878–1942) was a poet. Her *Midaregami* (Tangled Hair, 1901), her first collection which celebrated love and the female body, brought her fame. She was a frequent contributor to *Myōjō* (Venus), which was founded by Yosano Tekkan, her husband. Besides poetry, she wrote essays and stories for girls and women's magazines.

45. Ojima Kikuko (1879–1956) was a fiction writer from Toyama. At the age of seventeen, she came to Tokyo. While working as a teacher and typist, she started writing stories for *Shōjokai* and *Shōjo sekai*. With the support of her mentor, Tokuda Shūsei, she made her debut in the magazine *Bundan* (Literary Circle). She was also a member of the feminist group *Seitō*.

46. Takehisa Yumeji (1884–1934) was born in Okayama. His paintings of beautiful and vulnerable women became popular and were called *Yumeji bijinga* (Yumeji's pictures of beautiful women).

47. Fumiko, *Shōjo no tomo* 3, no. 2 (1910): 92–93.

48. Kitagawa Chiyo, *Shōjo no tomo* 3, no. 2 (1910): 102.

49. This debate is also discussed in Hiromi Tsuchiya Dollase's "Ribbons Undone: The Shōjo Story Debates in Prewar Japan" (see Dollase, "Ribbons Undone," *Girl Reading Girl in Japan*, 83).

50. Ibid.

51. K-ko, "Shōjo dokushokai," *Shōjo sekai* 5, no. 14 (1910): 75–77.

52. Quoted in Nagai, "Tanjō, shōjotachi no kaihōku," 301.

53. "Enishi: Jidō bungaku kobore banashi," http://www.iiclo.or.jp/06_respub/01_research/enishi/kagawa.htm.

54. By 1917, the number of girls' schools grew to 395 and the number of school girls had reached 100,000 ("Gakusei hyakunenshi," http://www.mext.go.jp/b_menu/hakusho/html/others/detail/1317659.htm).

55. Kyōko, "Jikatsu shinagara gakkō e iku shōjo," *Shōjo sekai* 9, no. 8 (1914): 44–49; *Shōjo sekai* 9, no. 9 (1914): 47–52.

56. "Ikkagetsu no gakuhi," *Shōjo sekai* 9, no. 3 (1914): 102.

57. Kyōko, "Jikatsu shinagara gakkō e iku shōjo," *Shōjo sekai* 9, no. 9 (1914): 50.

58. See Kadowaki Atsushi, "Nihonteki 'risshin, shusse' no imi hensen." *Kyōiku shakaigaku kenkyū* 24 (1969).

59. "*Kugaku*" (the struggle to study despite financial difficulty) was also a

popular term. See Takeuchi Yō, *Risshi, kugaku, shusse: jukensei no shakaishi* (Tokyo: Kōdansha, 1991), 134–38.

60. Barbara Sato, *The New Japanese Woman: Modernity, Media, and Women in Interwar Japan* (Durham: Duke University Press, 2003), 134.

61. *Shōjo sekai* 3, no. 2 (1908). This issue introduced readers to various occupations that they could pursue (such as nurse, teacher, educator, secretary, etc.).

62. "Keibo subeki fujin," *Shōjo sekai* 3, no. 2 (1908): 28–29.

63. Ibid., 28.

64. Sato, *The New Japanese Woman*, 139.

Chapter Three

1. Yoshiya Nobuko, "Sakusha no kotoba," in *Mittsu no hana* (Tokyo: Yumani Shobō, 2003), 3.

2. Yoshiya submitted "Suzuran" to *Shōjo gahō* because she admired Izawa Miyuki, who was a star writer of this magazine (Yoshiya, "Ichiryū no joryū sakka to naru niwa," 27).

3. Wada Kokō is also known for having served as chief editor of *Kodomo no kuni* (Country of Children).

4. *Hana monogatari* was published in book form by Rakuyōdō in 1920, while still being serialized in the magazine. Kami Shōichirō points out the similarity in narrative format between *Hana monogatari* and Louisa May Alcott's *A Garland for Girls*, which consists of seven episodes told by girls in the Mayflower Club. The stories deliver didactic messages related to womanhood, charity, and humanity. Although *A Garland for Girls* had never been translated before the publication of *Hana monogatari*, Kami speculates that Yoshiya might have heard about it (Kami Shōichirō, "Kindai nihon ni okeru *Hana monogatari* no keifu," in *Nihon jidō bungaku no shisō* vol. 1, ed. Kami Shōichirō [Tokyo: Kokudosha, 1976], 231). *Hana monogatari* was an instant success. Literary critic Ozaki Hotsuki (1928–1999) described the popularity of *Hana monogatari* as "Rakuyōdō's *dorubako* (dollar maker)" (quoted in Moriyama Yūko, "*Hana monogatari* ron: Nakahara Jun'ichi no sashie tono kanren ni tsuite," *Gakushūin daigaku kokugo kokubungaku kaishi* 56 [2013]: 31). For detailed original publication information of *Hana monogatari*, see Andō Kyōko, "Yoshiya Nobuko *Hana monogatari* ni okeru kyōkai kitei," *Nihon bungaku* 11, no. 46 (1997). Fifty tales are compiled in *Yoshiya Nobuko zenshū*, vol. 1, but some of the original tales are omitted from this collection.

5. *Kitagawa Chiyo bungaku shō* (The Kitagawa Chiyo Literary Award) was established in 1968 in honor of her contribution to Japanese juvenile literature (awarded through 1982).

6. Yoshiya Nobuko, "Suzuran," in *Yoshiya Nobuko zenshū*, vol. 1, *Hana monogatari, Yaneura no nishojo, dōwa* (Tokyo: Asahi Shinbunsha, 1975), 11.
7. Ibid., 12.
8. Ibid., 13.
9. Ibid.
10. As Yoshiya Nobuko continued to write *Hana monogatari*, the stories gradually became longer (sometimes published over two magazine issues) and more attention was paid to plot development.
11. See Kawamura, *Otome no inori*.
12. Yoshiya, "Wasurenagusa," in *Yoshiya Nobuko zenshū*, vol. 1, 34.
13. Shimizu Yoshio (1891–1954) was an illustrator for children's magazines. He illustrated *Hana monogatari*'s episodes in *Shōjo gahō*. He also drew pictures for *Akai tori* (Red Bird), a children's literary magazine.
14. Kametaka Fumiko (1886–1977) was born in Yokohama, the daughter of a traditional Japanese painter. She studied Western painting at Taiheiyōgakai kenkyūjo (Pacific Painting Society), where Takamura Chieko (1886–1938, the wife of poet Takamura Kōtarō and an artist for *Seitō* feminist magazine) was also a student. She is one of the founding members of *Shuyōkai* (Red Leaf Society), association for women painters.
15. Fukiya Kōji (1898–1979) was from Niigata prefecture. Having studied in France, he imported a modern and Western atmosphere into his drawings. The term *jojōga* was coined by Fukiya. He was friends with Murō Saisei (1889–1962), poet and fiction writer (including girls' fiction), and Fukiya also wrote poems. Fukiya published many *shiigashū*, collections of poems accompanied by illustrations.
16. Mizuki Takahashi, "Opening the Closed World of Shōjo Manga," in *Japanese Visual Culture: Explorations in the World of Manga and Anime*, Mark W. MacWilliams, ed. (New York: M. E. Sharpe, 2008), 117.
17. Nakahara Jun'ichi (1913–1988) was an illustrator, doll artist, and fashion designer. His illustrations accompanied stories by Yoshiya Nobuko and Kawabata Yasunari in *Shōjo no tomo*.
18. Michiko Suzuki, *Becoming Modern Women: Love and Female Identity in Prewar Japanese Literature and Culture* (Stanford: Stanford University Press, 2010), 40.
19. Anne-Marie Smith, *Julia Kristeva: Speaking the Unspeakable* (Sterling, VA: Pluto Press, 1998), 29.
20. Tsuboi Sakae (1900–1967) is known as the author of *Nijuyon no hitomi* (Twenty-Four Eyes, 1952). She was married to Tsuboi Shigeharu, a proletarian writer. She wrote many stories for *Shōjo kurabu*.
21. Tsuboi Sakae, "Shōjo shōsetsu no kotonado," *Shin nihon bungaku* 6 (1951): 84–87.

22. Yosano Akiko, "Shōnen shōjo no yomimono," in *Yosano Akiko zenshū* vol. 19, *Hyōron kansō shū* (Tokyo: Kōdansha, 1981), 452.
23. Yoshiya Nobuko, "Sazanka," *Shōjo gahō* 5, no. 10 (1916).
24. The story uses the term "*eta*" (a highly pejorative word, indicating the class of outcasts created in the Tokugawa era). This class system was abolished in 1871. The story is omitted from reprints of *Hana monogatari* including *Yoshiya Nobuko zenshū*, vol. 1.
25. Yoshiya, "Sazanka," 88.
26. A village of untouchables is indicated as *etamura* in Japanese. The term, *eta*, is blanked out in *Hana monogatari* published by Jitsugyō no Nihonsha in 1939 (Andō, "Yoshiya Nobuko," 33).
27. Yoshiya, "Sazanka," 91.
28. Andō, "Yoshiya Nobuko," 29.
29. Yoshiya, "Ukon zakura," in *Yoshiya Nobuko zenshū*, vol. 1, 33.
30. Yoshiya, "Fukujusō," in *Yoshiya Nobuko zenshū* vol. 1, 95.
31. Yoshiya, "Moyuru hana," in *Yoshiya Nobuko zenshū* vol. 1, 146.
32. Ibid., 148.
33. Honda Masuko compares the image of the imaginary world that Yoshiya constructs to that of "a cocoon" (Honda, *Ibunka to shite no kodomo*, 151). She explains that in this imaginary space, girl characters can spin their dreams, but when they grow up, they have to fly away.
34. Kurosawa Ariko discusses the fact that most of Yoshiya's characters do not have mothers, interpreting this as related to the author's resistance against her mothers' generation (Kurosawa Ariko, "Shōjotachi no chikadōmei: Yoshiya Nobuko no *Onna no Yūjō* o megutte," in *Onna to hyōgen: Feminizumu hihyō no genzai*, ed. Mizuta Noriko [Tokyo: Gakuyō Shobō, 1991]).
35. See Tompkins, *Sensational Designs*.
36. Kume, "Yoshiya Nobuko: 'Seido' no naka no rezubian sekushuaritī," *Josei sakka 'genzai,'* ed. Kan Satoko (Tokyo: Shibundo, 2004), 125.
37. Yoshiya, "Kuchinashi no hana," in *Yoshiya Nobuko zenshū*, vol. 1, 46.
38. Kawamura Kunimitsu, *Otome no karada: Onna no kindai to sekushuaritī* (Tokyo: Kinokuniya Shoten, 1994), 26. According to Kawamura Kunimitsu, in the Taishō period, cosmetics, perfumes, the consciousness of wrinkles and the concept of diet came from the West and permeated schoolgirl culture.
39. Ibid., 67.
40. Honda, *Ibunka to shite no kodomo*, 196–98.
41. Egusa Mitsuko, "Gendō to shintai no gensetsu," in *Jendā no nihon bungaku*, ed. Nakayama Kazuko et al. (Tokyo: Kanrin Shobō, 1998), 42.

42. Yoshiya, "Hikage no hana," in *Yoshiya Nobuko zenshū*, vol. 1, 203.
43. Ibid., 204.
44. Ibid.
45. Japanese girls' stories which deal with female-female romantic love are interesting in comparison with their American equivalent. In America around the turn of the twentieth century, there was also a fad of college girls' stories that dealt with same-sex love in school dormitories. However, the American stories taught readers the importance of growing up into well-rounded women and the characters eventually leave school to get married. See Sherrie A. Inness, *Intimate Communities: Representation and Social Transformation in Women's College Fiction, 1895–1910* (Bowling Green: Bowling Green University Press, 1995) and Shirley Marchalonis, *College Girls: A Century in Fiction* (New Brunswick: Rutgers University Press, 1995).
46. Lillian Faderman, "Lesbian Magazine Fiction in the Early Twentieth Century," *Journal of Popular Culture* 11, no. 4 (1978): 801.
47. Jennifer Robertson's *Takarazuka: Sexual Politics and Popular Culture in Modern Japan* explores women's culture from the perspective of the Takarazuka revue, which was first performed in 1914. Robertson emphasizes the fact that the original intention of Kobayashi Ichizō (1873–1957, the founder of Takarazuka revue and its associated girls' school) was to teach girls their gender roles: "he theorized that by performing as men, females learned to understand and appreciate males and the masculine psyche. Consequently, when they eventually retired from the stage and married . . . they would be better able to perform as 'Good Wives, Wise Mothers,' knowing exactly what their husbands expected of them" (Jennifer Robertson, *Takarazuka: Sexual Politics and Popular Culture in Modern Japan* [Berkeley: University of California Press, 1998], 67). Despite his conservative intentions, Japanese girls appreciated Takarazuka as a cultural space of their own.
48. See Lilian Faderman, *Surpassing the Love of Men: Romantic Friendship and Love between Women from the Renaissance to the Present* (New York: Morrow, 1981) and Smith-Rosenberg, "The Female World of Love and Ritual," *Signs* 1, no. 1 (1975).
49. Yoshiya Nobuko, *Sōsho joseiron*, vol. 35: *Shojo dokuhon* (Tokyo: Ōzorasha, 1997), 104.
50. Suzuki, *Becoming Modern Women*, 37.
51. Sappho (610–570 BC) was a lyric poet from the isle of Lesbos. Her poems circulated in the second and third centuries BC, but by the tenth century, her works disappeared and only fragments of verses remain.
52. Yoshiya, "Kibara," in *Yoshiya Nobuko zenshū*, vol. 1, 229. Translated by Sarah Frederick, *Yellow Rose* (Expanded Editions, 2016, Kindle edition), 532.
53. Ibid.
54. Yoshiya, *Sōsho joseiron*, vol. 35: *Shojo dokuhon*, 73.

55. Ibid., 74.
56. Yoshiya, "Nashi no hana," in *Yoshiya Nobuko zenshū*, vol. 1, 323.
57. Ibid., 256.
58. According to Inagaki Kyōko, even in 1920 only 9 percent of girls could afford to go to school (Inagaki, *Jogakkō to jogakusei*, 6).
59. Kitagawa, introduction to *Kinuito no zōri* (Tokyo: Kōdansha, 1931).
60. *Wakakusa* was created in 1925, when *Reijokai*'s readership requested the expansion of the popular submission page. Kitagawa Chiyo was among the supporters of the creation of *Wakakusa*. Although *Reijokai* was only for women, *Wakakusa* welcomed male contributors and attempted to grow as a literary magazine. See Odaira Maiko, "Bungei zasshi *Wakakusa* ni tsuite," in *Bungei zasshi Wakakusa: watashitachi wa bungei o aikō shiteiru*, ed. Odaira Maiko (Tokyo: Kanrin Shobō, 2018), 7.
61. *Akai tori* was an influential children's magazine founded by Suzuki Miekichi (1882–1936) in 1918. Many literary figures including Arishima Takeo (1878–1923), Akutagawa Ryūnosuke (1892–1927), Eguchi Kan (1887–1975), and Kitahara Hakushū (1885–1942) contributed to it. Suzuki Miekichi was impressed by Kitagawa Chiyo's "Sekai dōmei" (World Alliance), a story about a children's play in which each child represents a different country of the world and they create a peace treaty. Suzuki commented to Kitagawa, "You are welcome to submit your stories even every month" (Hamano Takuya, "Kitagawa Chiyo nenpu," in *Nihon jidō bungaku taikei*, vol. 22, *Kitagawa Chiyo Tsuboi Sakae shū* [Tokyo: Horupu Shuppan, 1978], 455).
62. Kitagawa used several pen names such as Eguchi Chiyoko and Matsudaira Kyōko. She was also interested in the theater, and under the name Shimizu Machiko she published several scripts in *Shōjo gahō*. She once studied under fiction writer and drama critic Okamoto Kidō (1872–1939) (Hamano, "Kitagawa Chiyo nenpu," 455).
63. Takabatake Kashō (1888–1966) studied Japanese traditional art at the Kyoto Municipal School of Art. He contributed illustrations to magazines for women, boys, and girls. He is known for his modern and melancholic drawing style.
64. Eguchi Kan (1887–1975) was a fiction writer and literary critic. Eguchi studied under prominent fiction writer Natsume Sōseki (1867–1916) and his "Rodōsha yūkai" (Kidnapped Workers) attracted critical attention. He was an active member of *Nihon proretaria sakka dōmei* (Japanese Proletarian Writers' Union).
65. Mikiso Hane, *Reflections on the Way to the Gallows: Rebel Women in Prewar Japan* (Berkeley: University of California Press, 1988), 126–27.
66. Vera Mackie, *Creating Socialist Women in Japan: Gender, Labour and Activism 1900–1937* (Cambridge, UK: Cambridge University Press 2002), 161.

67. Kitagawa Chiyo, "Kekkon no genmetsu," *Josei kaizō* 1, no. 3 (1922): 114.
68. Kitagawa Chiyo originally showed interest in the *Seitō* group. However, she felt the concerns of the labor movement to be more meaningful and urgent than the women's issues discussed by *Seitō* members, who were mostly from the bourgeois class (interview with the members of the *Kitagawa Chiyo kenshōkai* [Kitagawa Chiyo Study Group] in the city of Fukaya, Saitama, February 2004).
69. For decades throughout the late 1800s and early 1900s, there was strong opposition against Ashio Copper Mining's pollution of the environment in Tochigi prefecture.
70. Kitagawa Chiyo, "Kōfuku," in *Nihon jidō bungaku taikei*, vol. 22, 27.
71. Ibid.
72. Dorinne K. Kondo explains that *Yamanote* (the western part of Tokyo) and *Shitamachi* (the eastern part) are part of the same city, but culturally different. *Yamanote* has been seen as the modern ideal of Western civilization, while *Shitamachi*—literally Tokyo's downtown—has traditionally been dominated by small family businesses, merchants, and artisans. The two different areas and class associations come from hierarchical Tokugawa social structures. During the Edo period, the samurai and aristocrats mostly lived in *Yamanote*, while everyone else lived in *Shitamachi*. See Dorinne K. Kondo, *Crafting Selves: Power, Gender, and Discourses of Identity in a Japanese Workplace* (Chicago: University of Chicago Press, 1990).
73. Kitagawa, "Kōfuku," 31.
74. Ibid.
75. Ibid., 32.
76. Ibid.
77. Kitagawa Chiyo, "Mikan," in *Nihon jidō bungaku taikei* vol. 22, 40.
78. Ibid., 43.
79. Kitagawa Chiyo, "Tamago hitotsu," in *Nihon jidō bungaku taikei* vol. 22, 107.
80. Kitagawa, "Mikan," 43.
81. Kitagawa Chiyo, "Shunran," in *Nihon jidō bungaku taikei* vol. 22, 61.
82. Ibid., 64.
83. Kitagawa Chiyo, "Shōjo shōsetsu no kōsei to gijutsu," in *Nihon gendai bunshō kōza*, vol. 4, *Kōsei hen*, ed. Maemoto Kazuo (Tokyo: Kōseikaku, 1934), 104.
84. Kitagawa's "Na o mamoru" (Protecting My Name) is another criticism of Yoshiya and the girls' magazine community. The story is about a poor girl who, hiding her working class background, becomes a popular contributor of compositions. She eventually realizes that she can never belong to the *shōjo* community. See Dollase, "Ribbons Undone," in *Girl Reading Girl in Japan*.

85. Kitagawa Chiyo, "Kinuito no zōri," in *Nihon jidō bungaku taikei*, vol. 22, 100.
86. Ibid., 101.
87. Later Yoshiya's stories became didactic, teaching audiences the importance of understanding class differences. *Hana monogatari*'s flowery tone of voice disappeared from her later works which include *Chiisaki Hanabana* (Small Flowers), a collection of short tales published as a book in 1936.
88. *Uncle Tom's Cabin*, written by American fiction writer and abolitionist Harriet Beecher Stowe (1811–1896) in 1852, was influential on society and literature, but criticized for its overly sentimental tone.
89. Kitagawa Chiyo, "Kono monogatari ni tsuite," in *Ankuru Tomu monogatari* (Tokyo: Kōdansha, 1960), 1.

Chapter Four

1. *Hope* was one of the magazines published by *Shōjo dokushokai*. The passion of one of the group's members is evident in the poem she submitted to the inaugural issue: "Spring, an innocent traveler / gently walks toward me, goes through the gate, goes over the pavement, and approaches to kiss me / He finds 'hope' on my old Calico patterned desk / Oh, 'Hope,' the most beautiful maidens' friend / We, beautiful maidens dream of ancient spring / We sing with hope" (Morita Tama, "Wakai habataki," in *Zuihitsu kinuta* [Tokyo: Chūō Kōronsha, 1942], 68–69).
2. Hosokawa Takeko (1892–1956, fiction writer), Momma Chiyo (Yoshiya Nobuko's lifelong partner) and Kaneko (Yamataka) Shigeri (1899–1977, feminist journalist) were also the members of *Takane fujinkai*. See Morita, "Wakai habataki," 68.
3. Numata Rippō believed that it was good for women to have skills, but having an occupation should be secondary to domestic responsibilities (Numata Rippō, "Bōchū zakki," *Takane* 34 [1922]: 36).
4. In 1942 Kitagawa Chiyo, Yoshiya Nobuko, and Morita Tama contributed essays to a special edition of *Takane* commemorating Numata Rippō, who had passed away in 1936 (Hosokawa Takeko, ed., *Takane* [Chiba: Shōjo Sekai Kyū Shiyūkai, 1942]).
5. Morita Tama was elected to serve on the House of Councilors in 1962, and poured her energy into the improvement of Japanese education.
6. *Chi no hatemade* was serialized in *Asahi shinbun* beginning in January 1920.
7. This is based on an experience she had when she lived in a Baptist female dormitory. The dormitory had strict regulations. She was punished for having gone to see a movie. Yoshiya soon moved out of this place and started living in the YWCA

in Kanda (Matsumoto Tsuruo, "Yoshiya Nobuko nenpu," in *Yoshiya Nobuko*, ed. Matsumoto Tsuruo [Tokyo: Nihon Tosho Sentā, 1998], 267).

8. Yoshiya Nobuko, "Yaneura no nishojo," in *Yoshiya Nobuko zenshū*, vol. 1, 412.

9. *Nigorie* (Troubled Waters) was written by Higuchi Ichiyō (1872–1896) in 1895. Higuchi Ichiyō is the most prominent woman writer of the Meiji period. Her works depict the lives of women who live in the licensed pleasure quarters of Tokyo. *Nigorie* revolves around Oriki, one of the most popular prostitutes in a geisha house. Madly in love with her, Oriki's patron Genshichi spends his entire fortune on her. Meanwhile, Oriki starts to have a new warm relationship with a rich young man, Tomonosuke. The story mysteriously ends with Oriki's death. She seems to have been killed by Genshichi, who is also found dead by suicide near her.

10. Yoshiya, "Yaneura no nishojo," 380.

11. Ibid., 375.

12. Ibid., 419.

13. Ibid., 420.

14. Ibid., 439.

15. Akitsu Tamaki is modeled after Kikuchi Yukie, who was Yoshiya's roommate and lover at the YWCA. Fiction writer Tanabe Seiko finds contradictions in the image of fictional Tamaki compared with Kikuchi (Tanabe Seiko, *Yume haruka Yoshiya Nobuko*, vol. 1 [Tokyo: Asahi Shinbunsha, 1999], 338). In a letter to Yoshiya, Yukie shows her true voice: "In *Yaneura no nishojo*, you are described well, but I am described as if I [Tamaki] am just a doll dressed up beautifully for you" (ibid.).

16. Yoshiya, "Yaneura no nishojo," 428–30.

17. Ibid., 449.

18. Yoshikawa Toyoko, " 'Seitō' kara taishū shōsetsu sakka e no michi," in *Feminizumu hihyō e no shōtai: Kindai josei bungaku o yomu*, ed. Iwabuchi Hiroko et al. (Tokyo: Gakugei Shorin, 1995), 132.

19. Yoshiya, "Yaneura no nishojo," 433.

20. Raichō had a lesbian love affair with Otake Kōkichi (Beniyoshi), a *Seitō* member (Raichō writes an essay based on her relationship with Kōkichi in "Shigasaki e, Shigasaki e" published in *Seitō* magazine in August 1912), but soon met Okumura Hiroshi, a younger male artist and started to live with him. See Yoshikawa Toyoko, " 'Seitō' kara taishū shōsetsu sakka e no michi" and Kurosawa Ariko, "1912 nen no Raichō to Kōkichi," in *Bungaku, shakai e chikyū e*, ed. Nishida Masaru tainin taishoku kinen bunshū henshū iinkai (Tokyo: San'ichi Shobō, 1999).

21. Yoshiya, "Yaneura no nishojo," 478.

22. Ibid, 498.

23. Julia Kristeva, *Powers of Horror: An Essay on Abjection*, trans. Leon S. Roudiez (New York: Columbia University Press, 1982).

24. Yoshiya, "Yaneura no nishojo," 505.

25. Ibid., 511.

26. Critic Karatani Kōjin explains that when Western stories were introduced in Japan in the late nineteenth century, it was impossible to translate them into the Japanese written language system, which customarily did not use the subject "I." According to Karatani, the movement of *genbun icchi*, the agreement of written and spoken language, enabled Japanese not only to translate Western literature into Japanese but also to express Japanese inner minds. The system of *genbun icchi* invented "I," the consciousness of modern selfhood. See Karatani Kōjin, *Nihon kindai bungaku no kigen* (Tokyo: Kōdansha, 1988).

27. Quoted in Ishihara Chiaki, "Kiken shisō datta jiga," *Hon: Dokushojin no zasshi* 31, no. 11 (2006): 46.

28. Yoshiya, "Yaneura no nishojo," 503.

29. The model of a girl with strong selfhood is cultivated here, and continues to appear in Yoshiya's later girls' stories including *Beni suzume* (Red Sparrow) published in *Shōjo no tomo* (January–December 1930). *Yaneura no nishojo* is among her works, which signal the departure of her shy and sentimental *shōjo* heroine.

30. See Yoshikawa, " 'Seitō' kara taishū shōsetsu sakka e no michi."

31. Suzuki, *Becoming Modern Women*, 49. Also, see Sarah Frederick, "Not That Innocent: Yoshiya Nobuko's Good Girls," in *Bad Girls of Japan*, ed. Laura Miller et al. (New York: Palgrave Macmillan, 2005), 75.

32. Critic Kawasaki Kenko also points out that Yoshiya's depiction of sensual love is overshadowed by the message of *jiga* that she presents in the latter part of the story. Kawasaki argues that the idea "that *jiga* has to be recognized in human lives ... only exists outside *yaneura*" (Kawasaki, *Shōjo biyori* [Tokyo: Seikyūsha, 1990], 26).

33. Sarah Frederick, *Turning Pages: Reading and Writing Women's Magazines in Interwar Japan* (Honolulu: University of Hawai'i Press, 2006), 75.

34. Fukiya Kōji, "Kitagawa Chiyo san," in *Kitagawa Chiyo jidō bungaku zenshū*, vol. 2 (supplement) (Tokyo: Kōdansha, 1967), n.p.

35. Yoshiya's works written for a mature audience include *Otto no teisō* (Husband's Chastity), *Onna no yūjō* (Female Friendship), and *Atakake no hitobito* (People in the Ataka Family). Some of her stories were dramatized into movies and TV series.

36. See Kan Satoko, *Onna ga kokka o uragiru toki: Jogakusei, Ichiyō, Yoshiya Nobuko* (Tokyo: Iwanami Shoten, 2011).

37. Frederick, *Turning Pages*, 134.

38. Uno Chiyo (1897–1996) was a fiction writer. She gained her reputation in 1935 through her *Iro zange* (Confessions of Love), which is based on her relationship with the well-known painter Tōgō Seiji. She is also famous for *Ohan*, published in 1957, and known as a kimono designer and founder of *Style*, Japan's first fashion magazine.

39. William S. Clark (1826–1886) was an American botanical and biology professor who visited Hokkaido University as a foreign adviser in 1876.

40. Takeda Gendō, "Morita Tama-san no Sapporo" in *Watashi no Morita Tama*, quoted in Kōno Toshirō, "*Gakutō* o yomu," *Gakutō* 94, no. 4 (1997): 59.

41. Shiraki Shizu (1895–1918) was a fiction writer. She lost her right leg to tuberculosis arthritis after graduating from high school. Shiraki became a student of Morita Sōhei in 1913 ("Morita Tama," in *Hokkaido daijiten* [Sapporo: Hokkaido Bungakukan, 1985], 359). Her debut work was "Matsubazue o tsuku onna" (A Woman with a Crutch), published in *Shin shōsetsu* (New Fiction).

42. Morita Sōhei (1881–1949) was a fiction writer and a student of Natsume Sōseki. He is known for his translation of works by Henrik Ibsen, Fyodor Dostoyevsky, and so on. He is known to have had an affair with Hiratsuka Haru (Raichō), and their aborted double suicide is the basis of his *Baien* (Smoke) published in 1909.

43. Morita Tama, "Gonin onna," in *Zuihitsu kinuta*, 65.

44. "Morita Tama," in *Hokkaido daijiten*, 360.

45. Morita, "Odorizome," in *Zuihitsu saijiki* (Tokyo: Chūō Kōronsha, 1940), 9.

46. Ibid., 4.

47. Ibid.

48. Ibid., 7.

49. In the previous year, she serialized *Tōri no komichi* (The Path in the Peach Orchard) in *Reijokai*. This story is an autobiographical account of her girlhood. *Ishikari Otome* is the developed version of this work.

50. Endō Hiroko, "Kaisetsu," in *Shōnen shōsetsu taikei*, vol. 24, *Shōjo shōsetsu meisaku shū*, edited by Endō Hiroko (Tokyo: San'ichi Shobō, 1993), 615.

51. Ibid.

52. Hokkaido is the northern island of Japan and was originally called *ezochi*. Its indigenous occupants were the Ainu people. In 1869, *ezochi* was renamed into Hokkaido. The Japanese government established the *kaitakushi* (Development Commissioner), and Hokkaido became part of the Japanese nation-state. Hokkaido is often discussed in a colonial context.

53. Morita Tama, "Ishikari otome," in *Shōnen shōsetsu taikei*, vol. 24, 619.

54. Kunikida Doppo (1871–1908) was a fiction writer influenced by the works of Ivan Turgenev, Thomas Carlyle, and Ralph Waldo Emerson. His works include *Aru*

onna (A Certain Woman, 1919), *Musashino* (The Musashi Plain, 1898), *Gyūniku to bareisho* (Meat and Potatoes, 1901), and so forth.

55. Noriko Agatsuma Day, "The Outside Within: Literature of Colonial Hokkaido" (PhD diss. University of California, Los Angeles, 2012), 19.
56. Ibid., 1.
57. Simone de Beauvoir, *The Second Sex* (New York: Vintage Books, 1989), 315.
58. Morita "Ishikari otome," 442.
59. Ibid., 443.
60. Ibid., 448.
61. Ibid., 484.
62. Ibid., 485.
63. Watanabe, *Shōjozō no tanjō*, 80.
64. Morita, "Ishikari otome," 476.
65. Ibid., 457.
66. Ibid.
67. Ibid., 495.
68. Ibid.
69. Day, "The Outside Within: Literature of Colonial Hokkaido," 15.
70. Morita, "Ishikari otome," 496.
71. Ibid., 506.
72. Enchi Fumiko is known as a writer who depicted the darkness of domesticity and the sufferings of women. Her prize winning works include *Himojii tsukihi* (Days of Hunger, 1953), *Onnazaka* (Woman's Slope or Waiting Years. 1939), *Namamiko monogatari* (The Tale of Nagamiko, 1965). Her work often contains references to classical Japanese literature such as *The Tale of Genji* and *kabuki* works.
73. Morita, "Ishikari otome," 308.
74. Ibid., 521. In an oft-used folkloric motif, a fox transforms into a woman and tricks a man who lives in a village.
75. Morita, "Ishikari otome," 521.
76. Ibid., 522.
77. Ibid.
78. Ibid.
79. Michiko Suzuki states: "[A]lthough it is difficult to specify the exact age range, a 'virgin' (*shojo*) is commonly considered older than a 'girl' (*shōjo*) and is mature enough to marry" (Suzuki, *Becoming Modern Women*, 51). Watanabe Shūko states that an *otome* was over fifteen years old (Watanabe, *Shōjozō no tanjō*, 44). According to Kawamura Kunimitsu, the term *otome* eventually merged with *shojo* (Kawamura, *Otome no karada*, 16–17), giving *shojo* a cultural nuance beyond the merely

biological. The kanji word *shojo* (処女), therefore, sometimes had the katakana reading of *otome* (オトメ) next to the kanji characters.

80. For a detailed discussion of *shojo ronsō*, see Suzuki, *Becoming Modern Women*, 51–53.

81. Ibid., 52.

82. Yosano Akiko further supported the maintenance of physical purity until marriage.

83. Suzuki, *Becoming Modern Women*, 52.

84. In premodern Japan, it was not considered particularly important that a bride be a virgin. But eventually a new belief arose equating physical purity with "purity of blood." Physical virginity came to be taken as a significant element in keeping the patriarchal family line pure. In other words, virginity became an important condition for a bride. Incorporating societal, economic, and ethical values, the idea of virginity consequently came to control women's bodies and sexuality (Kawamura, *Otome no karada*, 223–24).

85. Frederick, "Not That Innocent," 76.

86. Catherine Driscoll, *Girls: Feminine Adolescence in Popular Culture and Cultural Theory* (New York: Columbia University Press, 2002), 134.

87. Autobiography was a popular literary genre in the 1900s. Early autobiographies described male success stories or the achievement of selfhood in Japan; they portrayed modern Japanese men who worked toward the modernization of Japan (Okano Sachie, " 'Jiden' to iu senryaku: Fukuda Eiko *Mekake no han shōgai*," in *Meiji josei bungakuron*, ed. Shin feminizumu hihyō no kai [Tokyo: Kanrin Shobō]). In female culture, autobiography became a popular literary style among *Seitō* members. This was actually influenced by magazine tradition in which women confessed their secrets on the pages of magazine, sharing their life stories in the closed protected space of women (ibid.).

Chapter Five

1. Uchiyama Motoi (1903–1982) started working at Jitsugyō no Nihonsha after graduating from Waseda University. He was assigned to be the chief editor of *Shōjo no tomo* in June, 1931, and from January 1932 his name started appearing in the magazine. He also worked on *Shinnyoen* (New Women's Garden) magazine, and founded *Watashi no kimono* (My Kimono) magazine (which later changed its name to *Modo e modo*). He later established Tōwasha publishing, which reprinted stories from before the war, including Yoshiya's works.

2. "*Shōjo no tomo* 45 nen no ayumi," *Shōjo no tomo* 45, no. 4 (1952): 223.

3. Uchiyama Motoi saw talent in Nakahara Jun'ichi, a young aspiring artist, and invited him to *Shōjo no tomo*. Nakahara was put in charge of cover illustrations for the magazine from January 1935. Like the work of Fukiya Kōji, Nakahara's drawings inherit the tradition of *jojōga*. See Takahashi, "Opening the Closed World of Shōjo Manga," 118–19.

4. Kawabata Yasunari (1899–1972) was a Japanese fiction writer. His works include *Yukiguni* (Snow Country, 1948), *Senbazuru* (Thousand Cranes, 1952), *Yama no oto* (The Sound of the Mountain, 1954), and so on. In 1968, he received the Nobel Prize for Literature. Kawabata was also involved in the field of juvenile literature; for *Shōjo no tomo*, not only did he contribute stories but also serve as a commentator on readers' compositions.

5. According to Inagaki Kyōko, by 1925, more than 1,000 movie theaters were constructed. However, moviegoing was prohibited at most girls' schools (Inagaki, *Jogakkō to Jogakusei*, 142).

6. *Wakakusa monogatari* (Stories of Young Grass), the Japanese title of George Cukor's 1933 film *Little Women*, was released in Japan in 1934 with Yoshiya Nobuko as a consultant, according to an advertisement in the October 1934 issue of *Shōjo no tomo*. The issue included a booklet devoted to *Little Women* that contained pictures from the movie.

7. *Anne of Green Gables* was introduced in *Shōjo gahō* 24, no. 5 (1935). This abbreviated translation was written by a woman named Minami Yoshiko and accompanied by pictures from the movie. The film was released in Japan in 1934 under the title, *Beni suzume* (Red Sparrow).

8. Shirley Temple, who played the role of Heidi, was popular in Japan. The film was released in Japan in 1939, and was featured in the February issue of *Shōjo no tomo*. *Heidi* was also serialized in *Shōjo no tomo* in 1935, with pictures by popular illustrator Matsumoto Katsuji (1904–1984).

9. The plot of Yoshiya's *Mittsu no hana* (Three Flowers) originally published in *Shōjo kurabu* (from April 1926 to June 1927) is also similar to that of *Little Women*.

10. Endō Hiroko, "Yuri Seiko," *Shōnen shōsetsu taikei*, vol. 24, 619.

11. *Daddy-Long-Legs* was written in 1912 by American writer Jean Webster. The film version was released in 1919. Today *Daddy-Long-Legs* is known as *Ashinaga Ojisan* in Japan. But the first translation is titled *Katonbo Sumisu* (Daddy Longlegs Smith) translated by Azuma Kenji (1889–1933) in 1919.

12. See Fukuda Ichiyo, "Shōjo shōsetsu no keifu," *Gakuen* 851 (2011).

13. It is known that Kawabata hired female fiction writer Nakazato Tsuneko to write his *Otome no minato*. The story is based on Nakazato's experience. *Kawabata Yasunari zenshū hokan*, vol. 2 publishes an exchange of letters between Kawabata

and Nakazato. Deborah Shamoon discusses *Otome no minato* in the context of *Shōjo no tomo* magazine culture. See Shamoon, *Passionate Friendship: The Aesthetics of Girls' Culture in Japan* (Honolulu: University of Hawai'i Press, 2012), 38–45.

14. Kobayashi Yoshihito, "Kawabata Yasunari," *Kokubungaku kaishaku to kanshō* 48, no. 14 (1983): 163.

15. Endō Hiroko, *Shōjo no tomo to sono jidai: henshūsha no yūki Uchiyama Motoi* (Tokyo: Hon no Izumisha, 2004), 28.

16. Uchida Shizue, "Zasshi no kōsei," in *Shōjo no tomo to sono jidai*, 175.

17. Wada Kokō, "Hana mo arashi mo," quoted in *Jitsugyō no Nihonsha hyakunenshi* (Tokyo: Jitsugyō no Nihonsha, 1997), 134.

18. Masui Takashi, "Naimushō toshoka 'Shōwa 13 nen jidō zasshi ken'etsubo' ni tsuite," *Kokusai jidō bungakukan kiyō* 12 (1997): 145. Nine educators and writers including Yamamoto Yūzō (1887–1974), Ogawa Mimei (1882–1961), and Tsubota Jōji (1890–1982) were involved in its creation (Satō "Jidō bunka seisaku to kyōiku kagaku," 86).

19. Satō Hiromi, "Jidō bunka seisaku to kyōiku kagaku," *Jinmon gakuhō, kyōikugaku* 28 (1993): 88.

20. *Jitsugyō no Nihonsha hyakunenshi*, 150.

21. Namekawa Michio, *Shōkokumin bungaku shiron*, published in 1942, quoted in Ōfuji Mikio, "Senchūki no jidō bungaku hyōron: Seikatsu dōwa kara shokokumin bungaku e no nagare o otte," *Gakudai kokubun* 29 [1986]: 154.

22. *Jitsugyō no Nihonsha hyakunenshi*, 150.

23. Imada Erika, *Shōjo no shakaishi* (Tokyo: Keisō Shobō, 2007), 167.

24. Quoted in Endō, *Shōjo no tomo to sono jidai*, 163. Endō Hiroko states that Uchiyama Motoi continued to work coolheadedly on the magazine. She believes that he never agreed with the government's policy, which was insulting to girls' culture (ibid.).

25. Miyamoto Saburō (1905–1974) was a Western-style painter who studied at Kawabata Art School. His first success was at the age of twenty-two when his work was selected for the Nika Exhibition. He is known for the importance he placed on life drawing.

26. Uchiyama Motoi, "Kurabushitsu dayori," *Shōjo no tomo* 33, no. 7 (1940): 244.

27. One girl supporting Uchiyama writes, "[I]t is sad that Nakahara-sensei's pictures are gone, but the new drawings are realistic and also beautiful" (Taga Noko, *Shōjo no tomo* 33, no. 9 [1940]: 237).

28. Miyamatsu Sayo, *Shōjo no tomo* 33, no. 9 (1940): 237.

29. Ibid. (Uchiyama's reply to Miyamatsu's letter.)

30. Uchiyama Motoi, "Henshū kōki," *Shōjo no tomo* 33, no. 9 (1940): 252.

31. Imada, *Shōjo no shakaishi*, 76.

32. According to Annika Culver, "Japanese policy makers in Manchukuo actively promoted the creation of a new national culture, art and literature in addition to a body of work describing the physical and symbolic construction of the new multi-ethnic nation.... [However,] culture in Manchukuo was in reality characterized by a primary focus on imperial Japan as the center" (Annika A. Culver, "Manchukuo and the Creation of a New National Literature: Kawabata Yasunari and 'Manchurian' Culture 1941–1942," *PAJLS* 9 [2008]: 255).

33. For more details, see Hiromi Tsuchiya Dollase, "Kawabata's Wartime Message in Beautiful Voyage (*Utsukushii tabi*)," in *Negotiating Censorship in Modern Japan*, ed. Rachael Hutchinson (New York: Routledge, 2013), 82.

34. For information on Yoshiya's works and involvement in *Shufu no tomo*, see Sarah Frederick's *Turning Pages*.

35. Writers like Kume Masao (1892–1952), Ozaki Shirō (1898–1964), and Hayashi Fumiko were embedded with the army, while Kikuchi Kan (1888–1948), Satō Haruo (1892–1964), Yoshikawa Eiji (1892–1962), and Yoshiya Nobuko were stationed with the navy.

36. Kameyama Toshiko, "Yoshiya Nobuko to Hayashi Fumiko no jūgunki o yomu: Pen butai no kō niten," in *Jūgoshi nōto fukkan*, vol. 2, *Nicchū kaisen sōdōinka no onnatachi*, ed. Kanō Mikiyo (Tokyo: JCA Shuppan, 1981), 79.

37. Ibid. Dying while serving as a *jūgun kangofu* (military nurse) was another way for women to be consecrated at the Yasukuni Shrine.

38. Yoshiya Nobuko, "Atarashiki seiki o tsukuru hitobito to shite," *Shōjo no tomo* 33, no, 4 (1940), n.p.

39. Yoshiya published a series of short stories in *Shōjo no tomo* in the 1940s including *Shōjoki* (Girlhood).

40. Uchiyama Motoi and Yoshiya Nobuko, "Shōjo ni okuru Yoshiya Nobuko sensei Uchiyama shuhitsu taidankai," *Shōjo no tomo* 31, no. 1 (1938): 87.

41. Ibid.

42. Ibid.

43. Yoshiya Nobuko, "Hitotsubu no mugi to mo naran," *Shōjo no tomo* 34, no. 3 (1941): 81.

44. Mabuchi Itsuo and Yoshiya Nobuko, "Seisen dai 5 nen: Mabuchi hōdō buchō, Yoshiya Nobuko, taidankai," *Shōjo no tomo* 34, no. 7 (1941): 65.

45. Ibid., 66.

46. Yoshiya Nobuko, "Senka no hokushi genchi o iku," in *Senka no hokushi genchi o iku* (Tokyo: Shinchōsha, 1937), 83.

47. Yoshiya Nobuko, "Senka no Shanhai kesshikō," *Shufu no tomo* 21, no. 11 (1937).

48. Ibid., 172–73.

49. Ibid., 173. The compassionate friendship between a Japanese woman and a Chinese woman amid the war is also depicted in her *Onna no kyōshitsu* (Women's Classroom, 1937), a story written for housewives.

50. Hayashi Fumiko was a fiction writer. She made her debut with *Hōroki* (Diary of a Vagabond, 1930), an autobiographical story written in the form of diary. Her stories were always written from the standpoint of working-class, struggling women. Hayashi's other works include *Bangiku* (Late Chrysanthemums, 1949) and *Ukigumo* (Floating Cloud, 1951). During the war, she joined the pen corps and traveled to China, where she enthusiastically reported the Japanese imperial army's war efforts.

51. See Hayashi Fumiko, *Hokugan butai* (Tokyo: Chūō Kōronsha, 1939).

52. Yoshiya's message seems to have borrowed from the concept of "international bonds of womanhood" discussed at the meetings of the Women's International League for Peace and Freedom (WILPF) (Leila J. Rupp, *Worlds of Women: The Making of an International Women's Movement* [Princeton: Princeton University Press, 1998]).

53. Yoshiya, "Senka no hokushi genchi o iku," 77.

54. See Rupp, *Worlds of Women*.

55. Kamiya Tadataka, "Jyūgun josei sakka: Yoshiya Nobuko o chūshin ni," *Shakai bungaku* 15 (2001): 57.

56. Takasaki Ryūji, *Senjō no joryū sakkatachi: Yoshiya Nobuko, Hayashi Fumiko, Sata Ineko, Masugi Shizue, Toyota Masako* (Tokyo: Ronsōsha, 1995), 39.

57. Yoshiya, "Senka no Shanhai kesshikō," in *Zuihitsu yuku michi* (Tokyo: Kyoritsu Shobō, 1947), 176.

58. Kan, *Onna ga kokka o uragiru toki*, 207–35.

59. Morita Tama, "Hitotsu no sōwa," in 176.

60. Hatori Tetsuya, for instance, states that "Kawabata did not encourage war. He could . . . do nothing but watch the sad fate of human beings" (Hatori Tetsuya, "Kawabata Yasunari to sensō," *Kokubungaku kaishaku to kanshō* 46, no. 4 [1981]: 157). After the war, Kawabata himself stated: "I am one of the Japanese who was affected least and suffered least because of the war. . . . I was never caught up in a surge of what is called divine possession, to become a fanatical believer in or blind worshiper of Japan" (*Tokyo shinbun* 1948; trans. Donald Keene, *Dawn to the West: Japanese Literature of the Modern Era [Fiction]* (New York: Holt, Rinehart and Winston, 1984, 823).

61. See Dollase, "Kawabata's Wartime Message in *Utsukushii tabi* (Beautiful Voyage)."

62. The *Tsuzurikata* movement was originally started by Suzuki Miekichi, the editor of *Akai tori* (Red Bird). For information on the *Tsuzurikata* movement, see Nakaya Izumi, "Tsuzurikata no keisei," *Nihon daigaku kokubun gakkai* 111, no. 12 (2001).

63. Kawabata Yasunari, "Senja no kotoba," *Shōjo no tomo*, 35, no. 1 (1942): 185.

64. *Utsukushii tabi* began serialization in July, 1939. Its sequel, *Zoku utsukushii tabi*, started from September 1941, but the story was never completed (the last episode was published in October 1942). For a discussion of this work, see Dollase, "Kawabata's Wartime Message in *Utsukushii tabi* (Beautiful Voyage)."

65. Endō, "Kaisetsu," 544.

66. Tsuda Katsuo, "Mihoko no shigoto," *Shōjo kurabu* 21, no. 11 (1943).

67. Kitagawa Chiyo contributed many stories to *Shōjo kurabu* and *Yōnen kurabu*. According to Kitagawa Sachihiko's chronology, she attended the inauguration ceremony of *Shōkokumin bunka kyōkai* (Children's Cultural Association), the governmental organization whose goals were the control of children's culture and the promotion of war efforts, in January, 1942 (Kitagawa Sachihiko, "Kitagawa Chiyo nenpu," in *Kitagawa Chiyo bungaku zenshū*, vol. 2 [Tokyo: Kōdansha, 1967], 357).

68. Kitagawa Chiyo, "Usagi o kau shōjo," *Shōjo kurabu* 20, no. 1 (1942).

69. Tsuboi Sakae, "Tsuyukusa," *Shōjo kurabu* 22, no. 11 (1944).

70. Muraoka Hanako (1893–1968) was a translator and educator. She translated many Western girls' stories, including *Anne of Green Gables*. She was also known as a radio personality who had a news program for children (1932–1942). She was close with writers such as Yoshiya Nobuko and Morita Tama, and when she founded a women's magazine, *Katei* (Home), Yoshiya and Kitagawa Chiyo contributed stories (Muraoka Eri, *An no yurikago: Muraoka Hanako no shōgai* [Tokyo: Magajin Hausu, 2008], 241).

71. Muraoka Hanako, "Jogakuseiron," *Shōjo no tomo* 34, no. 12 (1941): 106.

72. *Kageki*, founded in 1918, featured the Takarazuka Review.

73. *Shōjo no tomo* 34, no. 1 (1941): 227.

74. Uchiyama Motoi, "Kimitachi mo zensen no heishi da," *Shōjo no tomo* 36, no. 10 (1943): 24.

75. Takamura Kōtarō (1883–1956) was a sculptor and poet. He is known for his *Chiekoshō*, a collection of poems about his artist wife, Takamura Chieko, who suffered from symptoms of schizophrenia.

76. Takamura Kōtarō, "Shōjo tatakau," *Shōjo no tomo* 37, no. 1 (1944): 21.

77. Hazama Yuki, "Ajia taiheiyō sensōki no *shōjo no tomo*: Dokusha tōkōran no bunseki o chūshin ni," *Osaka jinken hakubutsukan kiyō* 9 (2006): 136.

78. Asami Fujiko, *Shōjo no tomo* 36.1 (1943): 162.

79. Tanabe Seiko, *Watashi no Osaka hakkei* (Tokyo: Iwanami Shoten, 2000), 162.
80. Honda Masuko, "Senjika no shōjo zasshi: Ikinobiru gensō," in *Shōjo zasshiron*, ed. Ōtsuka Eiji (Tokyo: Tōkyō Shoseki, 1991), 40–41.
81. Uchiyama Motoi, "Henshū kōki," *Shōjo no tomo* 37, no. 5 (1944): 76.
82. In 1941, however, Uchiyama encouraged readers to graduate from *Shōjo no tomo* quickly and become mature women (Uchiyama Motoi, "Kurabushitsu dayori," *Shōjo no tomo* 34, no. 4 [1941]: 229). He perhaps realized that there was no other choice but to feed his readers war propaganda. In the April 1945 issue the readers' column *"seikatsu kyōshitsu"* was finally discontinued.
83. *Shōjo no tomo* 34.9 (1941): 40.
84. Wakakuwa Midori, *Sensō ga tsukuru joseizō: Dainiji sekai taisenka no nihonjosei dōin no shikakuteki puropaganda* (Tokyo: Chikuma Shobō, 2000), 126.

Chapter Six

1. Uchiyama Motoi, "Saigo no hi," *Shōjo no tomo* 38, no. 8 (1945): 6–7.
2. SCAP is usually used to indicate both Douglas MacArthur and the whole institution of the occupation (Vera Mackie, *Feminism in Modern Japan: Citizenship, Embodiment and Sexuality* [Cambridge: Cambridge University Press, 2003], 212).
3. John W. Dower, *Embracing Defeat: Japan in the Wake of World War II* (New York: W. W. Norton & Company, 1999), 176.
4. Noriko Suzuki, *The Re-invention of the American West: Women's Periodicals and Gendered Geography in the Late Nineteenth-Century United States* (New York: Edwin Mellen Press, 2009), 212.
5. GHQ/SCAP presented the Japanese government with the following agenda of five necessary actions for the restoration of Japan: "the granting of full political rights to women; the granting of full political rights to workers, including the right to form unions; the democratisation of education; the abolition of the secret police (*tokkō keisatsu*); and the smashing of the *zaibatsu* conglomerate companies" (Mackie, *Feminism in Modern Japan*, 121).
6. Hiroshi Kitamura, *Screening Enlightenment: Hollywood and the Cultural Reconstruction of Defeated Japan* (Ithaca: Cornell University Press, 2010), 35.
7. Ibid., 33
8. Suzuki, *The Re-invention of the American West*, 213.
9. Ochi Hiromi, "What Did She Read?: The Cultural Occupation of Post-War Japan and Translated Girls' Literature," *GENS Journal* 5 (2006): 360.
10. Ibid., 361. Also, see Miyata Noboru, *Hon'yakuken no sengoshi* (Tokyo: Misuzu Shobō, 1999).
11. Ochi, "What Did She Read?," 360.

12. Jan Bardsley, *Women and Democracy in Cold War Japan* (London: Bloomsbury Publishing Plc, 2014), 11.
13. Ochi, "What Did She Read?" 360.
14. Okahara Miyako, *Amerika senryōki no minshuka seisaku: Rajio hōsō ni yoru nihon josei saikyōiku puroguramu* (Tokyo: Akashi Shoten, 2007).
15. Misaki Tomeko, "GHQ/CIE kyōiku eiga to sono eikyō," *Image & Gender* 7 (2007): 66.
16. Mackie, *Feminism in Modern Japan*, 123.
17. Mark McLelland, *Love, Sex, and Democracy in Japan during American Occupation* (New York: Palgrave Macmillan, 2012), 44.
18. Ibid., 45.
19. Mackie, *Feminism in Modern Japan*, 130.
20. Tsuchiya Yuka, *Shinbei nihon no kōchiku: Amerika no tainichi jōhō, kyōiku seisaku to nihon senryō* (Tokyo: Akashi Shoten, 2009), 219.
21. Ibid. Misaki Tomeko states, "Equality and democracy of men and women in the public sphere were far from realized and still had a long way to go" (Misaki, "GHQ/CIE kyōiku eiga to sono eikyō," 72).
22. Dower, *Embracing Defeat*, 407.
23. Sharalyn Orbaugh, *Japanese Fiction of the Allied Occupation: Vision, Embodiment, Identity* (Leiden: Brill, 2007), 42. In her book, Orbaugh discusses how works by such film directors as Mizoguchi Kenji, Kinoshita Keisuke, Kurosawa Akira, and Naruse Mikio were confiscated.
24. "Ishiusu no uta," was originally published in *Shōjo kurabu* 23, no. 6 (1945). Also see Tani Eiko, "Kaisetsu," in *Senryōki Zasshi shiryō taikei: Bungaku hen*, vol. 5, *Senryōki bungaku no tamensei*, ed. Yamamoto Taketoshi (Tokyo: Iwanami Shoten, 2010), 162–64.
25. Dower, *Embracing Defeat*, 408.
26. Jun Etō, *Tozasareta gengo kūkan: Senryōgun no ken'etsu to sengo nihon* (Tokyo: Bungei Shunjū, 1994).
27. Statement by a soldier named A. B. Chapman in a letter he sent to a senator from Arkansas who was on the naval affairs committee (Toshio Nishi, *Unconditional Democracy: Education and Politics in Occupied Japan 1945–1952* [Stanford: Hoover Institution Press, 1982], 188).
28. For a list of members of the mission, see Nishi, *Unconditional Democracy*, 190–91.
29. The report was submitted to the GHQ/SCAP on March 30, 1948. See Beauchamp and Vardaman, *Japanese Education since 1945*, 86.
30. Ibid., 87.
31. Nishi, *Unconditional Democracy*, 206.

32. Under the National School Order, which was instituted in 1941, elementary schools were called *Kokumin gakkō* (National Schools). Originally eight years of compulsory education were required, which was revised to six years with two optional years. *Kōtō jogakkō* (Girls' high schools), which was unified under the middle-level school, had four to five years of education. See "Japan's Modern Educational System," http://www.mext.go.jp/b_menu/hakusho/html/others/detail/1317220.htm.

33. Edward R. Beauchamp and James M. Vardaman Jr., *Japanese Education since 1945: A Documentary Study* (New York: M. E. Sharpe, 1994), 87.

34. Namekawa Michio, "Atarashii gakkōseido no hanashi," *Shōjo kurabu* 25, no. 4 (1947): 31.

35. During the occupation, Yoshiya published the serialized stories *Shōnen* (Boy) in 1949 and *Hana sorezore* (Various Flowers) in 1950 in *Shōjo no tomo*.

36. "Yoshiya sensei o kakomu zadankai," *Shōjo no tomo* 43, no. 8 (1950): 101.

37. "Jogakusei no yūjō," *Shōjo no tomo* 41, no. 12 (1948): 13.

38. Catherine Yoonah Bae, "Girl Meets Boy Meets Girl," *Asian Studies Review* 32, no. 3 (2008): 354.

39. Ibid., 354.

40. In 1946, Nakahara Jun'ichi created a fashion magazine called *Soleil*. After the success of *Soleil*, he founded his own publishing company, Himawariya, which printed the girls' magazine *Himawari* starting in January 1947.

41. Yoshiya Nobuko, "Seishun ni okuru," *Himawari* 1, no. 1 (1947): n.p.

42. Kitabatake Yao and Nakahara Jun'ichi, "Yoriyoki shōjo no hi no tameni," *Himawari* 2, no. 11 (1948): 20.

43. Kitabatake Yao, Kawakami Kikuko, and Takeuchi Teruyo, "Shōjo no sakuhin o megutte," *Himawari* 3, no. 2 (1949): 26.

44. *Yonin no shimai* was translated by Andō Ichirō (*Himawari* 1, no's. 1–8 [1947]). *Eren monogatari* (The Story of Ellen; English title, *The Wide, Wide World*) is another story serialized in *Himawari*, which puts the same emphasis on the value of domestic work as does *Little Women*. This story, written by Susan Warner (Elizabeth Wetherell) in 1850, was translated by Muraoka Hanako. American juvenile literature continued to influence Japanese girls' stories. Muraoka was active in introducing Western stories. She translated Louisa May Alcott's *Eight Cousins* (1875) and *Rose in Bloom* (1876) to show democratic relationships between boys and girls. She stated that these works teach readers how "boys and girls have proper relationships and work together" (Muraoka Hanako, "Kongetsu no dokusho kara," *Himawari* 2, no. 9 [1948], 30).

45. "Yonin no shimai," *Himawari* 1, no. 8 (1947): 32.

46. *Little Women*, directed by Mervyn LeRoy, was released in America by MGM in 1949. Jo March was played by June Allison.
47. Kitamura, *Screening Enlightenment*, 100.
48. Ibid., 104.
49. According to a poll conducted among Himawari's readers in 1951, the most popular movie was *Wakakusa monogatari* (*Little Women*), followed by *Kojika monogatari* (*The Yearling*, released in Japan in 1949) ("Eiga ni tsuite kangaete mimashou," *Himawari* 5, no. 3 [1951]: 98).
50. Ibid., 27.
51. "Nihon no wakakusa kyōdai," *Shōjo no tomo* 43, no. 5 (1950): n.p.
52. For the establishment of Mother's Day, see Kodama Ryōko, "Haha no hi no politics," in *Kyōikugaku nenpō 7 jendā to kyōiku*, ed. Fujita Hidenori, et al. (Yokohama: Seori Shobō). For a discussion of Mother's Day in postwar Japan, see Kodama Ryōko, " 'Haha no hi' ga seiji ni arawareru toki, kieru toki," *Jendāshi sensho*, vol. 2: *Kazoku to kyōiku*, ed. Ishikawa Teruko, et al. (Tokyo: Akashi Shoten, 2011).
53. In a *Himawari* fan event, a group of girls performed *Little Women* on stage under the instruction of Ashihara Kuniko, retired Takarazuka star and wife of Nakahara Jun'ichi ("Himawari aidokusha taikai no ki," *Himawari* 5, no. 4 [1951]: 74–75).
54. Nakahara Jun'ichi, "Anata wa donna shōjo?," *Himawari* 4, no. 2 (1950): 28–29.
55. Jō, *Himawari* 4, no. 11 (1950): 147.
56. Wakakusa, *Himawari* 5, no. 1 (1951): 118.
57. Ochi, "What Did She Read?," 361.
58. "Umi o wataru *Himawari*," *Himawari* 2, no. 5 (1948): 28.
59. Muraoka Hanako, "Kotoba ni tsuite," *Himawari* 1, no. 2 (1947): 35.
60. Kawabata Yasunari, "Utsukushii kotoba," *Himawari* 1, no. 3 (1947): n.p.
61. Tamai Tokutarō (1902–1986) studied at Kawabata Art School. He drew many illustrations for juvenile stories.
62. Nakazato Tsuneko (1909–1987) was a fiction writer. Her *Noriai basha* (Shared Stagecoach) received the Akutagawa Prize in 1939.
63. See Fukasawa Harumi, "*Shōjo kurabu, Shōjo no tomo* ni okeru Kawabata Yasunari," *Geijutsu shijōshugi bungei* 22 (1996).
64. Kawabata published three serialized stories in *Himawari*. According to Hirayama Jōji, *Kageki gakkō* (Musical School; July 1949–July 1950), was actually written by Hirayama's mother Morishita Miyako (Konoe Hisako), a Takarazuka actress, and was based on her experiences (Hirayama Jōji, *Kawabata Yasunari: Yohaku o umeru* [Tokyo: Kenbun Shuppan, 2003]). Also, fiction writer Satō

Midoriko mentions that she helped write Kawabata's *Manyō shimai* (Manyo Sisters), published in *Himawari* in 1951 (see Satō Midoriko, *Taki no oto: Kaikyū no Kawabata Yasunari* [Tokyo: Shirakawa Shoin, 1980], 356).

65. Ōmori Ikunosuke, "Kawabata Yasunari sengo shōjo shōsetsu shikan: Shōjozō no henbō," *Sapporo daigaku sōgō ronsō* 3 (1997): 53.

66. Kawabata, "Hana to kosuzu," *Himawari* 6, no. 3 (1952): 18.

67. Kawabata, "Hana to kosuzu," *Himawari* 6, no. 11 (1952): 19.

68. See Eiji Sekine, "Gender Differences in a Genealogy of Modern Love Stories," *PMAJLS* 2 (1996).

69. Kawabata, "Hana to kosuzu," *Himawari* 6, no. 9 (1952): 16.

70. Kawabata, "Hana to kosuzu," *Himawari* 6, no. 12 (1952): 30.

71. Kawabata, "Hana to kosuzu," *Himawari* 6, no. 11 (1952): 21.

72. Hamano Takuya, "Kawabata Yasunari ron: 'Niji' to shōjo shōsetsu 'Kageki gakkō,'" *Shōwa bungaku kenkyū* 9 (1984): 30.

73. Kobayashi Yoshihito, "Kawabata bungaku ni okeru seishōjo no keifu to sono tokuchō," *Kokubungaku kaishaku to kanshō* 62, no. 4 (1997): 64.

74. Kawabata Yasunari, "Aishū," in *Kawabata Yasunari sakuhinsen* (Tokyo: Chūō Kōronsha, 1968), 508.

75. After returning from France in 1952, Nakahara started a new magazine called *Junior Soleil*. Inspired by American *Seventeen* magazine, he wanted to create an entertainment magazine containing information on film, fashion, theater, singers, and so forth. Many well-known celebrities made their debut in this magazine.

Chapter Seven

1. Christopher Wood, *The Bubble Economy: Japan's Extraordinary Speculative Boom of the '80s and the Dramatic Burst of the '90s* (Jakarta: Solstice Publishing, 2006), 1.

2. The bubble economy was triggered by the Plaza Accord Agreement (in September 1985) between the United States, the United Kingdom, West Germany, and Japan designed to devalue the U.S. dollar with respect to other currencies. The end of the bubble economy was triggered by the stock market crash of 1990.

3. Barbara Molony, "Japan's 1986 Equal Employment Opportunity Law and the Changing Discourse on Gender," *Signs* 20, no. 2 (1995): 272.

4. "Chikushi tetsuya no kurara taidan: Genki jirushi no onnnatachi," *Asahi Journal* 28, no. 40 (1986).

5. *Za chenji* and *Nante suteki ni japanesuku* were made into *shōjo* manga drawn by Yamauchi Naomi.

6. *Genji monogatari*, consisting of fifty-four chapters, is the story of the tragic romantic entanglements of Imperial prince Genji, and was written by Murasaki Shikibu in early eleventh century.

7. Kan Satoko, "Watashitachi no ibasho: Himuro Saeko ron," in *Shōjo shōsetsu wandārando: Meiji kara Heisei made*, ed. Kan Satoko (Tokyo: Meiji Shoin, 2008), 75.

8. Iwasaki Mariko, "Junia shōsetsu," in *Nihon jidōbungaku daijiten*, vol. 2, 413.

9. Hasegawa Kei, "Haisengo kara 1960 nendai e," in *Shōjo shōsetsu jiten*, 13.

10. Nanba Kōji, "Sengo yūsu sabukaruchāzu ni tsuite 1: Taiyōzoku kara miyukizoku e," *Kansai gakuin daigaku shakaigakubu kiyō* 96 (2004): 163.

11. Furuichi Noritoshi, *Zetsubō no kuni no kōfuku na wakamonotachi* (Tokyo: Kōdansha, 2011), 41.

12. *Cobalt bukkusu* (Cobalt Books) later changed its name to *Cobalt bunko* (Cobalt Paperback Library).

13. Tomishima Takeo (1931–1998) was a fiction writer. His *Souka no inu* (Mourning Dog, 1953), which he wrote when he was a student at Waseda University, was nominated for the Akutagawa Prize. His works are known for his sensual depictions of the relationships between men and women. For a detailed study of Tomishima and his works, see Arakawa Yoshihiro, *Junia to kannō no kyoshō Tomishima Takeo den* (Tokyo: Kawade Shobō Shinsha, 2017).

14. Tomishima Takeo, "Junia shōsetsu wa bungaku ka," *Mainichi shinbun*, February 7, 1970.

15. Tomishima Takeo, *Osanazuma* (Tokyo: Shueisha, 1988).

16. *Asahi shinbun*, February 2, 1970, quoted in Iwata Yōko, "Junia shōstsu to kyoeishin: Tsumura Setsuko *Ajisaiiro no yume*, *Fukeyo kitakaze* o chūshin ni," *Kokubungaku* 97 (2013): 86.

17. Tomishima Takeo, " 'Junia shōsetsu' seishosetsu o warau," *Ushio* 124 (1970): 242.

18. Kaneda Junko, "Kyōiku no kyakutai kara sanka no shutai e: 1980 nendai no shōjomuke shōsetsu janru ni okeru shōjo dokusha," *Joseigaku* 9 (2001): 32.

19. Yokokawa Sumiko, "Posuto shōjo shōsetsu no genzai: Onnanoko wa otokonoko ni nani o motomete iruka," in *21seiki bungaku no sōzō 7: Danjo to iu seido*, ed. Saitō Minako (Tokyo: Iwanami Shoten, 2001), 213.

20. Tamura Yayoi, "Cobalt bunka to shōjotachi," in *Shōjo shōsetsu wandārando*, 115.

21. Tachihara Ayumi's *shōjo* manga *Baku-chan no ita sekusuarisu* (Baku's Vita Sexualis, published in the *Cobalt* paperback series from 1980–1982), a work that vividly portrayed teenage sex, was first serialized in this magazine.

22. Itō Saeko, *Shōsetsu junia* 6, no. 1 (1971): 494.

23. Tomishima Takeo, "Seishun no saigetsu," *Shōsetsu junia* 17, no. 6 (1982): 20.

24. See Jennifer S. Prough, *Straight from the Heart: Gender, Intimacy, and the Cultural Production of Shōjo Manga* (Honolulu: University of Hawai'i Press, 2011).
25. Tamura, "Cobalt bunka to shōjotachi," 116.
26. The first issue spotlighted writer and former radio personality Ochiai Keiko (1945–), known as the author of *Za reipu* (The Rape, 1982), a story that deals with a lawsuit brought by a young career woman who is a victim of rape. She appeared as an example of an independent woman.
27. Beside Himura Saeko, Arai Motoko, Kumi Saori, Tanaka Masami, and Masamoto Non appeared in this ad.
28. The judges included prominent writers and critics, including Miura Shumon (1926–2017), Tomishima Takeo, and Ozaki Hotsuki (1928–1999). They all praised Himuro's writing skills, although some pointed out the weakness of the stereotypical plot. "Sayōnara Arurukan" was published in the September issue of the same year.
29. Becoming a writer was not Himuro's original intention; she merely took on the challenge to test her writing ability. However, after college, she faced the job market "ice age" that resulted from the oil shock of 1979, and began to write to support herself.
30. Saga Keiko, *Kobaruto bunko de tadoru shōjo shōsetsu hensenshi* (Tokyo: Sairyūsha, 2016), 33.
31. Himuro used the term *shōjo shōsetsu* for the first time in her *Shōjo shōsetska wa shinanai* (Girls' Story Writer Never Dies, 1983), a comical portrayal of girls' story writers and the publishing scene of the 1980s, written with cynicism and sarcasm.
32. Barbara Molony writes that "the pressure to conform to international standards was a major factor in the creation of the EEOL" (Molony, "Japan's 1986 Equal Employment Opportunity Law and the Changing Discourse on Gender," 282).
33. Yoko Ogasawara states that "only 1 percent of all women employed are managers or officials" in 1995 (Yuko Ogasawara, Office Ladies and Salaried Men: Power, Gender, and Work in Japanese Companies [Berkeley: University of California Press, 1998], 19).
34. Karen Kelsky, "Postcards from the Edge: The 'Office Ladies' of Tokyo," *U.S.-Japan Women's Journal English Supplement* 6 (1944): 3.
35. Alexadra Hambleton, "Idol as Accidental Activist: Agnes Chan, Feminism and Motherhood in Japan," in *Idols and Celebrity in Japanese Media Culture*, ed. Patrick W. Galbraith (New York: Palgrave Macmillan, 2012), 159–60. See also Molony, "Japan's 1986 Equal Employment Opportunity Law and the Changing Discourse on Gender," 270.
36. Molony, "Japan's 1986 Equal Employment Opportunity Law and the Changing Discourse on Gender," 287.

37. Agnes Chan (1955–) studied at Stanford University and obtained a PhD in education. The debate took place on the pages of such magazines as *Sandē mainichi* (Sunday Mainichi), *Uīkurī asahi* (Weekly Asahi), *Shūkan bunshun* (Weekly Bunshun), and *Chūō kōron*. Opinions were expressed by Hayashi Mariko (fiction writer), Nakano Midori (essayist), Ueno Chizuko (feminist scholar), and so on.

38. Hayashi Mariko's (1954–) made her debut as a writer in 1982 with *Run run o katte ouchi ni kaerō* (Buy Runrun and Go Home), which became a best seller. Her works include award winning *Byakuren renren* (a biographical account of poet Yanagiwara Byakuren, 1995) and *Minna no himitsu* (Everyone's Secret, 1998).

39. Hambleton, "Idol as an Accidental Activist," 160.

40. Keichi Kumagai, "An Observation Floating Young Men: Globalization and the Crisis of Masculinity in Japan," *HAGAR Studies in Culture, Policy and Identities* 10, no. 2 (2012): 158.

41. Ogura Chikako, *Kekkon no jōken* (Tokyo: Asahi Shinbun Shuppan, 2007), 136.

42. Ibid., 139.

43. Ogura Chikako, *Taidan: Giakusha no feminizumu* (Tokyo: Gakuyō Shobō, 1991), 162.

44. Himuro grew up reading *shōjo* manga, including her favorite, *Berusaiyu no bara* (Rose of Versailles, 1972–73) by Ikeda Riyoko, a story about a girl who is raised as a boy and grows up to become a member of the Royal Guard, eventually taking part in the French Revolution (Himuro Saeko, *Himuro Saeko dokuhon* [Tokyo: Tokuma Shoten, 1993], 150). Himuro's interest in the topic of the gender bending, as featured in *Torikaebaya*, might have come from her interest in *shōjo* manga.

45. In the original *Torikaebaya monogatari*, it is hard to identity which sibling is older. Kuwahara Hiroshi, who translated *Torikaebaya Monogatari* into modern language, interprets the boy to be older and the girl to be younger.

46. Himuro Saeko, *Za chenji*, vol. 2, 52.

47. See Judith Butler, *Gender Trouble: Feminism and the Subversion of Identity* (New York: Routledge, 1990).

48. Yukari Fujimoto, "Transgender: Female Hermaphrodites and Male Androgynies," *U.S.-Japan Women's Journal* 27 (2004): 79–80.

49. *Genpuku* is a Japanese coming-of-age ceremony for aristocratic male children between the ages of ten and twenty. From the ages of three or four, the boys began studying key court ceremonies, Buddhist doctrine, and proper ethics. *Genpuku* is the culmination of their studies. At the ceremony, they wore ceremonial court caps. *Mogi* is the ceremony for girls. It was timed to take place when they were ready for marriage. To indicate their having come of age, each girl wore a pleated skirt

and changed her hairstyle to a traditional bun. For the ceremony, both males and females changed their names to new adult names.

50. Kuwabara Hiroshi, *Torikaebaya monogatari* (Tokyo: Kōdansha, 1978), 44.

51. Gregory M. Pflugfelder, "Strange Fates: Sex, Gender, and Sexuality in *Torikaebaya Monogatari*," *Monumenta Nipponica* 47, no. 3 (1992): 368.

52. Himuro, *Za chenji*, vol. 2, 87.

53. Kataoka Asami, "Murasaki no yukari to Himuro Saeko: *Za chenji* ni miru koten juyō no ichiyōsō," *Kenkyū to shiryō* 47 (2002): 56.

54. In the Original *Torikaebaya Monogatari*, the siblings' names are not identified. They are called by their social ranks and titles; for instance, the heroine, after the coming-of-age ceremony, serves in the court and is called by her rank, Jijyū, and later is promoted to, and referred to as Chūnagon.

55. In the original version, Sanno-miya, the wife, is older than Chūnagon (the heroine); she feels she deserves to be the wife of the emperor and is not happy about being the wife of Chūnagon. Their awkward relationship reminds us of Genji and Aoi (his first wife).

56. See Aiko Ōgoshi, "Women and Sexism in Japanese Buddhism: A Reexamination of Shinran's View of Women," *Japan Christian Review* 59 (1993).

57. Baba Junko, "*Imatorikaebaya* no onna chūnagon: Danjo heiritsu kara michibiki dasareru onna no tsumi to jubaku," *Atomi gakuen joshi daigaku kokubun gakkahō* 26 (2004), 181.

58. Ibid.

59. Himuro, *Za chenji*, vol. 2, 240.

60. Hayashi Mariko, *Run run o katte ouchi ni kaerō* (Tokyo: Kadokawa Shoten, 2005), 107.

61. Drama producer Tōru Ōta states that "while there is no clear-cut definition of this notion, 'trendy drama' often refers to a specific type of drama, which was produced only from the late 1980s to 1990" (Tōru Ōta, "Producing [Post-] Trendy Japanese TV Dramas," trans. Midori Nasu, in *Feeling Asian Modernities: Transnational Consumption of Japanese TV Dramas*, ed. Koichi Iwabuchi [Hong Kong: Hong Kong: University Press, 2004], 72). They "feature fashion, music, and trendy places where they [women] would want to go on a date" (ibid., 70).

62. Ibid.

63. Ushikubo Megumi, *Ren'ai shinai wakamonotachi: Konbinikasuru sei to kosupasuru kekkon* (Tokyo: Discover Twenty One, 2015), 13.

64. Ogura, *Kekkon no jōken*, 28.

65. The average marriage age for a woman was 24.4 in 1986.

66. Himuro Saeko, *Ippashi no onna* (Tokyo: Chikuma Shobō, 1992), 214.

67. Himuro's relationship with her mother is comically narrated in her collection of essays *Saeko no hahakogusa* (Saeko's Mother Daughter Grass, 1996).
68. Himuro Saeko, "Atogaki," in *Nante suteki ni japanesuku* vol. 1 (Tokyo: Shūeisha, 2012), 291.
69. Tamakazura's childhood name Fujiwara no Rurigimi is mentioned only once in *The Tale of Genji*.
70. Himuro, *Nante suteki ni japanesuku*, vol. 1, 86–87.
71. Ibid., 87.
72. Ibid., 8.
73. Ibid., 10.
74. Himuro, *Nante suteki ni japanesuku*, vol. 2, 35.
75. The latter half of Genji's life is believed to have been modeled after that of Fujiwara Michinaga, the father of Princess Shōshi, the princess whom the author of *The Tale of Genji*, Murasaki Shikibu, served.
76. Himuro, "Kaisetsu," in Setouchi Jakuchō, *Nyonin genji monogatari*, vol. 1, Kiritsubo–Shien (Tokyo: Shūeisha, 1997), 259.
77. Himuro, *Nante suteki ni japanesuku*, vol. 3, 14.
78. Lady Kiritsubo is Genji's mother in *The Tale of Genji*. Despite her modest family background, she becomes the emperor's favorite. She eventually dies due to suffering harassment from the emperor's first wife, Lady Kokiden.
79. Saitō Shōichi states that "in contrast to men, who put weight on public matters, women's values are placed on affection" (Saitō Shōichi, "Himuro Saeko Nante suteki ni japanesuku ron," *Shindai kokugo kyōiku* 5 [1996]: 27).
80. Himuro, *Himuro Saeko dokuhon*, 120.
81. Yamashita Etsuko, *Josei no jidai to iu shinwa* (Tokyo: Seikyūsha, 1991), 8.
82. See Saga, *Kobaruto bunko de meguru shōjo shōsetsu hensenshi*, 66–73.
83. Himuro, *Himuro Saeko dokuhon*, 20.
84. Ibid., 121.
85. Tomoko Aoyama and Barbara Hartley, introduction to *Girl Reading Girl in Japan*, 2.
86. Yanabu Akira, "Shōjo shōsetsu no shōgeki," *Shisō no kagaku* 7, no. 145 (1991): 28.
87. Himuro, *Himuro Saeko dokuhon*, 204.
88. Treat, "Yoshimoto Banana Writes Home," 356.
89. Saitō Minako, "Yoshimoto Banana and Girl Culture," trans. Eiji Sekine, in *Woman Critiqued*, 172.
90. Light novelist Konno Oyuki's *Maria-sama ga miteiru* (Maria Watches over Us), published in the Cobalt book series from 1998 to 2012, is inspired by Yoshiya

Nobuko's sentimental tales. Unfortunately, in January 2016, Shūeisha announced the termination of *Cobalt* magazine due to the deterioration of sales; in April of the same year, *Cobalt* became a free web magazine.

91. Saga, *Kobaruto bunko de tadoru shōjo shōsetsu hensenshi*, 90.

92. For a discussion of women writers who emerged in the mid-1980s, see Hiromi Tsuchiya Dollase, "Choosing Your Family," *Journal of Popular Culture* 44, no. 4 (2011).

Chapter Eight

1. Tanabe Seiko, *Yume haruka Yoshiya Nobuko*.
2. Tanabe Seiko, *Hoshigarimasen katsumadewa* (Tokyo: Popurasha, 2009), 23–24.
3. Tanabe Seiko, "Sara," *Shōjo no tomo* 36, no. 7 (1943): 117.
4. Tanabe, *Hoshigarimasen katsumadewa*, 85.
5. Ibid., 296.
6. The Tanabe Seiko Literature Museum was built on the Shōin College campus in 2007, to celebrate Tanabe's great contribution to Japanese literature. In the following year, the Tanabe Seiko Museum Junior Literary Prize was created, with the goal of helping nurture the creativity of young people of the next generation.
7. Kan Satoko, "Sensō dokushin josei e no manazashi: 'Hai misu' mono no haikei ni arumono," in ed. Kan Satoko, *Tanabe Seiko: Sengo bungaku e no shinshikaku* (Tokyo: Shibundō, 2006), 150–51.
8. Tanabe Seiko, *Shihon genji monogatari*, in ed. Kan Satoko, *Tanabe Seiko zenshū* Vol. 17, *Ubazakari shirīzu, Shihon genji monogatari shirīzu* (Tokyo: Shueisha, 2005), 533–59.
9. Ibid., 586–612.
10. Ariyoshi Sawako (1931–1984) was a fiction writer. She made her debut with her "Jiuta" (Ballad), which was nominated for the *Bungakukai* (Literary World) Newcomer's Prize and the Akutagawa Prize in 1956. She is known as the author of *Kinokawa* (The River Ki, 1964), which depicts three generations of women living in Japanese tradition; *Hanaoka Seishū no tsuma* (The Doctor's Wife, 1967); and *Hishoku* (Without Color, 1964), which deals with racism.
11. The word *kaigo* (elder care) made its first appearance in the *Kōjien* dictionary in 1983. In the eighties, society and the government realized the necessity of being prepared for the aging society that would soon arrive.

12. Kan Satoko, "Yūmoa to hihyō seishin: 'Ubazakari' shirīzu, 'Shihon genji monogatari' shirīzu o megutte," in *Tanabe Seiko zenshū*, vol. 17 (Tokyo: Shūeisha, 2005), 696.
13. See Kurata Yōko, "Jishisuru rōjo tachi: Kazoku, jendā, eijingu," in *Josei sakka: genzai*, ed. Kan Satoko (Tokyo: Shibundō, 2004).
14. *Ubazakari* was produced by Kansai television. The role of Utako was played by respected actress Kyō Machiko.
15. Tanabe Seiko, *Ubazakari* (Tokyo: Shinchōsha, 2009), 42.
16. Ibid., 43.
17. Ibid.
18. Ibid., 20.
19. Tanabe Seiko, *Ubatokimeki* (Tokyo: Shinchōsha, 2010), 184.
20. Ibid.
21. Tanabe, *Ubagatte* (Tokyo: Shinchō Sha, 2007), 190.
22. Kasuga Kisuyo, "Kazoku kaigo no mirai," *Shōsetsu Tripper* (Spring, 1998): 31.
23. Tanabe, *Ubagatte*, 187.
24. Ibid., 194.
25. "Futarizake" (lyrics by Taka Takashi, music by Gen Tetsuya) released in 1980, was sung by Kawanaka Miyuki.
26. Ibid., *Ubagatte*, 193.
27. Ibid., 214.
28. Ibid., 230.
29. Saitō Minako, "Tanabe Seiko ni manabu otona no onna no tame no essei kōza," in *Tanabe Seiko*, 192.
30. The *ubasute* practice is depicted in *Narayama bushikō* (Ballad of Narayama), written by Fukazawa Shichirō, which was adapted into a film directed by Imamura Shōhei in 1983.
31. Tanabe, "Sekiyō kagirinaku yoshi," *Tanabe Seiko zenshū*, vol. 17, 678.
32. The facts that their names, "kin" (gold) and "gin" (silver) symbolize happiness and that they were healthy and lively at one hundred contributed to their great popularity. Utako, however, expresses cynicism toward the Kin-san Gin-san boom, saying, "[W]hat is so great about them? They just had long lives" (Tanabe, *Ubagatte*, 114).
33. Īda Yūko, "Tanabe Seiko to feminizumu: Kasanari to chigai to," in *Tanabe Seiko*, 178.
34. Ibid., 176.
35. Tanabe, "Sekiyō kagirinaku yoshi," 670.

36. Emphases are Radway's original. Janice A. Radway, "Women Read the Romance: The Interaction of Text and Content," *Feminist Studies* 9, no. 1 (1983), 72.

Epilogue

1. Matsumoto Yuko (1963–) is a fiction writer and translator. She debuted with her *Kyoshokushō no akenai yoake* (Anorexia, the Dawn that Never Breaks, 1987), which received the Subaru Literary Prize. Besides her translation of the full *Anne of Green Gables* series, her recent works include *Koi no Hotaru: Yamazaki Tomie to Dazai Osamu* (Love Fireflies, 2010) and *Misuzu to Gasuke* (Misuzu and Gasuke [a biography of poet Kaneko Misuzu], 2017). In our conversation, she said that when she was a child she read *Daddy-Long-Legs* and realized that girls can choose "fiction writer" as a future occupation like Jerusha Abbott did.

2. These anime titles were shown as *Sekai meisaku gekijō* (World Masterpiece Theater), which aired on Fuji TV every Sunday night from 1969 to 2009.

3. *Candy Candy* was serialized in *Nakayoshi* (Good Friends) from 1975 to 1979.

4. Masami Toku, "Shōjo Manga! Girls' Comics! A Mirror of Girls' Dreams," *Mechademia* 2 (2007): 20.

5. Prough, *Straight from the Heart*, 139.

6. Sullivan Catherine and Masami Toku, *Girl Speak: Shōjo Manga and Women's Prints from the Turner*, Nov. 12–Dec. 14, 2015, The Janet Turner Print Museum, California State University, Chico, 2013.

7. *World of Shōjo Manga! Mirror of Girls' Desires* was Masami Toku's second world exhibition tour. The first tour, *Shōjo Manga Girl Power!*, visited nine venues in North America, and displayed works by twenty-three *shōjo* manga artists.

8. See *World of Shōjo Manga!: Mirrors of Girls' Desires*, California State University, Chico, 2013.

9. The illustration of *Little Women* was drawn by Maki Miyako (1935–) for a calendar of a monthly magazine.

10. Higuchi Ichiyō's "Takekurabe" (Child's Play) was published intermittently in *Bungakukai* (Literary World) from 1895 to 1896. It is the coming-of-age story of Midori, who grew up in the *yoshiwara* pleasure quarter following her gradual acceptance of her future as a courtesan. The story also depicts her interaction with and separation from a group of adolescents with whom she grew up.

11. For a discussion of Yanagi Miwa's art, see Emily Jane Wakeling, "Girls Are Dancin': Shōjo Culture and Feminism in Contemporary Japanese Art," *New Voices* 5 (2011).

12. Laura Steiner, "Gothic Lolita Fashion Makes Its Way from Japan to Mexico," *Huffington Post*, May 30, 2013, http://www.huffingtonpost.com/2012/05/06/gothic-lolita-fashion-style-mexico_n_1479029.html.

13. Jun Kaminishikawara, " 'Cute Ambassadors' Roam Globe to Promote Japan's Pop," *Japan Times*, June 17, 2009, http://www.japantimes.co.jp/news/2009/06/17/national/cute-ambassadors-roam-globe-to-promote-japans-pop-culture/.

14. Prough, *Straight from the Heart*, 145.

WORKS CITED

Aeba Kōson. "Jo," in *Shōfujin*. Translated by Kitada Shūho. Tokyo: Saiunkaku, 1906.

Alcott, Louisa May. *A Garland for Girls*. Boston: Little Brown, 1908.

———. *Little Women*. New York: Signet Classic, 1983.

———. *Shōfujin*. Translated by Kitada Shūho. Tokyo: Saiunkaku, 1906.

———. "Yonin no shimai." Translated by Andō Ichirō. *Himawari* 1, no. 1–8 (1947): 14–17, 22–23, 28–32, 36–45, 40–47.

Anderson, Benedict. *Imagined Communities: Reflections on the Origin and Spread of Nationalism*. New York: Verso, 1991.

Andō Kyōko. "Yoshiya Nobuko *Hana monogatari* ni okeru kyōkai kitei." *Nihon bungaku* 11, no. 46 (1997): 21–33.

Anonymous. "Eiga ni natta yonin no shimai: *Wakakusa monogatari*." *Himawari* 4, no. 2 (1950): n.p.

———. "Eiga ni tsuite kangaete mimashou." *Himawari* 5, no. 3 (1951): 96–99.

———. "Ikkagetsu no gakuhi." *Shōjo sekai* 9, no. 3 (1914): 102–3.

———. "Shōjo no tomo 45 nen no ayumi." *Shōjo no tomo* 45, no. 4 (1952): 222–23.

———. "*Himawari* aidokusha taikai no ki." *Himawari* 5, no. 4 (1951): 74–75.

———. "Jogakusei no yūjō." *Shōjo no tomo* 41, no. 12 (1948): 10–17.

———. "Keibo subeki fujin." Shōjo sekai 3, no. 2 (1908): 28–29.

———. "Morita Tama." In *Hokkaido daijiten*, 359–60. Sapporo: Hokkaido Bungakukan, 1985.

———. "Nihon no wakakusa kyōdai: Haha no hi no ichinichi." *Shōjo no tomo* 43, no. 5 (1950): n.p.

———. "Shōjo no chikara." *Shōjo sekai* 4, no. 2 (1909): 100–2.

———. "Shōjo no sekai." *Shōjo sekai* 3, no. 2 (1908): 40–45.

———. "Umi o wataru Himawari." *Himawari* 2, no. 5 (1948): 28.

———. "Yoshiya sensei o kakomu zadankai: Shōnen to shōjo wa dou otsukiai surunoga ichiban iika?" *Shōjo no tomo* 43, no. 8 (1950): 94–103.

Aoyama, Tomoko. "The Genealogy of the 'Girl' Critic Reading Girl." In *Girl Reading Girl in Japan*, edited by Tomoko Aoyama and Barbara Hartley, 38–49. New York: Routledge, 2009.

Aoyama, Tomoko, and Barbara Hartley. "Introduction." In *Girl Reading Girl in Japan*, edited and translated by Tomoko Aoyama and Barbara Hartley, 1–14. New York: Routledge, 2009.

Arakawa Yoshihiro. *Junia to kannō no kyoshō Tomishima Takeo den*. Tokyo: Kawade Shobō Shinsha, 2017.

Asami Fujiko. *Shōjo no tomo* 36, no. 1 (1943): 162.

Asō Shōzō. "Beikoku no jogakusei." *Shōjo sekai* 2, no. 14 (1907): 32–38.

Atomi Kakei. "Joshi no shūyō." *Shōjo sekai* 1, no. 1 (1906): 49–51.

Baba Junko. "*Imatorikaebaya* no onna chūnagon: Danjo heiritsu kara michibiki dasareru onna no tsumi to jubaku." *Atomi gakuen joshi daigaku kokubun gakkahō* 26 (2004): 175–87.

Bardsley, Jan. *Women and Democracy in Cold War Japan*. London: Bloomsbury Publishing, 2014.

Beauvoir, Simone de. *The Second Sex*. New York: Vintage Books, 1989.

Butler, Judith. *Gender Trouble: Feminism and the Subversion of Identity*. New York: Routledge, 1990.

Bae, Catherine Yoonah. "Girl Meets Boy Meets Girl: Heterosocial Relations, Wholesome Youth, and Democracy in Postwar Japan." *Asian Studies Review* 32, no. 3 (2008): 341–60.

Beauchamp, Edward R., and James M. Vardaman Jr. *Japanese Education Since 1945: A Documentary Study*. New York: M. E. Sharpe, 1994.

Brownstein, Michael C. "*Jogaku zasshi* and the Founding of *Bungakukai*." *Monumenta Nipponica* 35, no. 3 (1980): 319–36.

Cart, Michael. *From Romance to Realism: 50 Years of Growth and Change in Young Adult Literature*. New York: Harper Collins Publishers, 1996.

Chikushi Tetsuya, and Himuro Saeko. "Chikushi Tetsuya no kurara taidan: Genki jirushi no onnnatachi." *Asahi Journal* 28, no. 40 (1986): 49–53.

Copeland, Rebecca. *Lost Leaves: Women Writers of Meiji Japan*. Honolulu: University of Hawai'i Press, 2000.

Culver, Annika A. "Manchukuo and the Creation of a New National Literature: Kawabata Yasunari and 'Manchurian' Culture 1941–1942." *PAJLS* 9 (2008): 253–63.

Daio. "Shasetsu." *Jokgaku zasshi* 172 (1889): 387–93.

Day, Noriko Agatsuma. "The Outside Within: Literature of Colonial Hokkaido." PhD diss., University of California, Los Angeles, 2012.

Dollase, Hiromi Tsuchiya. "Choosing Your Family: Reconfiguring Gender and Familial Relationships in Japanese Popular Fiction." *Journal of Popular Culture* 44, no. 4 (2011): 755–72.

———. "Kawabata's Wartime Message in *Utsukushii tabi* (Beautiful Voyage)." In *Negotiating Censorship in Modern Japan*, edited by Rachael Hutchinson, 74–92. New York: Routledge, 2013.

———. "Ribbons Undone: Shōjo Story Debates in Prewar Japan." In *Girl Reading Girl in Japan*, edited by Tomoko Aoyama and Barbara Hartley, 80–91. New York: Routledge, 2009.

Dower, John W. *Embracing Defeat: Japan in the Wake of World War II*. New York: W. W. Norton & Company, 1999.

Driscoll, Catherine. *Girls: Feminine Adolescence in Popular Culture and Cultural Theory*. New York: Columbia University Press, 2002.

Egusa Mitsuko. "Gendō to shintai no gensetsu." In *Jendā no nihon kindai bungaku*, edited by Nakayama Kazuko, Egusa Mitsuko, and Fujimori Kiyoshi, 39–45. Tokyo: Kanrin Shobō, 1998.

Endō Hiroko. "Kaisetsu." In *Shōnen shōsetsu taikei*. Vol. 24, *Shōjo shōsetsu meisaku shū*, edited by Endō Hiroko, 607–23. Tokyo: San'ichi Shobō, 1993.

———. *Shōjo no tomo to sono jidai: Henshūsha no yūki Uchiyama Motoi*. Tokyo: Hon no Izumisha, 2004.

———. "Yuri Seiko." In *Shōnen shōsetsu taikei*. Vol. 24, *Shōjo shōsetsu meisaku shū*, edited by Endō Hiroko, 619. Tokyo: San'ichi shobō, 1993.

Enchi Fumiko. *Onnazaka*. Tokyo: Kadokawa Shoten, 1957.

The International Institute for Children's Literature. "Enishi: Jidō bungaku kobore banashi." http://www.iiclo.or.jp/06_respub/01_research/enishi/kagawa.htm.

Etō Jun. *Tozasareta gengo kūkan: Senryōgun no ken'etsu to sengo nihon*. Tokyo: Bungei Shunjū, 1994.

Faderman, Lillian. "Lesbian Magazine Fiction in the Early Twentieth Century." *Journal of Popular Culture* 11, no. 4 (1978): 800–17.

———. *Surpassing the Love of Men: Romantic Friendship and Love between Women from the Renaissance to the Present*. New York: Morrow, 1981.

Frederick, Sarah. *Turning Pages: Reading and Writing Women's Magazines in Interwar Japan* Honolulu: University of Hawai'i Press, 2006.

———. "Not That Innocent: Yoshiya Nobuko's Good Girls." In *Bad Girls of Japan*, edited by Laura Miller and Jan Bardsley, 65–80. New York: Palgrave Macmallan, 2005.

Fujimoto, Yukari. "Transgender: Female Hermaphrodites and Male Androgynes." *U.S.-Japan Women's Journal* 27 (2004): 76–117.

Fukasawa Harumi. "*Shōjo kurabu*, *Shōjo no tomo* ni okeru Kawabata Yasunari." *Geijutsu shijōshugi bungei* 22 (1996): 70–85.

Fukaya Masashi. *Ryōsai kenbo shugi no kyōiku*. Nagoya: Reimei Shobō, 1998.

Fukiya Kōji. "Kitagawa Chiyo san." In *Kitagawa Chiyo jidō bungaku zenshū*. Vol. 2 (supplement), n.p. Tokyo: Kōdansha, 1967.
Fukuda Ichiyo. "Shōjo shōsetsu no keifu: *Shōjo gahō* to Izawa Miyuki." *Gakuen* 851 (2011): 9–18.
Fumiko. *Shōjo no tomo* 3, no. 2 (1910): 92–93.
Furuichi Noritoshi. *Zetsubō no kuni no kōfuku na wakamonotachi*. Tokyo: Kōdansha, 2011.
Haga Noboru. *Ryōsai kenboron*. Tokyo: Yūzankaku, 1990.
Hamano Takuya. "Kawabata Yasunari ron: 'Niji' to shōjo shōsetsu 'Kageki gakkō.'" *Shōwa bungaku kenkyū* 9 (1984): 24–36.
———. "Kitagawa Chiyo nenpu." In *Nihon jidō bungaku taikei*. Vol. 22, *Kitagawa Chiyo Tsuboi Sakae shū*, 453–62. Tokyo: Horupu Shuppan, 1978.
Hambleton, Alexandra. "Idol as Accidental Activist: Agnes Chan, Feminism, and Motherhood in Japan." In *Idols and Celebrity in Japanese Media Culture*, edited by Patrick W. Galbraith, 153–65. New York: Palgrave Macmillan, 2012.
Hane, Mikiso. *Reflections on the Way to the Gallows: Rebel Women in Prewar Japan*. Berkeley: University of California Press, 1988.
Hasegawa Kei. "Haisengo kara 1960 nendai e." In *Shōjo shōsetsu jiten*, edited by Iwabuchi Hiroko, Kan Satoko, Kume Yoriko, and Hasegawa Kei, 12–13. Tokyo: Tokyodō Shuppan, 2015.
Hatori Tetsuya. "Kawabata Yasunari to sensō." *Kokubungaku kaishaku to kanshō* 46, no. 4 (1981): 152–57.
Yamaguchi Hatsuko. *Shōjo sekai* 1, no. 1 (1906): 111.
Hayashi Fumiko. *Hokugan butai*. Tokyo: Chūō Kōronsha, 1939.
Hayashi Mariko. *Run run o katte ouchi ni kaerō*. Tokyo: Kadokawa Shoten, 2005. Originally published in 1982.
Hazama Yuki. "Ajia taiheiyō sensōki no *shōjo no tomo*: Dokusha tōkōran no bunseki o chūshin ni." *Osaka jinken hakubutsukan kiyō* 9 (2006): 125–39.
Higuchi Ichiyō. "Nigorie." In *Higuchi Ichiyō shōsetsu shū*. Tokyo: Chikuma shobō, 2005.
Himuro Saeko. "Atogaki." In *Nante suteki ni japanesuku*. Vol. 1, 289–93. Tokyo: Shūeisha, 2012.
———. *Himuro Saeko dokuhon*. Tokyo: Tokuma Shoten, 1993.
———. *Ippashi no onna*. Tokyo: Chikuma Shobō, 1992.
———. "Kaisetsu." In Setouchi Jakuchō, *Nyonin genji monogatari*. Vol. 1, Kiritsubo–Shien, 258–65. Tokyo: Shūeisha, 1997.
———. *Nante suteki ni japanesuku*. Vols. 1–10. Originally published from 1987 to 1991. Tokyo: Shūeisha, 2012.
———. *Shōjo shōsetsuka wa shinanai*. Tokyo: Shūeisha, 1983.
———. *Za chenji*. Vols. 1–2. Tokyo: Shūeisha, 1985. Originally published in 1983.

Hirayama Jōji. *Kawabata Yasunari: Yohaku o umeru*. Tokyo: Kenbun Shuppan, 2003.
Honda Masuko. *Ibunka to shite no kodomo.* . Tokyo: Chikuma Shobō, 1998. Originally published in 1982.
———. *Jogakusei no keifu: Saishoku sareru meiji*. Tokyo: Seidosha, 1990.
———. "The Genealogy of *Hirahira*: Liminality and the Girl." In *Girl Reading Girl in Japan*, edited and translated by Tomoko Aoyama and Barbara Hartlety, 19–37. New York: Routledge, 2009.
———. "Senjika no shōjo zasshi: Ikinobiru gensō." In *Shōjo zasshiron*, edited by Ōtsuka Eiji, 8–43. Tokyo: Tōkyō Shoseki, 1991.
Hosokawa Takeko, ed. *Takane*. Chiba: Shōjo Sekai Kyū Shiyūkai, 1942.
Īda Yūko. "Tanabe Seiko to feminizumu: Kasanari to chigai to." In *Tanabe Seiko: Sengo bungaku e no shinshikaku*, edited by Kan Satoko, 172–79. Tokyo: Shibundō, 2006.
Imada Erika. "Jendāka sareru kodomo: 1985–1945 nen no shōnen shōjo zasshi hyōshie bunseki kara." *Soshiorojī* 48 (2003): 57–74.
———. *Shōjo no shakaishi*. Tokyo: Keisō Shobō, 2007.
———. " 'Shōnen' kara shōnen, shōjo e: Meiji no kodomo tōkō zasshi *Eisai shinshi* ni okeru jendā no henyō." *Kyōikugaku kenkyū* 71, no. 2 (2004): 62–75.
———. "Shōnen zasshi ni okeru senchimentarizumu no haijo: 1930 nendai no *Nihon shōnen*, *Shōjo no tomo* tōkōran no hikaku kara." *Nihon joseigaku* 11 (2003): 86–106.
Inagaki Kyōko. *Jogakkō to jogakusei: Kyōyō, tashinami, modan bunka*. Tokyo: Chūō Kōronsha, 2007.
Inness, Sherrie A. *Intimate Communities: Representation and Social Transformation in Women's College Fiction, 1895–1910*. Bowling Green, OH: Bowling Green State University Popular Press, 1995.
Igarashi Yumiko, and Mizuki Kyōko. *Kyandī kyandī*. Vols. 1–2. Tokyo: Chūō kōronsha, 1991.
Ishihara Chiaki. "Kikenshisō datta jiga." *Hon: Dokushojin no zasshi* 31, no. 11 (2006): 46–53.
Itō Saeko, *Shōsetsu junia* 6, no. 1 (1971): 494.
Iwasaki Mariko. "Junia shōsetsu." In *Nihon jidō bungaku daijiten*. Vol. 2, *Jinmei na–wa*, edited by Osaka kokusai jidō bungakukan, 413–14. Tokyo: Dainihon Tosho, 1993.
Iwata Yōko. "Junia shōstsu to kyoeishin: Tsumura Setsuko *Ajisaiiro no yume*, *Fukeyo kitakaze* o chūshin ni." *Kokubungaku* 97 (2013): 85–93.

Ministry of Education, Culture, Sports, Science, and Technology. "Japan's Modern Educational System." http://www.mext.go.jp/b_menu/hakusho/html/others/detail/1317220.htm.

Jitsugyō no Nihonsha hyakunenshi. Tokyo: Jitsugyō no Nihonsha, 1997.

Jō, *Himawari* 4, no. 11 (1950): 147.

Kadowaki Atsushi. "Nihonteki 'risshin, shusse' no imi hensen: Kindai nihon no seishin keisei kenkyū oboegaki." *Kyōiku shakaigaku kenkyū* 24 (1969): 94–110.

Kaiga Hentetsu. "Ame." *Shōjo sekai* 1, no. 3 (1906): 17–27.

Kameyama Toshiko. "Yoshiya Nobuko to Hayashi Fumiko no jūgunki o yomu: Pen butai no kō niten." In *Jūgoshi nōto fukkan*. Vol. 2, *Nicchū kaisen sōdōinka no onnatachi*, edited by Kanō Mikiyo, 78–89. Tokyo: JCA Shuppan, 1981.

Kami Shōichirō. "Kindai nihon ni okeru *Hana monogatari* no keifu." In *Nihon jidō bungaku no shisō*. Vol. 1, edited by Kami Shōichirō, 226–50. Tokyo: Kokudosha, 1976.

Kaminishikawara, Jun. " 'Cute Embassadors' Roam Globe to promote Japan's Pop." *Japan Times*, June 17, 2009. http://www.japantimes.co.jp/news/2009/06/17/national/cute-ambassadors-roam-globe-to-promote-japans-pop-culture/.

Kamiya Tadataka. "Jyūgun josei sakka: Yoshiya Nobuko o chūshin ni." *Shakai bungaku* 15 (2001): 49–58.

Kan Satoko. *Media no jidai: Meiji bungaku o meguru jōkyō*. Tokyo: Sōbunsha Shuppan, 2001.

———. *Onna ga kokka o uragiru toki: Jogakusei, Ichiyō, Yoshiya Nobuko*. Tokyo: Iwanami Shoten, 2011.

———. "Sensō dokushin josei e no manazashi: 'Hai misu' mono no haikei ni arumono." In *Tanabe Seiko: Sengo bungaku e no shinshikaku*, edited by Kan Satoko, 150–59. Tokyo: Shibundō, 2006.

———. "Yūmoa to hihyō seishin: 'Ubazakari' shirīzu, 'Shihon genji monogatari' shirīzu o megutte." In *Tanabe Seiko zenshū*. Vol. 17, *Ubazakari shirīzu Shihon genji monogatari shirīzu*, 692–700. Tokyo: Shūeisha, 2005.

———. "Watashitachi no ibasho: Himuro Saeko ron." In *Shōjo shōsetsu wandārando: Meiji kara Heisei made*, edited by Kan Satoko, 75–84. Tokyo: Meiji Shoin, 2008.

Kaneda Junko. "Kyōiku no kyakutai kara sanka no shutai e: 1980 nendai no shōjomuke shōsetsu janru ni okeru shōjo dokusha." *Joseigaku* 9 (2001): 25–46.

Karatani Kōjin. *Nihon kindai bungaku no kigen*. Tokyo: Kōdansha, 1988.

Kasson, Joy S. Introduction to *Work: A Story of Experience*, ix–xxxi. New York: Penguin, 1994.

Kasuga Kisuyo. " 'Kazoku kaigo' no mirai." *Shōsetsu Tripper* (Spring 1998): 30–72.

Kataoka Asami. "Murasaki no yukari to Himuro Saeko: *Za chenji* ni miru koten juyō no ichiyōsō." *Kenkyū to shiryō* 47 (2002): 51–61.

Kawabata Yasunari. "Aishū." In *Kawabata Yasunari sakuhinsen*, 506–11. Tokyo: Chūō Kōronsha, 1968.

———. "Hana to kosuzu." *Himawari* 6, no. 2–12 (1952): 4–9, 14–19, 12–22, 20–31, 66–73.

———. "Manyō shimai." *Himawari* 5, no. 1–12 (1951): 4–9, 6–11, 22–27, 29–41, 44–60.

———. "Otome no minato." In *Kawabata Yasunari zenshū*. Vol. 20, *Shonen shōjo shōsetsu*, 9–183. Tokyo: Shinchōsha, 1981.

———. "Senja no kotoba." *Shōjo no tomo* 35, no. 1 (1942): 185.

———. "Utsukushii kotoba." *Himawari* 1, no. 3 (1947): n.p.

———. "Utsukushii tabi." In *Kawabata Yasunari zenshū*. Vol. 20, *Shonen shōjo shōsetsu*, 401–658. Tokyo: Shinchōsha, 1981.

———. "Zoku utsukushii tabi." In *Kawabata Yasunari zenshū*. Vol. 20, 659–733. Tokyo: Shinchōsha, 1981.

Kawamura Kunimitsu. *Otome no inori: Kindai josei imēji no tanjō*. Tokyo: Kinokuniya Shoten, 1995.

———. *Otome no karada: Onna no kindai to sekushuaritī*. Tokyo: Kinokuniya Shoten, 1994.

Kawato Michiaki. "Wakamatsu Shizuko to shoki no hon'yaku jidō bungaku: Nihon ni okeru kindai jidō bungaku no shuppatsuten." In *Meiji no joryū bungaku, hon'yaku hen*. Vol. 1, *Wakamatsu Shizuko shū*, edited by Kawato Michiaki and Sakakibara Takanori, 271–90. Tokyo: Gogatsu Shobō, 2000.

Keene, Donald. *Dawn to the West: Japanese Literature of the Modern Era*. New York: Holt, Rinehart, and Winston, 1984.

Kelsky, Karen. "Postcards from the Edge: The 'Office Ladies' of Tokyo." *U.S.-Japan Women's Journal*, English Supplement 6 (1944): 3–26.

Kawasaki Kenko. *Shōjo biyori*. Tokyo: Seikyūsha, 1990.

Kishida, Toshiko. "Daughters in Boxes." In *The Modern Murasaki: Writing by Women of Meiji Japan*, edited By Rebecca L. Copeland, translated by Rebecca L. Copeland and Aiko Okamoto MacPhail, 62–71. New York: Columbia University Press, 2006.

Kitabatake Yao, Kawakami Kikuko, and Takeuchi Teruyo. "Shōjo no sakuhin o megutte." *Himawari* 3, no. 2 (1949): 24–27.

Kitabatake Yao and Nakahara Junichi. "Yoriyoki shōjo no hi no tameni." *Himawari* 2, no. 11 (1948): 18–21.

Kitagawa Chiyo. Introduction to *Kinuito no zōri*. Tokyo: Kōdansha, 1931.

———. "Kekkon no genmetsu." *Josei kaizō* 1, no. 3 (1922): 108–24.
———. "Kinuito no zōri." In *Nihon jidō bungaku taikei*. Vol. 22, 91–101. Tokyo: Horupu Shuppan, 1978.
———. "Kōfuku." In *Nihon jidō bungaku taikei*. Vol. 22, *Kitagawa Chiyo Tsuboi Sakae shū*, 26–32. Tokyo: Horupu Shuppan, 1978.
———. "Kono monogatari ni tsuite." In *Ankuru Tomu monogatari* 1–2. Tokyo: Kōdansha, 1960.
———. "Mikan." In *Nihon jidō bungaku taikei*. Vol. 22, 39–42. Tokyo: Horupu Shuppan, 1978.
———. *Shōjo no tomo* 3, no. 2 (1910): 102.
———. "Shōjo shōsetsu no kōsei to gijutsu." In *Nihon gendai bunshō kōza*. Vol. 4, *Kōsei hen*, edited by Maemoto Kazuo, 103–5. Tokyo: Kōseikaku, 1934.
———. "Shunran." In *Nihon jidō bungaku taikei*. Vol. 22, *Kitagawa Chiyo Tsuboi Sakae shū*, 58–64. Tokyo: Horupu Shuppan, 1978.
———. "Tamago hitotsu." In *Nihon jidō bungaku taikei*. Vol. 22, *Kitagawa Chiyo Tsuboi Sakae shū*, 102–6. Tokyo: Horupu Shuppan, 1978.
———. "Usagi o kau shōjo." *Shōjo kurabu* 20, no. 1 (1942): 51–58.
Kitagawa Sachihiko. "Kitagawa Chiyo nenpu." In *Kitagawa Chiyo bungaku zenshū*. Vol. 2, 346–62. Tokyo: Kōdansha, 1967.
Kitamura, Hiroshi. *Screening Enlightenment: Hollywood and the Cultural Reconstruction of Defeated Japan*. Ithaca, NY: Cornell University Press, 2010.
Kobayashi Yoshihito. "Kawabata Yasunari." *Kokubungaku kaishaku to kanshō* 48, no. 14 (1983): 161–64.
———. "Kawabata bungaku ni okeru seishōjo no keifu to sono tokuchō." *Kokubungaku kaishaku to kanshō* 62, no. 4 (1997): 62–67.
Kodama Ryōko. "'Haha no hi' ga seiji ni arawareru toki, kieru toki: Shōwa 23 nen no 'shukusaijitsu no kaisei' no giron kara." In *Jendāshi sensho*. Vol. 2, *Kazoku to kyōiku*, edited by Ishikawa Teruko and Takahashi Yūko, 52–76. Tokyo: Akashi Shoten, 2011.
———. "Haha no hi no poritikkusu: Sono seiritsu to fukyū ni tsuite no hikakushi teki kentō." In *Kyōikugaku nenpō 7 jendā to kyōiku*, edited by Fujita Hidenori, Kurosaki Isao, Katagiri Yoshio, and Sato Manabu, 243–66. Yokohama: Seori Shobō.
K-ko. "Shōjo dokushokai." *Shōjo sekai* 5, no. 14 (1910): 75–77.
Kondo, Dorinne K. *Crafting Selves: Power, Gender, and Discourses of Identity in a Japanese Workplace*. Chicago: University of Chicago Press, 1990.
Kōno Toshirō. " 'Gakutō' o yomu: Morita Tama." *Gakutō* 94, no. 4 (1997): 58–63.

Kotani Kanako. "Wakakusa monogatari no Meijiki hon'yaku no shomondai: Shōfujin ni mirareru sakujo." *Baika jidō bungaku* 7 (1999): 22–39.
Koyama Shizuko. *Katei no seisei to josei no kokuminka*. Tokyo: Keisō Shobō, 1999.
———. *Ryōsai kenbo to iu kihan*. Tokyo: Keisō Shobō, 2004.
Kristeva, Julia. *Powers of Horror: An Essay on Abjection*. Translated by Leon S. Roudiez. New York: Columbia University Press, 1982.
Kumagai, Keichi. "An Observation Floating Young Men: Globalization and the Crisis of Masculinity in Japan." *HAGAR Studies in Culture, Policy and Identities* 10, no. 2 (2012): 3–15.
Kume Yoriko. "Kōsei sareru shōjo." *Kindai nihon bungaku* 68 (2003): 1–15..
———. "Shōjo shōsetsu no shuppatsu to hensen: Meiji, Taishōki." In *Shōjo shōsetsu jiten*, edited by Iwabuchi Hiroko, Kan Satoko, Kume Yoriko, and Hasegawa Kei, 7–9. Tokyo: Tōkyōdō Shuppan, 2015.
———. "Shōjo shōsetsu: Sai to kihan no gensetsu sōchi." In *Media, hyōshō, ideorogī: Meiji sanjū nendai no bunka kenkyū*, edited by Komori Yōichi, Kōno Kensuke, Takahashi Osamu, 195–222. Tokyo: Ozawa Shoten, 1997.
———. "Yoshiya Nobuko: 'Seido' no naka no rezubian sekushuaritī." *Josei sakka: genzai*, edited by Kan Satoko, 121–30. Tokyo: Shibundo, 2004
———. *Shōjo shōsetsu no seisei: jendā poritikkusu no seiki*. Tokyo: Seikyūsha, 2013.
Kurata Yōko. "Jishisuru rōjo tachi: Kazoku, jendā, eijingu." In *Josei sakka: genzai*, edited by Kan Satoko, 141–51. Tokyo: Shibundō, 2004.
Kurosawa Ariko. "1912 nen no Raichō to Kōkichi: 'Josei kaihō' to rezubianizumu o megutte." In *Bungaku, shakai e chikyū e*, edited by Nishida Masaru tainin taishoku kinen bunshū henshū iinkai, 309–27. Tokyo: San'ichi Shobō, 1999.
———. "Shōjotachi no chikadōmei: Yoshiya Nobuko no Onna no Yūjō o megutte." In *Onna to hyōgen: Feminizumu hihyō no genzai*, edited by Mizuta Noriko, 81–95. Tokyo: Gakuyō Shobō, 1991.
Kuwabara Hiroshi. *Torikaebaya Monogatari*. Tokyo: Kōdansha, 1978.
Kyōko. "Jikatsu shinagara gakkō e iku shōjo." *Shōjo sekai* 9, no. 8 (1914): 44–49; *Shōjo sekai* 9, no. 9 (1914): 47–52.
Mabuchi Itsuo, and Yoshiya Nobuko. "Seisen dai 5 nen: Mabuchi hōdō buchō, Yoshiya Nobuko, taidan kai." *Shōjo no tomo* 34, no. 7 (1941): 62–78.
Mackie, Vera. *Creating Socialist Women in Japan: Gender, Labour and Activism 1900–1937*. Cambridge, UK: Cambridge University Press, 2002.
———. *Feminism in Modern Japan: Citizenship, Embodiment and Sexuality*. Cambridge, UK: Cambridge University Press, 2003.

Marchalonis, Shirley. *College Girls: A Century in Fiction*. New Brunswick, NJ: Rutgers University Press, 1995.
Masui Takashi. "Naimushō toshoka 'Shōwa 13 nen jidō zasshi ken'etsubo' ni tsuite." *Kokusai jidō bungakukan kiyō* 12 (1997): 141–71.
Matsui Yuriko. "Yūbe no hoshi." *Shōjo sekai* 5, no. 7 (1910): 34–37.
Matsumoto Tsuruo. "Yoshiya Nobuko nenpu." In *Yoshiya Nobuko*, edited by Matsumoto Tsuruo, 265–72. Tokyo: Nihon Tosho Sentā, 1998.
McLelland, Mark. *Love, Sex, and Democracy in Japan during American Occupation*. New York: Palgrave Macmillan, 2012.
Misaki Tomeko. "GHQ/CIE kyōiku eiga to sono eikyō." *Image & Gender* 7 (2007): 64–83.
Miyamatsu Sayo. *Shōjo no tomo* 33, no. 9 (1940): 237.
Miyasako Chizuru. *Chō shōjo e*. Tokyo: Shūeisha, 1989.
Miyata Noboru. *Hon'yakuken no sengoshi*. Tokyo: Misuzu Shobō, 1999.
Moi, Toril. *Sexual/Textual Politics: Feminist Literary Theory*. New York: Routledge, 1985.
Molony, Barbara. "Japan's 1986 Equal Employment Opportunity Law and the Changing Discourse on Gender." *Signs* 20, no. 2 (1995): 268–302.
Morinaga Matsue. *Shōjo sekai* 2, no. 12 (1909): 114.
Morita Tama. "Gonin onna." In *Zuihitsu kinuta*, 60–65. Tokyo: Chūō Kōronsha, 1942.
———. "Hitotsu no sōwa." In *Zuihitsu yuku michi*, 18–30. Tokyo: Kyōritsu Shobō, 1947.
———. "Ishikari otome." Tokyo: Jitsugyō no Nihonsha, 1940. Reprinted in *Shōnen shōsetsu taikei*. Vol. 24, *Shōjo shōsetsu meisaku shū*, 439–524. Tokyo: San'ichi Shobō, 1993.
———. "Odorizome." In *Zuihitsu saijiki*, 1–17. Tokyo: Chūō Kōronsha, 1940.
———. "Wakai habataki." In *Zuihitsu kinuta*, 66–76. Tokyo: Chūō Kōronsha, 1942.
———. *Zuihitsu kinuta*. Tokyo: Chūō Kōronsha, 1938.
Moriyama Yūko. "Yoshiya Nobuko Hana monogatari ron: Nakahara Jun'ichi no sashie tono kanren ni tsuite." *Gakushūin daigaku kokugo kokubungaku kaishi* 56 (2013): 29–43.
Mukōgawa Mikio. "Yōranki no shōjo shōsetsu: Shōjokai o chūshin ni." *Gengo hyōgen kenkyū* 12 (1996): 1–12.
Muraoka Eri. *An no yurikago: Muraoka Hanako no shōgai*. Tokyo: Magajin Hausu, 2008.
Muraoka Hanako. "Jogakusei ron." *Shōjo no tomo* 34, no. 12 (1941): 104–7.

———. "Kongetsu no dokusho kara." *Himawari* 2, no. 9 (1948): 30.

———. "Kotoba ni tsuite." *Himawari* 1, no. 2 (1947): 35.

Murasaki Shikibu. *Genji monogatari*, Vols. 1–10, edited by Tamagami Takuya. Tokyo: Kadokawa Shoten, 1964–1975.

Muta, Kazue. "Images of the Family in Meiji Periodicals: The Paradox Underlying the Emergence of the 'Home.'" *U.S.-Japan Women's Journal*, English Supplement 7 (1994): 53–71.

Nagai Kiyoko. "Tanjō, shōjotachi no kaihōku: Shōjo sekai to Shōjo dokushokai." In *Onna to otoko no jikū: Nihon joseishi saikō*. Vol. 9, *Semegiau onna to okoto kindai*, edited by Okuda Akiko, 278–311. Tokyo: Fujiwara Shoten, 1995.

Nakahara Jun'ichi. "Anata wa donna shōjo?" *Himawari* 4, no. 2 (1950): 28–29.

Nakamura Tetsuya. "Shōjo shōsetsu o yomu." In *Nihon jidō bungakushi o toinaosu: Hyōgenshi no shiten kara*, edited by Nihon jidō bungakukai, 249–64. Tokyo: Tōkyō Shoseki, 1995.

Nakane, Chie. *Kinship and Economic Organization in Rural Japan*. London: Athlone Press, 1967.

Nakaya Izumi. "'Tsuzurikata' no keisei: Toyoda Masako Tsuzurikata kyōshitsu o megutte." *Nihon daigaku kokubun gakkai* 111, no. 12 (2001): 43–54.

Namekawa Michio. "Atarashii gakkōseido no hanashi." *Shōjo kurabu* 25, no. 4 (1947): 30–31.

Nanba Kōji. "Sengo yūsu sabukaruchāzu ni tsuite 1: Taiyōzoku kara miyukizoku e." *Kansai gakuin daigaku shakaigakubu kiyō* 96 (2004): 163–78.

Nishi, Toshio. *Unconditional Democracy: Education and Politics in Occupied Japan 1945–1952*. Stanford, CA: Hoover Institution Press, 1982.

Nishikawa, Yōko. "The Changing Form of Dwellings and the Establishment of the Katei (home) in Modern Japan." *U.S.-Japan Women's Journal*, English Supplement 8 (1995): 3–36.

Nolte, Sharon H., and Sally Ann Hastings. "The Meiji State's Policy toward Women, 1890–1910." In *Recreating Japanese Women, 1600–1945*, edited by Gail Lee Bernstein, 151–74. Berkeley: University of California Press, 1991.

Numata Rippō. "Aidokusha taikai no ki." *Shōjo sekai* 3, no. 4 (1908): 83–87.

———. "Bōchū zakki." *Takane* 34 (1922): 36.

———. "Kokoro no ane." *Shōjo sekai* 4, no. 1 (1909): 34–53.

———. "Kongetsu no tōsho." *Shōjo sekai* 6, no. 12 (1911): 192.

———. "Mannikanen." *Shōjo sekai* 3, no. 12 (1908): 20–23.

———. "Shōjo kyōshitsu." *Shōjo sekai* 2, no. 3 (1907): 110–11.

O'Brien, Sharon. "Tomboyism and Adolescent Conflict: Three Nineteenth-Century Case Studies." In *Woman's Being, Woman's Place: Female Identity and Vocation*

in American History, edited by Mary Kelly, 351–72. Boston: G. K. Hall and Co., 1977.
Ochi, Hiromi. "What Did She Read? The Cultural Occupation of Post-War Japan and Translated Girls' Literature." *GENS Journal* 5 (2006): 359–63.
Odaira Maiko. "Bungei zasshi Wakakusa ni tsuite." In *Bungei zasshi Wakakusa: watashitachi wa bungei o aikō shiteiru*, edited by Odaira Maiko, 7–24. Tokyo: Kanrin Shobō, 2018.
Ōfuji Mikio. "Senchūki no jidō bungaku hyōron: Seikatsu dōwa kara shōkokumin eno nagare o otte." *Gakudai kokubun* 29 (1986): 153–69.
Ogasawara, Yuko. *Office Ladies and Salaried Men: Power, Gender, and Work in Japanese Companies*. Berkeley: University of California Press, 1998.
Ōgoshi, Aiko. "Women and Sexism in Japanese Buddhism: A Reexamination of Shinran's View of Women." *Japan Christian Review* 59 (1993): 19–25.
Ogura Chikako. *Kekkon no jōken*. Tokyo: Asahi Shinbunsha, 2007.
———. *Taidan: Giakusha no feminizumu*. Tokyo: Gakuyō Shobō, 1991.
Okahara Miyako. *Amerika senryōki no minshuka seisaku: Rajio hōsō ni yoru nihon josei saikyōiku puroguramu*. Tokyo: Akashi Shoten, 2007.
Okano Sachie. " 'Jiden' to iu senryaku: Fukuda Eiko Mekake no han shōgai." In *Meiji josei bungakuron*, edited by Shin feminizumu hihyō no kai, 197–213. Tokyo: Kanrin Shobō.
Ōmori Ikunosuke. "Kawabata Yasunari sengo shōjo shōsetsu shikan: Shōjozō no henbō." *Sapporo daigaku sōgō ronsō* 3 (1997): 340–66.
Orbaugh, Sharalyn. *Japanese Fiction of the Allied Occupation: Vision, Embodiment, Identity*. Leiden, The Netherlands: Brill, 2007.
Oshikawa Shunrō. "Shōjo bōkentan." *Shōjo sekai* 1, no. 2 (1906): 66–70.
Ōta, Tōru. "Producing (Post-)Trendy Japanese TV Dramas." In *Feeling Asian Modernities: Transnational Consumption of Japanese TV Dramas*, edited by Koichi Iwabuchi, translated by Midori Nasu, 69–86. Hong Kong: Hong Kong University Press, 2004.
Ōtsuka Eiji. *Shōjo minzokugaku*. Tokyo: Kōbunsha, 1997. Originally published in 1989.
Pflugfelder, Gregory M. "Strange Fates: Sex, Gender, and Sexuality in Torikaebaya Monogatari." *Monumenta Nipponica* 47, no. 3 (1992): 347–68.
Plath, David W. "The Japanese Popular Christmas: Coping with Modernity." *American Folklore* 76, no. 302 (1963): 309–17.
Prough, Jennifer S. *Straight from the Heart: Gender, Intimacy, and the Cultural Production of Shōjo Manga*. Honolulu: University of Hawai'i Press, 2011.
Radway, Janice A. "Women Read the Romance: The Interaction of Text and Content." *Feminist Studies* 9, no. 1 (1983): 53–78.

Robertson, Jennifer. *Takarazuka: Sexual Politics and Popular Culture in Modern Japan*. Berkeley: University of California Press, 1998.
Rupp, Leila J. Worlds of Women: The Making of an International Women's Movement. Princeton: Princeton University Press, 1998.Saga Keiko. Kobaruto bunko de tadoru shōjo shōsetsu hensenshi. Tokyo: Sairyūsha, 2016.
Saitō Minako, ed. *L bungaku kanzen dokuhon*. Tokyo: Magajin Hausu, 2002.
———. "Tanabe Seiko ni manabu otona no onna no tame no essei kōza." In *Tanabe Seiko: Sengo bungaku e no shinshikaku*, edited by Kan Satoko, 180–92. Tokyo: Shibundō, 2006.
———. "Yoshimoto Banana and Girl Culture." In *Woman Critiqued: Translated Essays on Japanese Women's Writings*, edited by Rebecca L. Copeland, translated by Eiji Sekine, 167–84. Honolulu: University of Hawai'i Press, 2006.
Saitō Shōichi. "Himuro Saeko Nante suteki ni japanesuku ron." *Shindai kokugo kyōiku* 5 (1996): 22–23.
Sand, Jordan. "At Home in the Meiji Period: Inventing Japanese Domesticity." In *Mirror of Modernity: Invented Traditions of Modern Japan*, edited by Stephen Vlastos, 191–207. Berkeley: University of California Press, 1998.
Sato, Barbara. *The New Japanese Woman: Modernity, Media, and Women in Interwar Japan*. Durham, NC: Duke University Press, 2003.
Satō Hiromi. "Jidōbunka seisaku to kyōiku kagaku: Naimushō 'Jido yomimono kaizen ni kansuru shishiyōkō' (1938, October) o megutte." *Jinmon gakuhō, kyōikugaku* 28 (1993): 83–118.
Satō Midoriko. *Taki no oto: Kaikyū no Kawabata Yasunari*. Tokyo: Shirakawa Shoin, 1980.
Sekine, Eiji. "Gender Differences in a Genealogy of Modern Love Stories." *PMAJLS* 2 (1996): 313–44.
Shamoon, Deborah. *Passionate Friendship: The Aesthetics of Girls' Culture in Japan*. Honolulu: University of Hawai'i Press, 2012.
Showalter, Elaine, ed. *Scribbling Women: Short Stories by 19th Century American Women*. New Brunswick, NJ: Rutgers University Press, 1996.
———. *Sister's Choice: Tradition and Change in American Women's Writing*. New York: Oxford University Press, 1994.
Smith, Anne-Marie. *Julia Kristeva: Speaking the Unspeakable*. Sterling, VA: Pluto Press, 1998.
Smith, Daniel Scott. "Family Limitation, Sexual Control, and Domestic Feminism in Victorian America." *Feminist Studies* 1, no. 3–4 (1973): 40–57.

Smith-Rosenberg, Carroll. *Disorderly Conduct: Visions of Gender in Victorian America*. New York: A. A. Knopf, 1985.

———. "The Female World of Love and Ritual." *Signs* 1, no. 1 (1975): 1–29.

Steiner, Laura. "Gothic Lolita Fashion Makes Its Way from Japan to Mexico." *Huffington Post*, May 30, 2013. http://www.huffingtonpost.com/2012/05/06/gothic-lolita-fashion-style-mexico_n_1479029.html.

Sullivan, Catherine, and. *Girl Speak: Shōjo Manga and Women's Prints from the Turner*, Nov. 12–Dec. 14, 2015. The Janet Turner Print Museum, California State University, Chico, 2013.

Suzuki, Michiko. *Becoming Modern Women: Love and Female Identity in Prewar Japanese Literature and Culture*. Stanford, CA: Stanford University Press, 2010.

Suzuki, Noriko. *The Re-invention of the American West: Women's Periodicals and Gendered Geography in the Late Nineteenth-Century United States*. New York: The Edwin Mellen Press, 2009.

Taga Noko, *Shōjo no tomo* 33, no. 9 (1940): 237.

Takahara Eiri. *Shōjo ryōiki*. Tokyo: Kokusho Kankōkai, 1999.

———. "The Consciousness of the Girl: Freedom and Arrogance." In *Woman Critiqued: Translated Essays on Japanese Women's Writing*, edited by Rebecca L. Copeland, translated by Tomoko Aoyama and Barbara Hartley, 185–93. Honolulu: University of Hawai'i Press, 2006.

Takahashi, Mizuki. "Opening the Closed World of Shōjo Manga." In *Japanese Visual Culture: Explorations in the World of Manga and Anime*, edited by Mark W. MacWilliams, 114–36. New York: M. E. Sharpe, 2008.

Takamura Kōtarō. "Shōjo tatakau." *Shōjo no tomo* 37, no. 1 (1944): 20–21.

Takasaki Ryūji. *Senjō no joryū sakkatachi: Yoshiya Nobuko, hayashi Fumiko, Sata Ineko, Masugi Shizue, Toyota Masako*. Tokyo: Ronsōsha, 1995.

Takeda Gendō. "Morita Tamasan no Sapporo." *Watashi no Morita Tama. Gakutō* 94, no. 4 (1997): 59.

Takeuchi Yō. *Risshi, kugaku, shusse: jukensei no shakaishi*. Tokyo: Kōdansha, 1991.

Tamura Yayoi. "Interview: Cobalt bunka to shōjotachi." In *Shōjo shōsetsu wandārando*, edited by Kan Satoko, 114–21. Tokyo: Meiji Shoin, 2008.

Tanabe Seiko. *Hoshigarimasen katsumadewa*. Tokyo: Popurasha, 2009.

———. "Sara." *Shōjo no tomo* 36, no. 7 (1943): 116–17.

———. "Sekiyō kagirinaku yoshi." In *Tanabe Seiko zenshū*. Vol. 17, *Ubazakari shirīzu, Shihon genji monogatari shirīzu*, 669–81. Tokyo: Shūeisha, 2005.

———. Shihon genji monogatari. In *Tanabe Seiko zenshū*. Vol. 17, *Ubazakari shirīzu, Shihon genji monogatari shirīzu*, 377–666. Tokyo: Shūeisha, 2005.

———. *Ubazakari*. Tokyo: Shinchōsha, 2009. Originally published in 1981.

———. *Ubatokimeki*. Tokyo: Shinchōsha, 2010. Originally published in 1984.
———. *Ubagatte*. Tokyo: Shinchōsha, 2007. Originally published in 1993.
———. *Yume haruka Yoshiya Nobuko*. Vols. 1–2. Tokyo: Asahi Shinbunsha, 1999.
———. *Watashi no Osaka hakkei*. Tokyo: Iwanami Shoten, 2000.
Tani Eiko. "Kaisetsu." In *Senryōki Zasshi shiryō taikei: Bungaku hen*. Vol. 5, *Senryōki bungaku no tamensei*, edited by Yamamoto Taketoshi, 159–95. Tokyo: Iwanami Shoten, 2010.
Toku, Masami. "Shojo Manga! Girls' Comics! A Mirror of Girls' Dreams." *Mechademia* 2 (2007): 19–32.
———. *World of Shojo Manga! Mirrors of Girls' Desires*. Chico, CA: Dept. of Art and Art History, California State University, 2013. Traveling exhibition.
Tomishima Takeo. "'Junia shōsetsu' seishosetsu o warau." *Ushio* 124 (1970): 240–45.
———. "Junia shōsetsu wa bungaku ka." *Mainichi Shinbun*, February 7, 1970.
———. *Osanazuma*. Tokyo: Shueisha, 1988.
———. "Seishun no saigetsu." *Shōsetsu junia* 17, no. 6 (1982): 17–23.
Tompkins, Jane. *Sensational Designs: The Cultural Work of American Fiction*. New York: Oxford University Press, 1985.
Treat, John Whittier. "Yoshimoto Banana Writes Home: Shōjo Culture and the Nostalgic Subject." *Journal of Japanese Studies* 19, no. 2 (1993): 353–87.
Tsuboi Sakae. "Ishiusu no uta." *Shōjo kurabu* 23, no. 6 (1945): 24–29.
———. "Shōjo shōsetsu no kotonado." *Shin nihon bungaku* 6 (1951): 84–87.
———. "Tsuyukusa." *Shōjo kurabu* 22, no. 11 (1944): 18–25.
Tsuchiya Yuka. *Shinbei nihon no kōchiku: Amerika no tainichi jōhō, kyōiku seisaku to nihon senryō*. Tokyo: Akashi Shoten, 2009.
Tsuda Katsuo. "Mihoko no shigoto." *Shōjo kurabu* 21, no. 11 (1943): 72–77.
Tsugihashi Tatsuo. "Numata Ryūhō." *Nihon jidō bungaku daijiten*. Vol. 1, *Jinmei a–to*, edited by Osaka kokusai jidō bungakukan, 52–54. Tokyo: Dainihon Tosho, 1993.
Uchida Shizue. "Zasshi no kōsei." In *Shōjo no tomo to sono jidai: Henshūsha no yūki Uchiyama Motoi*, edited by Endō Hiroko, 174–76. Tokyo: Hon no Izumi Sha, 2004.
Uchiyama Motoi. "Henshū kōki." *Shōjo no tomo* 33, no. 9 (1940): 252.
———. "Henshū kōki," *Shōjo no tomo* 37, no. 5 (1944): 76.
———. "Kimitachi mo zensen no heishi da: Kaigun hōdōbu kachō Kurihara taisa ni kiku." *Shōjo no tomo* 36, no. 10 (1943): 14–27.
———. "Kurabushitsu dayori." *Shōjo no tomo* 33, no. 7 (1940): 244.
———. "Kurabushitsu dayori." *Shōjo no tomo* 34, no. 4 (1941): 229.
———. "Saigo no hi." *Shōjo no tomo* 38, no. 8 (1945): 4–7.

———. *Shōjo no tomo* 34, no. 1 (1941): 227.
Uchiyama Motoi, and Yoshiya Nobuko. "Shōjo ni okuru Yoshiya Nobuko sensei Uchiyama shuhitsu taidankai." *Shōjo no tomo* 31, no. 1 (1938): 84–95.
Uno, Kathleen S. "Women and Changes in the Household Division of Labor." In *Recreating Japanese Women, 1600–1945*, edited by Gail Lee Bernstein, 17–41. Berkeley: University of California Press, 1991.
Ushikubo Megumi. *Ren'ai shinai wakamonotachi: Konbinikasuru sei to kosupasuru kekkon*. Tokyo: Discover Twenty One, 2015.
Wakakusa Tsubomi. *Himawari* 5, no. 1 (1951): 118–19.
Wakakuwa Midori. *Sensō ga tsukuru joseizō: Dainiji sekai taisenka no nihonjosei dōin no shikakuteki puropaganda*. Tokyo: Chikuma Shobō, 2000.
Wakeling, Emily Jane. "Girls Are Dancin': Shōjo Culture and Feminism in Contemporary Japanese Art." *New Voices* 5 (2011): 130–46.
Watanabe Shūko. *Shōjozō no tanjō: Kindai nihon ni okeru shōjo kihan no keisei*. Tokyo: Shinsensha, 2007.
Wood, Christopher. *The Bubble Economy: Japan's Extraordinary Speculative Boom of the '80s and the Dramatic Burst of the '90s*. Jakarta: Solstice Publishing, 2006.
Yamashita Etsuko. *"Josei no jidai" to iu shinwa*. Tokyo: Seikyūsha, 1991.
Yanabu Akira. "Shōjo shōsetsu no shōgeki." *Shisō no kagaku* 7, no. 145 (1991): 17–28.
Yokokawa Sumiko. "Posuto shōjo shōsetsu no genzai: Onnanoko wa otokonoko ni nani o motomete iruka." In *21seiki bungaku no sōzō 7: Danjo to iu seido*, edited by Saitō Minako, 205–30. Tokyo: Iwanami Shoten, 2001.
———. *Shochō toiu kirifuda: Shōjo hihyō josetsu*. Tokyo: JICC Shuppankyoku, 1991.
———. "Shōjo shōsetsu." In *Nihon jidō bungaku daijiten*. Vol. 2, *Jinmei na–wa*, edited by Osaka kokusai jidō bungakukan, 416–17. Tokyo: Dainihon Tosho, 1993.
Yosano Akiko. "Shōnen shōjo no yomimono." *Kaizō* (August 1926): 123. Reprinted in *Yosano Akiko zenshū*. Vol. 19, *Hyōron kansō shū*, 452–53. Tokyo: Kōdansha, 1981.
Yoshikawa Toyoko. "'Seitō' kara taishū shōsetsu sakka e no michi." In *Feminizumu hihyō e no shōtai: Kindai josei bungaku o yomu*, edited by Iwabuchi Hiroko, Kōra Rumiko, and Kitada Sachie, 121–48. Tokyo: Gakugei Shorin, 1995.
Yoshiya Nobuko. "Atarashiki seiki o tsukuru hitobito to shite." *Shōjo no tomo* 33, no. 4 (1940): n.p.
———. "Fukujusō." In *Yoshiya Nobuko zenshū*. Vol. 1, *Hana monogatari, Yaneura no nishojo, dōwa*, 93–100. Tokyo: Asahi Shinbunsha, 1975.

———. "Hikage no hana." In *Yoshiya Nobuko zenshū*. Vol. 1, *Hana monogatari, Yaneura no nishojo, dōwa*, 202–4. Tokyo: Asahi Shinbunsha, 1975.
———. "Hitotsubu no mugi tomo naran." *Shōjo no tomo* 34, no. 3 (1941): 78–85.
———. "Ichiryū no joryū sakka to naru niwa." *Shōjo no tomo* 42, no. 4 (1949): 26–31.
———. "Kibara." In *Yoshiya Nobuko zenshū*. Vol. 1, *Hana monogatari, Yaneura no nishojo, dōwa*, 219–32. Tokyo: Asahi Shinbunsha, 1975.
———. "Kuchinashi no hana." In *Yoshiya Nobuko zenshū*. Vol. 1, *Hana monogatari, Yaneura no nishojo, dōwa*, 45–48. Tokyo: Asahi Shinbunsha, 1975.
———. "Moyuru hana." In *Yoshiya Nobuko zenshū*. Vol. 1, *Hana monogatari, Yaneura no nishojo, dōwa*, 141–58. Tokyo: Asahi Shinbunsha, 1975.
———. "Nashi no hana." In *Yoshiya Nobuko zenshū*. Vol. 1, *Hana monogatari, Yaneura no nishojo, dōwa*, 322–24. Tokyo: Asahi Shinbunsha, 1975.
———. "Sakusha no kotoba." In *Mittsu no hana*. Tokyo: Kōdan Sha, 1927. Reprinted in *Mittsu no hana*, 3–5. Tokyo: Yumani Shobō, 2003.
———. "Sazanka." *Shōjo gahō* 5, no. 11 (1914): 86–91.
———. "Seishun ni okuru." *Himawari* 1, no. 1 (1947): n.p.
———. "Senka no shanhai kesshikō." *Shufu no tomo* 21, no. 11 (1937): 134–75.
———. "Senka no hokushi genchi o iku." In *Senka no hokushi genchi o iku*, 1–96. Tokyo: Shinchōsha, 1937.
———. *Shojo dokuhon*. Tokyo: Kenbunsha, 1936. Reprinted in *Sōsho joseiron*. Vol. 35, *Shojo dokuhon*. Tokyo: Ōzorasha, 1997.
———. "Suzuran." In *Yoshiya Nobuko zenshū*. Vol. 1, *Hana monogatari, Yaneura no nishojo, dōwa*, 11–12. Tokyo: Asahi Shinbunsha, 1975.
———. "Ukon zakura." *Yoshiya Nobuko zenshū*. Vol. 1, *Hana monogatari, Yaneura no nishojo, dōwa*, 30–33. Tokyo: Asahi Shinbunsha, 1975.
———. "Wasurenagusa." *Yoshiya Nobuko zenshū*. Vol. 1, *Hana monogatari, Yaneura no nishojo, dōwa*, 34–37. Tokyo: Asahi Shinbunsha, 1975.
———. "Yaneura no nishojo." *Yoshiya Nobuko zenshū*. Vol. 1, *Hana monogatari, Yaneura no nishojo, dōwa*, 412. Tokyo: Asahi Shinbunsha, 1975.
———. *Yellow Rose*. Translated by Sarah Frederick. Los Angeles and Tokyo: Expanded Editions, 2016. Kindle edition.

INDEX

A Doll's House (Ibsen), 55
A Little Princess (Burnett), xi, 67, 127, 131n2
Adolescence, xv; discomfort of, 58, 59; maturation during, 13, 36, 37, 41, 95; preservation of, 95; realistic portrayal of, 57; resistance against growing up, 41; sexuality during, 99
Aeba Kōson, 2, 4–5, 134n18, 134n19
Age of Women, 97, 102, 123
aged, positive portrayal of, 120
aging society, 115; media focus on, 119
Agnes Debate (*Agunesu ronsō*), 103
Agunesu ronsō. *See* Agnes debate
aidokusha taikai (readers' event), 24
aikoku shōjo (patriotic girl), *see under shōjo*
"Aishū" (Melancholy) (Kawabata), 95
Akai tori (Red Bird), 42, 142n13, 145n61, 156n62
akogare no kimi (the boy of love), 87
Alcott, Louisa May, xv, 1, 4–6, 22, 31, 55, 57, 137n77, 141n4; description of Jo March,13–14; *Eight Cousins*,127, 160n44; feminism and, 134n23; *Hospital Sketches*, 138n22; idea of home,8–9; influence on Japanese women, 127; *Rose in Bloom*, 127, 160n44
"Ame" (Rain), 21
American Culture, xviii; embrace of, 89; presentation of, 81–83; values, 84, 88; literary scene, 1; magazines, 84

Americanism, resistance to, 92
Anime, 129, 170n2
Anne of Green Gables (Montgomery), xi, xvii, 66, 132n27, 157n70, 169n1; influence on Japanese women, xix, 127; introduction in Japan, 153n7
Aoyama, Tomoko, x, xiv, 114, 132n20
Ariyoshi, Sawako, 168n10. See also *Kōkotsu no hito* (A Man in a Trance)
Asahi Journal, 97, 162n4
Asahi shinbun, 50, 92, 147n6
Ashio Copper Mining Incident, 43, 146n69
Atomi Jogakkō (Atomi Girls' Schools), 20
Atomi Kakei, 20, 30
autobiography, xvi, 152n87; Kitagawa Chiyo, 44; Louisa May Alcott, 1; Morita Tama, 63; Tanabe Seiko, 115; Yoshiya Nobuko, 49, 63

Beauvoir, Simon de, 58
Beni suzume (Red Sparrow) (Yoshiya), 149n29
Better Homes and Gardens, 84
biiku (cultivation of beauty), 13
Blackboard Jungle, 98
boke rōjin (Senile Old People), 119
bubble economy, 97, 115, 162n2; materialism during, 108
Buddhism, 106, 165n49
bungei eiga (literary and artistic film), 89
Bungei kurabu (Literary Club), 15, 139n33

191

Bunshō sekai (Composition World), 24
Burnett, Frances Hodgson, influence in Japan, xi. See also *Little Lord Fauntleroy*; *A Little Princess*

CCD (Civil Censorship Detachment), 85
censorship, 68, 69, 85
Chan, Agnes, 103, 164n34
Chi no hate made (To the Furthest Ends of the World) (Yoshiya), 50
Chibikun monogatari (Story of Chibi) (Yuri), 67
Chiisaki hanabana (Small Flowers) (Yoshiya), 147n87
Chikushi Tetsuya, 97
Chōshōjo e (Miyasako), xiii
chū (loyalty), 14
chūkan shosetsu (midway fiction), 118
Chūō kōron (Central Review), 6, 164n37
CIE (Civil Information and Education), 83, 85, 88, 92
Civil War, American, 11, 138n22
Clark, William S., 56, 150n39
CMPE (Central Motion Picture Exchange), 89
Cobalt, 100–2, 114, 132n25, 167n90; book series, 99, 163n12; Cobalt fresh five, 101; creation of xviii
comedy essay genre, 119
Confucianism, 4, 6, 14, 22, 29, 88, 123
Cult of Domesticity, 4, 5
Cult of Productivity, 4
Culver, Annika, 155n32

Daddy-Long-Legs (Webster), xi, 84; influence on Japanese women, 127; influence on Yuri Seiko, 67; introduction in Japan, 170n1; translation, 153n11
"Daughters in Boxes" (Kishida), 9

daughters of domesticity (*ie no musume*), 4, 17, 21, 63
democracy, 49, 86, 159n21; value of, xvii; in Japan, 81, 83
didacticism, 21, 23, 78, 147n87
différance, 137n77
domestic fiction (*katei shōsetsu*), xv, 138n9
domesticity, 4, 5, 15,21, 30, 40; as woman's space, 84, 88; education, 16; responsibility, 7, 36; wife's role, 62; women's leadership, 6

education: system, 159n32; adolescent, 39; Americanization of, 93; coeducation, 86, 98, 137n3; health and, 11; home, 8; ideology 1; Japanese girls,' xii, 17, 135n34; Japanese language, xvii; postwar, 83, 85, 86; wartime, 68; Western girls,' xix; women's 4, 5, 8
Eguchi Kan, 42–43,145n61, 145n64
Eight Cousins (Alcott), 127, 160n44
Enchi, Fumiko, 62, 114, 119, 151n72. See also *Onnazaka* (Waiting Years)
Endō Hiroko, 57, 154n24
Endō Shūsaku, 119
enka (sentimental ballad), 122–123
Equal Employment Opportunity Law, 97, 102, 103

Faderman, Lillian, 39
fantasy, xii, xiii, xix, 128, 129; fiction, 22, 125; adventure, 22; danger of, 118; influence on Tanabe, 115; in Kawabata's work, 93–95; in Tanabe's work, 124–125; in Yoshiya's work, 31, 32, 37, 46, 50, 51; *shōjo*, 94; power of, 129; wartime, 78–79
father, absence of, 88, 89
feminism, 49, 103, 123, 134n23; American literature, 37; domestic,

5, 7; in Tanabe's work, 123, 124; in Yoshiya's work, 52, 53, 56, 63; organizations, xvi; wartime, 73
Frederick, Sarah, 56, 63
Fujin no jikan (Women's Time), 84
fujoshi (young women and children), 5
Fukiya Kōji, ix, 33–34, 42, 55, 83, 142n15, 153n3; Illustration style, 33
Fukuda Ichiyo, 67
Furuichi Noritoshi, 99
"Futari zake" (Couple's Wine), 122

geisha, 50, 93–94, 148n9
genbun icchi (The Agreement of Written and Spoken Languages), 149n26
gender, 36, 165n44; equality, 86; feminization of male characters, 108, 111; Japanese traditional gender norms, 91; normativity, xvi; roles, 4, 144n47; roles in Heian period, 98; performative nature of, 104, 108; traditional role, xviii
Genji monogatari (The Tale of Genji): Genji, 167n75, 167n78; parody of, 119; relation to Himuro's work, 97, 104–6, 109, 111–13; relation to Tanabe's work, 119, 129
"Genki jirushi no onnatachi" (Women Marked by Energy), 97
genpuku, 104–5, 165n49
ghost writing, 92, 153n13, 161n64
GHQ/SCAP, 81, 85, 158n2, 158n5, 159n29
girls' fiction. *See shōjo shōsetsu*
girls' magazines, xvii, 16, 19, 41, 65, 128; culture, 17, 48, 115, 66
girls: control of body, 63; future roles as women, 36; physicality, 38; rebellion against responsibility, 63; resistance against authority, 71; responsibilities as Japanese citizens, 78; social obligations, xiii; women's culture, as opposed to girls' culture, 97
girls' culture (*shōjo bunka*), xi, xiv, xix, 130, 132n15; community, 25, 41, 68; creation of, 19; rebelliousness of, 71
girls' study (*shōjo kenkyū*), xiv
Good Housekeeping, 84
Good Wife, Wise Mother (*ryōsai kenbo*), xii, xv, 1, 3, 5, 8, 13, 20, 22, 28–30, 60, 133n8, 135n34; origin of, 4
gunkoku shōjo (a girl of the military nation), xvii, 65, 78–79, 117–18
gyokusui (death for honor), 118

Hana monogatari (Flower Tales) (Yoshiya), 50–52, 141n4, 142n10, 142n13, 143n24, 143n26, 147n87; antithesis of, 46; cultural resistance, 36–37; end of, 40–41; sexuality 38–40; *shōjo* image in, 33. See also "Hikage no hana" (Shaded Flower); "Kibara" (Yellow Rose); "Sazanka"; "Suzuran" (Lily of the Valley); "Ukon zakura" (Saffron Cherry Blossoms). See also under Yoshiya Nobuko, writing style, 32, 34–35
Hana to kosuzu (Flower and Small Bell) (Kawabata), xvii, 83, 92–96
Hanako, 108
Harabayashi Taiko, 56
Hartley, Barbara, 114
Hasegawa Shigure, 28
Hastings, Sally A., ix, 3
Hatori Tetsuya, 156n60
Hayashi Fumiko, 56, 75, 155n35, 156n50
Hayashi Mariko, 103, 164n37, 164, 38; comments on materialism, 108
Heian period, xviii, 97, 98; court culture, 106
Heidi (Spyri), xi, 66, 127, 153n8

Helen Keller, 77
Higuchi Ichiyō, 15, 50, 129, 148n9, 170n10. *See also* "Nigorie" (Troubled Waters); "Takekurabe" (Child's Play)
"Hikage no hana" (Shaded Flower) (Yoshiya), 38
Himawari (Sunflower), 83, 87–92, 160n40, 160n44, 161n64; educational goals, 81; end of, 96. *See also Hana to kosuzu* (Flower and Small Bell)
Himuro Saeko, xviii, 97–98, 132n26, 164n28, 164n29, 164n31, 165n44; comments on bubble era, 108–9; comments on marriage, 111; criticism of Heian literature, 110; early life, 102; humor, xix, 98; opinion of feminism, 103; thoughts on Agnes debate, 103; thoughts on girls' fiction, 113–14. *See also Nante suteki ni japanesuku* (How Splendid Japanesque); "Sayōnara arurukan" (Farewell Arurukan); *Za chenji* (The Change)
Hirabayashi Taiko, 114
"Hirahira no keifu" (The Genealogy of Hirahira) (Honda), xiii, 131n10
Hiratsuka, Raichō, 28, 52–53, 63, 73, 87, 148n20, 150n42
Hiroshima, 85
hisabetsu buraku (outcast communities), 35, 143n24
Hokkaido, 56, 150n52; literary importance of, 58
home: as girls' space, 87; comparison between West and Japan, 5, 6, 8; *katei* (home), 7, 44, 88; postwar, 83; sphere of, 9
hōmu no jōō (queen of the home), 7
Honda Masuko, xiii, 25, 38, 79, 132n20, 139n40, 143n33

honne (True Feelings), 61, 119, 123, 125
Hōpu (Hope), 28, 147n1
Hosokawa Takeko, 147n2

Ibsen, Henrik Johan, 150n42. *See also A Doll's House*
Īda Yūko, 124
ie (stem-family household), 4, 6–7
ie no musume. *See* daughters of domesticity
Igarashi Yumiko. *See Kyandī kyandī* (Candy dandy)
ikiokure (old maid), 118
Ikuta Hanayo, 63
imagined community, 25, 31, 34, 37, 69; power of, 128
immaturity: writings, xv, 57, 128; power of, 70, 110, 128; *shōjo*, xiv
Inagaki Kyoko, 137n2, 145n58, 153n5
ippashi no onna (mature independent woman), 109
Ishihara Shintarō. *See Taiyō no kisetsu* (Season of the Sun)
Ishikari otome (Ishikari Maiden) (Morita), xvi, 49, 56–58, 63, 150n49
Ishiusu no uta (Song of the Stone Mill) (Tsuboi), 85, 159n24
Iwamoto Yoshihasu, xi, 6, 131n2
Iwaya Sazanami, 19, 24, 138n11
Izawa Miyuki, 24, 139n30, 141n2
"Izu no odoriko" (The Dancing Girl of Izu) (Kawabata), 94

Japanese culture: contemporary, xviii; disappearance of, 83; family, xviii; family system, changes in, 122; modern family system, xix; nostalgia for, 92, 95; refutation of, 58; role of women, 49; romance, collapse of, 109; traditional gender norms, 91; wives, suffering of, 62

Japanese government, 130; colonization of Asia, xvii, 72, 77; control, 65; *kazoku kokka* (familial nationhood), 4; *kokka* (unified state), 20; *kokumin* (Japanese citizens), 20, 30; propaganda, xvii, 3, 65
Jean Webster. See *Daddy-Long-Legs*
jiga (selfhood), 43, 49, 54–55, 87, 149n32
"Jijisute no tsuki" (the Moon to Watch on the Day to Abandon Elderly Men) (Tanabe), 123
jō (sympathy and compassion), 111–13
Jogaku sekai (School Girls' World), 24, 33, 138n9, 139n38
Jogaku zasshi (Women's Educational Journal), xi, 1, 6–7, 131n2, 131n3
jojō shōsetsu (lyrical stories), 87
jojōga (lyrical painting), 153n3
jūgo no onna (women behind shields), 77
jun bungaku (pure literature), 118
Junia bungei (Junior Literary Art), 99
Junia raifu (Junior Life), 99
junia shōsetsu. See junior fiction
junior fiction (junia shōsetsu), 98; change in, 102; debate surrounding, 99, 100

Kageki (Opera), 78
Kaiga Hentetsu. *See* "Ame" (Rain)
kaigo (elder care), 168n11
Kakuta Mitsuyo, 114
Kametaka Fumiko, 33, 142n14
Kan Satoko, x, 15, 55, 76, 118–19
Kaneda Junko, 100
Kaneko (Yamataka) Shigeri, 147n2
Karatani Kōjin, 149n26
Kasuga Kisuyo, 122
Kataoka Asami, 105
"Katase made" (To Katase) (Morita), 56–57
Katei (Home), 54, 157n70

katei (home). *See under* home
katei kyōiku (domestic education), 4
katei no yomimono (home novel), 4
katei shōsetsu. See domestic fiction
Katō Masao, 42
Kawabata, Yasunari, xvii, 66, 79, 153n4, 156n60, 161n64; comment on Tanabe Seiko, 117; ghost writing, 153n13; wartime conflict, 76–77, *Yukiguni* (Snow Country), 93. *See also* "Aishū" (Melancholy); *Hana to kosuzu* (Flower and Small Bell); "Izu no odoriko" (The Dancing Girl of Izu); *Manyō shimai* (Manyō Sisters); *Mizuumi* (The Lake); *Otome no minato* (Maiden's Harbor); *Utsukushii tabi* (Beautiful Voyage); *Yama no oto* (The Sound of the Mountain)
Kawaii (cute), 129, 132n15
Kawamura Kunimitsu, 25, 33, 38, 139n38, 139n40, 143n38, 151n79
Kawasaki Kenko, 149n32
kazoku kokka (familial nationhood), 4
keishū sakka (talented literary women), 15, 25
Kelsky, Karen, 103
"Kibara" (Yellow Rose) (Yoshiya), 39
Kicchin (Kitchen) (Yoshimoto), 114
kigyō senshi (corporate warriors), 103
Kikuchi Dairoku, 133n8
"Kinuito no zōri" (Silk Sandals) (Kitagawa), 41–42, 46
Kishida Toshiko. *See* "Daughters in Boxes"
Kita Morio, 119
Kitabatake Yao, 88
Kitada Shūho, 1, 3, 5, 11, 133n6; translation decisions, 7–10, 13–15
Kitagawa Chiyo, xvi, xvii, 128, 140n42, 145nn60–62, 157n67; class consciousness, 31, 41, 47, 49; early life, 24–25, 26–28, 41–43, socialism, 30, 17. *See also* "Kinuito no zōri" (Silk Sandals); "Kōfuku"

(Happiness); "Na o mamoru" (Protecting My Name); "Sekai domei" (World Alliance); "Shunran" (The Noble Orchid); "Tamago hitotsu" (One Egg); "Usagi o kau shōjo" (A Girl Who Raises Rabbits)
kitsunebi (foxfire), 94
kiyoku tadashiku utsukushiku (Pure, Proper, and Beautiful), 120
kō (duty to the parents), 14, 21
Kobayashi Yoshihito, 95
"Kōfuku" (Happiness) (Kitagawa), 43–44
kokka (unified state), 20
"Kokoro no ane" (Sister of My Heart) (Numata), 23
Kōkotsu no hito (A Man in a Trance) (Ariyoshi), 119
kokumin (Japanese citizens), 20, 30
Komiya Toyotaka, 57
Kondō Masahiko, 100
Kondo, Dorinne, 146n72
kōtō jogakkō rei (Women's Higher School Act), 19, 135n34
Kristeva, Julia; abjection, 54; *joissance*, 39, 54
Kubota Mantarō, 57
Kume Yoriko, xii, 11, 21, 37
Kumi Saori, 102, 164n27
kuni no musume (daughters of the nation), 4
Kunikida Doppo, 58, 60, 150n54
kuon no josei (eternal women), 55
Kurosawa Ariko, 143n34
Kuwabara Hiroshi, 104
Kyandī kyandī (Candy Candy) (Igarashi and Mizuki), 127
kyōiku rei (The order on Education), 137n3

Ladies Home Journal, 84
Little Lord Fauntleroy (Burnett), xi, 131n2

Little Women (Alcott), xi, 30, 84, 129, 133n1, 135n44, 153n9, 161n53; 1933 film version, 153n6; 1949 film version, 89–90, 160n49; 1906 translation, 1–16 *passim*; 1917 translation, 137n77; 1947 translation, 89, 160n44; translators of, 133n7; importance in Japan, xv; influence on Japanese women, 127; influence on Yoshiya Nobuko, 66–67

MacArthur, Douglas, 81, 85, 158n2
magazine readers: gatherings, xvi, 24; submissions, xii, 23, 24, 27, 33, 67, 68, 100, 145n60, 158n82; magazine section, 19
Manchukuo, 72, 155n32; five ethnic groups, 72; Japanese language, education in, 76
Manchurian Incident, 68
Manyō shimai (Manyō Sisters) (Kawabata), 95, 161n64
Marginality, 115, 128; of aged, 115, 119; male characters, 113; power of, 128; social marginality, *shōjo*, xiv
Masamoto Non, 102, 164n27
masculinity, 14, 12–14; Heian portrayal of, 104
materialism, 6, 129
Matsuda Seiko, 100
Matsui Yuriko (Numata Fuku), 23–24, 28, 139n30
Matsumoto Katsuji, 153n8
Matsumoto Yūko, 127, 169n1
Meiji period, xi, 1, 14, 15, 74, 127, 128, 135n44; Christmas, 135n30; gender division of labor 4; idea of "home," 6, 9; literary style, 25; *keishū sakka* (talented literary women), 15, 25; Meiji Restoration, xv; translation convention,

137n77; values, 21; Westernization of Japan, 20
Midaregami (Tangled Hair) (Yosano), 38, 140n44
Miki Sumiko, 99
Militarism, 65–80 *passim*; removal of, 83
Minshushugi (Primer of Democracy), 84
Mittsu no hana (Three Flowers) (Yoshiya), 153n9
Miyake Kaho, 15
Miyamoto Saburō, 69, 71, 154n25
Miyamoto Yuriko, 114
Miyasako Chizuru, xiii, xiv
Mizuki Kyōko. See *Kyandī kyandī* (Candy Candy)
Mizuumi (The Lake) (Kawabata), 95
Modan shōkōjo (Modern Little Princess) (Yuri), 67
mogi, 104, 165n49
Momen zuihitsu (Cotton Essays) (Morita), 57
Momma Chiyo, 147n2
Morita, Sōhei, 56, 150n41
Morita, Tama, 17, 24, 30, 63, 117, 128, 147n4, 157n70; early life, 56–57; educational interest, 147n5; influence of *Seitō* on, xvi; opinion on war, 76; postwar, 84; *shōjo dokushokai* (Girls' Book Reading Circle), 27, 49; wartime, 76. See also *Ishikari otome* (Ishikari Maiden); "Katase made" (To Katase); *Momen zuihitsu* (Cotton Essays); *Tōri no komichi* (The Path in the Peach Orchard)
Mother's Day, 89, 161n52
Muraoka Hanako, xvii, 78, 83, 92, 132n27, 157n70, 160n44
murasaki no yukari (the purple linkage), 105–6

"Na o mamoru" (Protecting My Name) (Kitagawa), 146n84

naichi (Japanese main land), symbolic image of, 61
Nakahara Jun'ichi, xvii, xix, 142n17, 160n40, 161n53, 162n75; *Hana monogatari* (Flower Tales), 33; *Himawari* (Sunflower), 87, 88, 96; illustration style, 33; *jojōga* (lyrical painting),153n3; *Shōjo sekai* (Girls' World), 66; Tanabe Seiko comment on, 117; traditional beliefs, 88; return of, 81, 83; wartime removal of, 69–71
Nakazato Tsuneko, 92, 153n13, 161n62
Nante suteki ni japanesuku (How Splendid Japanesque) (Himuro), xviii, 97, 107–10, 113–15; marriage, 111
narcissism, 34, 38, 39
National Mobilization Law, xvii
nationalism, 4, 19, 20
netakiri (bed-ridden), 119, 122
"Nigorie" (Troubled Waters) (Higuchi), 50, 148n9
Nihon no katei (Japanese Home), 20, 138n12
Nolte, Sharon H., 3
Numata Fuku. See Matsui Yuriko
Numata Rippō, xv, 17, 30, 49, 56, 67, 147nn4; assistance to readers, 28–29; biographical information, 138n12; education goals, 20–21, 24, 147nn3; readers' events, 24; readers' submissions, 24–25; wife, 23. See also "Kokoro no ane" (Sister of My Heart); "Yūbe no hoshi" (Evening Star)

Ōba Minako, 119
obāchan (granny), 121
obasan (middle-aged woman), 110
occupation, xvii, xviii, 81 121, 128; end of, 96
Office Ladies (OL), 103
Ogura Chikako, 103

Ojima Kikuko, 27, 140n45
Okamoto Kanoko, 119
Okamoto Kidō, 145n62
Ōmachi Keigetsu, 139 ,25n33
Ōmori Ikunosuke, 92
Onēsama (bosom sister), 23, 36, 87
Onna no kaikyū (Women's Class) (Yoshiya), 124
onna rashisa (mature women's conventional femininity), 20
Onnazaka (Waiting Years) (Enchi), 62
Ōru yomimono (All Reading), 115
ōrudo misu (old miss), 118
Osanazuma (Young Bride) (Tomishima), 99
Oshikawa Shunrō, 22, 138n23
Otome (maiden), xvi, 38, 63, 139n40, 151n79
Otome no minato (Maiden's Harbor) (Kawabata), 67, 92, 153n13
Ōtsuka Eiji, xiii, 132n15
Otto no teisō (Husband's Chastity) (Yoshiya), 124, 149n35

Patriarchy, xvi, 6, 15, 21, 49, 57, 86, 106, 128; family system, 10, 84; rebellion against, xiv, xvi, 37, 48; women's role, 63
Patriotism, 72, 76; propaganda, 3
pen butai. *See* pen corps
pen corps (*pen butai*), 72
pen names, 33, 68
Pollyanna (Porter), xi, 84, 91, 127
Prough, Jennifer, 129

Rebel without a Cause, 98
Reijokai (Lady's World), 33, 42, 45, 145n60, 150n49
ren'ai kekkon (marriage by love), 86
risshin shusse (establishment and advancement of the public self), 15, 19, 29–30
Robertson, Jennifer, 144n47

rōjo (elderly women), xviii, 115, 129
rōmaji, 85–86, 93
Rose in Bloom (Alcott), 127, 160n44
Russo–Japanese war, 11
Ryōsai kenbo. *See* Good Wife; Wise Mother

Sagi musume (Heron Girl), 94
Saitō Minako, 114, 119, 123, 132n20
Same-sex love, xvi, 38–40, 51; changing portrayal of, 55; in America, 144n45; S-relationship, 39, 67, 86, 98
sankō (three highs), 109
Sappho, 39, 144n51
Sasayaki, 28
Sata Ineko, 56, 114
Satō Aiko, 99
Satō Kōroku, 77
Sato, Barbara, 29–30
"Sayōnara arurukan" (Farewell Arurukan) (Himuro), 102, 164n28
"Sazanka" (Yoshiya), 35, 45
scribbling girls, 17, 117, 128
scribbling women, 14, 16, 30, 57, 136n69
seika (wise governance of family affairs), 5
seikatsu kyōshitsu (Lifestyle Classrooms), 78–79, 157–58n82
seishōjo (sublime girl), 95
Seitō, xvi, 43, 54, 55, 140n45, 142n14; autobiographical style,152n87; contrast with *Shōjo dokushokai* (Girls' Book Reading Circle), 28, 49; discourse, 49; parody of, 53; Hiratsuka Raichō, 52, 148n20; *jiga* (selfhood), 88; Kitagawa, 146n68; *shojo ronsō* (virgin debate), 63; Yoshiya, 49, 52
"Sekai dōmei" (World Alliance) (Kitagawa), 145n61
Sekirankai (Red Wave Society), 17, 42, 46, 49

Self-Help (Smile), 29
Semi-autobiography, 1, 49
Senchimentaru jānī (Sentimental Journey) (Tanabe), 118
sentimentalism, xvi, 21, 128; criticism of, 35, 46; imagined community, 25, 31, 65; in America, 11, 37; sentimental style, xiii, 23, 34
sexuality, 10, 59, 60, 63, 63, 119; Chastity, 10, 63, 131n3; denaturalization of, 37; girls: sexualization of, 59–60, 63; girls' stories, 87; heterosexuality, non-acceptance of, xiv, 55; lesbianism, as pathology, 39; virginity, 63, 152n84
Shamoon, Debra, 153n13
shashin monogatari (photo stories), 89
Shihon genji monogatari (My Original Tale of Genji) (Tanabe), 119
Shimake no kodomobeya (Children's Room of the Shima Family) (Yoshiya), 66–67
Shimizu Yoshio, 33, 142n13
Shimoda Utako, 29–30, 54
Shiraki Shizu, 56, 150n41
shitamachi (eastern part of Tokyo), 43, 146n72
Shōfujin (Little Women), xv, 1, 3–5, 7–17, 21, 30, 133n5, 134n19; Kitada Shūho's statement, 133n6
shojo (virgin), xvi, 151n79
shōjo bunka. *See* girls' culture
Shōjo dokushokai (Girls' Book Reading Circle), 27–28, 49
Shōjo gahō (Girls' Illustrated), 19, 24, 31, 42, 43, 139n30, 141n2, 142n13, 145n62; *Anne of Green Gables*, 153n7; Fukiya Kōji, 33; *Little Women*, 137n77
shōjo kenkyū. *See* girls' study
Shōjo kurabu (Girls' Club), 19, 31, 42, 117, 142n20, 153n9, 157n67, 159n24; end of, 98; postwar, 81, 85, 86; wartime, xvii, 72, 77–78

shōjo manga, xi, xviii, xix, 113, 129, 163n21, 165n44; emergence of, 100; gender in, 104
shōjo meisaku (girls' fiction masterpieces), 91
shōjo narratives, xiv
Shōjo no tomo (Girls' Friend), xvii, 19, 27, 57, 65, 66, 87, 92, 132n23, 139n30, 140n42, 153n8; contrast with *Himawari*, 89; contrast with *Shōjo kurabu*, 77–78; educational goals, 67, 86; end of, 98; Kawabata Yasunari, 76–77, 152n4; Mother's Day, 89; Naharaha Jun'ichi, 33, 69, 83, 142n17, 152n3, 154n27; postwar, 81, 83; relationship with government, 77–79; Tanabe Seiko, 115, 117; Uchiyama Motoi,152n1, 154n24; wartime, 68–79 *passim*; Yoshiya Nobuko, 73, 149n29, 153n6
shōjo rashisa (conventional girls' quality), 20
shojo ronsō (virgin debate), 63
Shōjo Sekai (Girls' World), xv, 60, 67, 117, 132n22; American girls comments on, 11; creation of 17, 19; educational goals, 20–22, 29–30; end of, 66; Kitagawa Chiyo, 27, 31, 42; Morita Tama, 56; Numata Rippō, 138n12; readers' community, 25; readers' event, 24; *shōjo dokushokai* (Girls' Book Reading Circle), 27–28; Yoshiya Nobuko, 32
shōjo shōsetsu (girls' fiction), xii, xvi, 16, 22, 46, 113, 115, 128; commodification of, 113; criticism of, 99; cultural resistance of, 128, 129; evolution of, 127; genre,57; girls' fiction writers (*shōjo shōsetsuka*), 113, 115; modern, 98; new age of, 102; genre, xvi; as opposed to *junia shōsetsu* (junior fiction), 102; Westernization of, 67

shōjo, xi–xix, 27, 30, 130; ambition, 29, 30; community, xii, 30, 17, 23–25; concept of, 19–21; contrast with *onna* (woman), 36; cultural identity, 128; definition of, xii, 30; feminism, 49, 53; wartime roles, 72, 78, 79; comparison between America and Japan, 11, 12; future responsibilities of, 60; health of, 11, 22, 69; identity 17; in *Hana monogatari* (Flower Tales), 33–38, 40–41; *aikoku shōjo* (patriotic girl), 76–79; postwar image of, 83; relationship to *rōjo* (elderly women), xviii; sexualization of, 93–97; shift in image, 66–69; spirit, xvi, 113, 115; values, 125, 129
"Shōjogata ishiki" (consciousness of the girl) (Takahara), xiv
Shōjokai (Girls' Society), 19, 32, 42, 140n45
Shōkokumin Bunka Kyōkai (Children's Cultural Association), 157n67
shōnen (young children), xii, 19, 131n6
Shōsetsu gendai (Contemporary Fiction), 115
Shōsetsu junia (Fiction Junior): conventions of, 100; creation of, 98; focus on women's issues, 100–1; end of, 100–1; Himuro Saeko, 102; *seishun shōsetsu shinjin shō* (Youth Fiction Newcomers' Prize), 102; Tanabe Seiko, 115
Shōsetsu shinchō (New Tide Fiction), 115, 120
Shufu no tomo (Housewives' Friend), 55–56, 72, 75
"Shunran" (The Noble Orchid) (Kitagawa), 42, 45–46
shūshin (morals), 5, 135n34
shusse (social advancement), 111
Sino–Japanese war, 3, 72
Smile, Samuel, 29
Smith, Daniel Scott, 5
soft power, xi,

Soga Keiko, 102
S-relationship. *See* same-sex love
Stowe, Harriet Beecher, 31. See also *Uncle Tom's Cabin*
Suzuki, Michiko, 34, 39, 55, 63, 151n79
"Suzuran" (Lily of the Valley) (Yoshiya), 31–32, 47, 141n2

Tadataka Kamiya, 75
Taisho period, 29
Taiyō no kisetsu (Season of the Sun) (Ishihara), 98
Taiyōzoku (Sun Tribe), 99
Takabatake Kashō, 42, 145n63
Takahara Eiri, xiv, xv. *See also* "Shōjogata ishiki" (consciousness of the girl)
Takamura Kōtaro, 79, 142n14, 157n75
Takane fujinkai (Takane Women's Group), 49, 147n2
Takane, 28
Takano Matsutarō, 43
Takarazuka, 39, 66, 68, 74, 120, 144n47; Ashihara Kuniko, 161n53
Takasaki Ryūji, 75
Takehisa Yumeji, 27, 33, 140n46
Takeuchi Teruyo, 88
"Tamago hitotsu" (One Egg) (Kitagawa), 44
Tamai Tokutarō, 92, 161n61
Tamura Toshiko, 28
Tanabe, Seiko, xviii–xix, 99, 148n15, 168n6; admiration for Yoshiya, 115–17; early life, 117; feminism, 123–24; parody of Genji, 119; portrayal of elderly, 118, 119, 120; wartime, 79. *See also* "Jijisute no tsuki" (the Moon to Watch on the Day to Abandon Elderly Men); *Senchimentaru jānī* (Sentimental Journey); *Shihon genji monogatari* (My Original Tale of Genji); "Ubagatte" (Selfish Old Woman); "Ubatokimeki" (Old Woman's

Fluttering Heart); "Ubaukare" (Joyful Old Woman); *bazakari* (Blooming Old Woman) (Tanabe); *Watashi no Osaka hyakkei* (Eight Views of My Osaka); *Yume haruka Yoshiya Nobuko* (Far Away Dream, Yoshiya Nobuko)
Tanaka Masami, 102, 164n27
Teenagers, 99
The Equal Employment Opportunity Law, 97, 102–3
The Long Winter (Wilder), 84
The Wide, Wide World (Wetherell), 160n44
Toku, Masami, x, 129, 170n6
Tokutomi Roka, 25, 139n32
Tomishima Takeo, 99–100, 163n13, 164n28. See also *Osanazuma* (Young Bride)
tonarigumi (neighborhood association),77
Tōri no komichi (The Path in the Peach Orchard) (Morita), 150n49
Torikaebaya monogatari (The Changelings), 97, 104, 106, 165n45, 166n54
Tozasareta gengo kūkan (Closed Linguistic Space) (Etō), 85
Transcendentalism, 133nn1–2
Treat, John Whittier, xiii
trendy drama, 108, 166n61
Tsuboi, Sakae, xvii, 34, 77, 85, 142n20. See also *Ishiusu no uta* (Song of the Stone Mill)
Tsubouchi Shōyō, 2, 4–5, 134n17, 134n19
Tsuda Katsuo, 77
Tsumura Setsuko, 99
tsuzurikata undō (composition movement), 76, 117, 156n62

"Ubagatte" (Selfish Old Woman) (Tanabe), 120

ubasute (abandoning elderly women), 123, 169n30
"Ubatokimeki" (Old Woman's Fluttering Heart) (Tanabe), 120
"Ubaukare" (Joyful Old Woman) (Tanabe), 120
Ubazakari (Blooming Old Woman) (Tanabe), xviii, 115–16, 119–20, 123–25, 168n8, 168n12. See also "Jijisute no tsuki" (the Moon to Watch on the Day to Abandon Elderly Men); "Ubagatte" (Selfish Old Woman); "Ubatokimeki" (Old Woman's Fluttering Heart); "Ubaukare" (Joyful Old Woman)
Uchiyama Motoi, 66, 79, 87; biographical information, 152n1; educational goals, 67; Nakahara Jun'ichi, 69, 153n3; postwar, 81; relationship to readers, 67–68; wartime, 70, 74, 78, 154n24; Yoshiya Nobuko, 72
Ueno Chizuko, 103, 164n37
Uncle Tom's Cabin (Stowe), 47, 147n88
universal sisterhood, 65, 75
Uno Chiyo, 56–57, 150n38
Uno, Kathleen S., 4
US education mission, 85
"Usagi o kau shōjo" (A Girl Who Raises Rabbits) (Kitagawa), 77
Ushikubo Megumi, 109
Utsukushii tabi (Beautiful Voyage) (Kawabata), 77, 157n64

Vassar College, 127

Wada Kokō, 141n3
Wakakusa (Young Grass), 1, 42, 44
Wakakusa monogatari (Story of Young Grass), 1, 66, 89, 91, 153n6, 156n6, 160n49. See also *Little Women*
Wakamatsu Shizuko, xi, xii, 15, 131n2

Watashi no Osaka hyakkei (Eight Views of My Osaka) (Tanabe), 79
way of *shōjo*, xi, xviii, xi, 17, 65, 128, 129, 130; emotional power of, 31, 112, 113
Webster, Jean, 127, 153n11
Western culture, 5, 16; Christmas, 135n30; films, 66; home, xi, 84; ideals, 4; imagery and language, xvii, 33, 37, 66; literature, xi, 127, 130; relation to women's culture, 74; values, contrast with *ie* system, 66; writers, status of, 114
What Katy Did (Woolsey), 84
Women: absence of obligation, 115; beauty, 13, 93, 94; body, 38, 69; Childrearing, 4, 7; career opportunities, xviii; consumerist, 108; economic strength, xviii; function 52; lack of capability, 121; modern womanhood, xvi ; mother, role of, 7, 8; new women, xvi, 98; *onna rashisa* (mature women's conventional femininity), 20; opposed to girls' culture, 97; physical purity, 10, 152n82; reproduction, 4, 69; responsibility, xiii, 4, 28, 109; wives, suffering of, 62
women's age, xviii, 98; marketing strategy, 113; relation with girls' age, 113
Women's International League for Peace and Freedom, 75, 156n52
World War II, xvii, 65, 128, 129; end of, 81
writing style: ellipses, 23, 34, 39, 41; colloquial language, xviii; emotional style, 51; epistolary style,67, 73, 74; flowery, 23; non-verbal symbols, 34; sentimental, 24; *shōjo* literary style, xviii

Yama no oto (The Sound of the Mountain) (Kawabata), 95

Yamakawa Kikue, 42
Yamamoto Fumio, 114
yamanote (western part of Tokyo), 146n72
Yamashita Etsuko, 113
Yanabu Akira, 114
Yanagi Miwa, 129
Yaneura no nishojo (Two Virgins in the Attic) (Yoshiya), xvi, 49–50, 52, 55–56, 63, 148n15; lesbianism, 56
Yasukuni shrine, 72, 155n37
Yokokawa Sumiko, xiv, 132n15
Yonin no shimai (Four Sisters), 89, 160n44. *See also Little Women*
Yosano Akiko, 27–8, 35, 38, 63, 140n44, 152n82. See also *Midaregami* (Tangled Hair)
Yoshikawa Toyoko, 52, 148n20
Yoshimoto Banana. *See Kicchin* (Kitchen)
Yoshiya, Nobuko, xvi, xvii, xviii, 17, 31, 49, 56, 57, 63, 66, 79, 128, 139n30, 141n4, 142n17, 147n2, 147n4, 147n7, 148n15, 153n6, 156n52, 157n70, 167n90; contrast with Kitagawa Chiyo, 45–48; early life, 25, 32; career beginning, 50; change in style of 55, 147n87, 149n29; collaboration with government 75; commentary on anti-west movement, 73–74; comment on anti-west,74; comment on sentimentality,72; criticism of men, 53; desire for acceptance, 55; disillusionment, 55; fantasy, 37; Hiratsuka Raichō, 52; inaugural essay for *Himawari*, 87; lesbianism, 39, 56; Numata Rippō, 28, 30, political naiveté of, 75–76; resistance against society, 36, 40–41, 143n34; Tanabe Seiko, 115, 124; postwar, 83, 86–88; *shōjo*, 33, 55; trip to china, 72, 74–75; wartime, 65, 72–76; writing style, xiii, 34–35,

75. See also *Beni suzume* (Red Sparrow); *Chiisaki hanabana* (Small Flowers); *Chi no hate made* (To the Furthest Ends of the World); *Hana monogatari* (Flower Tales); "Hikage no hana" (Shaded Flower); "Kibara" (Yellow Rose); *Mittsu no hana* (Three Flowers); *Onna no kaikyū* (Women's Class); *Otto no teisō* (Husband's Chastity); "Sazanka"; *Shimake no kodomobeya* (Children's Room of the Shima Family); "Suzuran" (Lily of the Valley); "Ukon zakura" (Saffron Cherry Blossoms); *Yaneura no nishojo* (Two Virgins in the Attic)

youth culture, postwar, 98

"Yūbe no hoshi" (Evening Star) (Numata), 23

Yuikawa Kei, 114

Yukiguni (Snow Country) (Kawabata), 93

Yume haruka Yoshiya Nobuko (Far Away Dream, Yoshiya Nobuko) (Tanabe), 115, 148n15

yumemiru shōjo (dreamy girl), xvii, 78

Yuri Seiko. See *Chibikun monogatari* (Story of Chibi); *Modan shōkōjo* (Modern Little Princess)

YWA, 50, 54

Za chenji (The Change) (Himuro), xviii, 97, 104–5

www.ingramcontent.com/pod-product-compliance
Ingram Content Group UK Ltd.
Pitfield, Milton Keynes, MK11 3LW, UK
UKHW021845140426
5217IPUK00022B/1599